THE WORLD OF FREEDOM

THE WORLD OF FREEDOM

HEIDEGGER, FOUCAULT,
AND THE POLITICS OF HISTORICAL ONTOLOGY

ROBERT NICHOLS

STANFORD UNIVERSITY PRESS

STANFORD, CALIFORNIA

Stanford University Press
Stanford, California

©2014 by the Board of Trustees of the Leland Stanford Junior University. All rights reserved.

No part of this book may be reproduced or transmitted in any form or by any means, electronic or mechanical, including photocopying and recording, or in any information storage or retrieval system without the prior written permission of Stanford University Press.

Printed in the United States of America on acid-free, archival-quality paper

Library of Congress Cataloging-in-Publication Data

Nichols, Robert, 1979- author.
 The world of freedom : Heidegger, Foucault, and the politics of historical ontology / Robert Nichols.
     pages cm
 Originally presented as the author's thesis (doctoral)--University of Toronto.
 Includes bibliographical references and index.
 ISBN 978-0-8047-8875-5 (cloth : alk. paper)--
 ISBN 978-0-8047-9264-6 (pbk. : alk. paper)
 1. Heidegger, Martin, 1889-1976. 2. Foucault, Michel, 1926-1984. 3. Ontology. 4. Liberty--Philosophy. 5. Political science--Philosophy. 6. Continental philosophy. 7. Philosophy, European--20th century. I. Title.
 B3279.H49N525 2014
 193--dc23
                            2014023173
 ISBN 978-0-8047-9271-4 (electronic)

Typeset by Bruce Lundquist in 10/14 Palatino

For my father

CONTENTS

	Acknowledgments	ix
	Abbreviations	xi
ONE	Overview of the Problematic	1
TWO	Potentiality and Authenticity: Heidegger's Preparatory Existential Analytic in *Being and Time*	27
THREE	The Field of Freedom: Heidegger from Fundamental to Historical Ontology	57
FOUR	Foucault Contra Heidegger	99
FIVE	Foucault's "Autocritique": Three Equivocations of Conduct, Experience, and Thought	129
SIX	The Subject of Spirituality	161
SEVEN	Objectification, Reification, Subjectification: Historical Ontology and Social Criticism	199
	Notes	225
	Works Cited	259
	Index	269

ACKNOWLEDGMENTS

This book began at the University of Toronto, where Ronald Beiner and James Tully offered me unwavering support, prompting, and constructive criticism. For that I owe them thanks. I was fortunate enough to spend some time as a visitor at the University of Victoria as well, which afforded me an additional opportunity to work closely with Jim. Jim is the person most responsible for any decent ideas that can be found here and, more importantly, is an exemplar of how to combine intellectual acumen with generosity and humility.

The manuscript was then reworked at the University of Alberta, where I was fortunate enough to land in the midst of a community of smart, supportive, and welcoming colleagues. Conversations with Cressida Heyes, Catherine Kellogg, Marie-Eve Morin, and Chloë Taylor have been particularly helpful in reformulating the thinking that went into this work. Also at the University of Alberta, Connor Morris gave me great help with the editing and preparation of the manuscript.

The book then traveled with me and was completed during my year at the Humboldt Universität zu Berlin before I took up my current position at the University of Minnesota. I owe a debt to Rahel Jaeggi and Martin Saar for their roles in making Berlin a fantastic intellectual home away from home, and to Joan Tronto and Nancy Luxon for welcoming me to Minneapolis–St. Paul. During the past few years, I have also spent shorter research stints at Columbia University and the University of Cambridge, and I thank colleagues and staff at those institutions for giving me temporary bases from which to think and work.

Finally, there is a collection of people who, even when they have not read much of the work here, have probably contributed all the more just by keeping me going and not letting me take it all too seriously. Without the insistence of Johanna Oksala this would have likely died in a desk drawer. Isabel Altamirano-Jiménez, Rita Dhamoon, Johnny Mack, John Monroe, Dory Nason, Shiri Pasternak, Audra Simpson, and Jakeet Singh are all good friends who keep showing me how to be fun and serious all at once. Glen Coulthard has been my most important intellectual sparring/drinking partner and, together with Amanda, Hayden and Tulita, has been there for me from the beginning . . . and then again, and again, and again. At the foundation of my broader, nonprofessional world, I am fortunate enough to get enormous support and love from my family and my partner, Travis. Thank you all.

Financial support for this project was provided by the Fulbright, Humboldt, Killam and Trudeau Foundations, as well as the Social Sciences and Humanities Research Council of Canada.

ABBREVIATIONS

HEIDEGGER: ORIGINAL TEXTS

GA1–77   *Gesamtausgabe*. 77 vols. Frankfurt am Main: Vittorio Klostermann, 1975–2000.

SZ   *Sein und Zeit*. Tübingen: Max Niemeyer, 1967.

HEIDEGGER: TRANSLATIONS

BTa   *Being and Time*. Trans. John Macquarrie and Edward Robinson. New York: Harper and Row, 1962.

BTb   *Being and Time*. Trans. Joan Stambaugh. Albany: New York Press, 1996.

BW   *Basic Writings*. Ed. David Farell Krell. New York: Harper and Row, 1977.

EHF   *The Essence of Human Freedom*. Trans. Ted Sadler. London: Continuum, 2002.

FCM   *The Fundamental Concepts of Metaphysics: World, Finitude, Solitude*. Trans. William McNeill and Nicholas Walker. Bloomington: Indiana University Press, 1995.

IM   *An Introduction to Metaphysics*. Trans. James Manheim. New Haven, Conn.: Yale University Press, 1984.

KPM   *Kant and the Problem of Metaphysics.* Trans. Richard Taft. 5th ed. Bloomington: Indiana University Press, 1997.

MFL   *The Metaphysical Foundations of Logic.* Trans. Michael Heim. Bloomington: Indiana University Press, 1984.

N1–4   *Nietzsche.* Vols. 1–4. Trans. David Farrell Krell. San Francisco: Harper and Row, 1991.

OBT   *Off the Beaten Track.* Ed. and trans. Julian Young and Kenneth Haynes. Cambridge: Cambridge University Press, 2002.

OHF   *Ontology: The Hermeneutics of Facticity.* Trans. John van Buren. Bloomington: Indiana University Press, 1999.

P   *Pathmarks.* Ed. William McNeil. Cambridge: Cambridge University Press, 1998.

TB   *Of Time and Being.* Trans. Joan Stambaugh. New York: Harper and Row, 1972.

FOUCAULT: ORIGINAL TEXTS

A   *Les anormaux.* Paris: Gallimard, 1999.

AS   *L'archéologie du savoir.* Paris: Gallimard, 1969.

DE1–2   *Dits et écrits.* Vols. 1–2. Paris: Gallimard, 1994.

FDS   *Il faut défendre la societé.* Paris: Gallimard, 1997.

HF   *Histoire de la folie à l'âge classique.* Paris: Gallimard, 1972.

HS   *L'herméneutique du sujet.* Paris: Gallimard, 2001.

MC   *Les mots et les choses.* Paris: Gallimard, 1966.

MMP   *Maladie mentale et psychologie.* 4th ed. Paris: Quadridge/Puf, 2005.

NC   *Naissance de la clinique.* Paris: Presses Universitaires de France, 1963.

OD   *L'ordre du discours.* Paris: Gallimard, 1971.

SP   *Surveiller et punir: Naissance de la prison.* Paris: Gallimard, 1975.

SS *Histoire de la sexualité, vol. III: Le souci de soi.* Paris: Gallimard, 1984.
STP *Sécurité, territoire, population.* Paris: Gallimard, 2004.
UP *Histoire de la sexualité, vol. II: L'usage des plaisirs.* Paris: Gallimard, 1984.
VS *Histoire de la sexualité, vol. I: La volonté de savoir.* Paris: Gallimard, 1976.

FOUCAULT: TRANSLATIONS

A2 *Abnormal.* Trans. Graham Burchell. New York: Picador, 2003.
AK *The Archaeology of Knowledge.* Trans. Alan Sheridan Smith. London: Routledge, 2002.
BC *The Birth of the Clinic: An Archaeology of Medical Perception.* Trans. Alan Sheridan. London: Routledge, 1989.
CS *The History of Sexuality, vol. 3: The Care of the Self.* Trans. Robert Hurley. New York: Vintage, 1986.
DI "Dream, Imagination and Existence." *Review of Existential Psychology and Psychiatry* 19.1 (1986): 31–78.
DL *Death and the Labyrinth: The World of Raymond Roussel.* Trans. Charles Ruas. Garden City, N.J.: Doubleday, 1986.
DP *Discipline and Punish: The Birth of the Prison.* Trans. Alan Sheridan. New York: Vintage, 1977.
EW1 *Essential Works of Foucault.* Vol. 1, *Ethics, Subjectivity, and Truth.* Ed. Paul Rabinow. New York: New Press, 1997.
EW2 *Essential Works of Foucault.* Vol. 2, *Aesthetics, Method, and Epistemology.* Ed. James D. Faubion. New York: New Press, 1998.
EW3 *Essential Works of Foucault.* Vol. 3, *Power.* Ed. James D. Faubion. New York: New Press, 2000.
FL *Foucault Live: Collected Interviews, 1961–1984.* Trans. Sylvère Lotringer. New York: Semiotext(e), 1989.

FR	*The Foucault Reader*. Ed. Paul Rabinow. New York: Pantheon, 1984.
Herm.	*The Hermeneutics of the Subject*. Trans. Graham Burchell. New York: Picador, 2005.
HM	*History of Madness*. Trans. Jonathan Murphy and Jean Khalfa. London: Routledge, 2006.
HP	"Interview with Michael Bess." *History of the Present* 4 (Spring 1988): 11–13.
HS1	*The History of Sexuality, vol. 1: An Introduction*. Trans. Robert Hurley. New York: Vintage, 1978.
MIP	*Mental Illness and Psychology*. Trans. Alan Sheridan. Berkeley: University of California Press, 1987.
OT	*The Order of Things*. London: Routledge, 1989.
PT	*The Politics of Truth*. Ed. Sylvère Lotringer. New York: Semiotext(e), 1997.
RC	*Religion and Culture: Michel Foucault*. Ed. Jeremy R. Carrette. New York: Routledge, 1999.
RM	*Remarks on Marx: Conversations with Duccio Trombadori*. Trans. R. James Goldstein and James Cascaito. New York: Semiotext(e), 1991.
SMD	*"Society Must Be Defended."* Trans. David Macey. New York: Picador, 2003.
STP2	*Security, Territory, Population*. Trans. Graham Burchell. New York: Palgrave Macmillan, 2007.
TS	*Technologies of the Self: A Seminar with Michel Foucault*. Ed. Luther Martin, Huck Gutman, and Patrick Hutton. Amherst: University of Massachusetts Press, 1988.
UP2	*The History of Sexuality, vol. 2: The Use of Pleasure*. Trans. Robert Hurley. New York: Vintage, 1985.

THE WORLD OF FREEDOM

ONE

OVERVIEW OF THE PROBLEMATIC

> No idea is so generally recognized as indefinite, ambiguous, and open to the greatest misconceptions (to which it therefore actually falls a victim) as the Idea of Liberty.... When individuals and nations have once got in their heads the abstract concept of full-blown liberty, there is nothing like it in its uncontrollable strength.
>
> G. W. F. Hegel

ALTHOUGH THE CONCEPT OF FREEDOM is nearly universally praised, it is also highly abstract and thus deeply contested. The combination of these factors has given the term tremendous mobilizing force for competing political projects. Numerous critics and commentators of the French Revolution noted this (including Burke and Kant), but it was perhaps not until Hegel that it was given a full philosophical analysis. As the passage above attests, Hegel understood well that the idea of freedom was at once vague, powerful, and necessary. He also recognized that modern philosophy is thus burdened by the demands of freedom: the demand not only of its articulation but its realization. Unlike Classical thought, for instance, in which philosophy must first and foremost meet the demands of truth, modernity has imposed the additional expectation that thought be *liberating*. In a recent polemic, Peter Sloterdijk bemoans this historical transition, lamenting that "'knowledge is power.' This is the sentence that dug the grave of philosophy in the nineteenth century.... This sentence brings to an end the tradition of a knowledge that, as its name indicates, was an erotic theory—the love of truth and the truth through love (*Liebeswahrheit*).... Those who utter the sentence reveal the truth. However, with the utterance they want to achieve more than truth: They want to intervene in the game of power."[1] Setting aside Sloterdijk's longing for a prelapsarian philosophical love affair with truth unsullied by the problem of power, perhaps we can invert this lament, turn it into a positive and future-oriented impulse. Can we read our desire to "achieve more than truth" as something other than a closure, as perhaps even an opening to new horizons?

If philosophic activity can no longer be confined to the rather solitary pursuit of truth, a modern focus on freedom is related to a certain resocialization of thought as well. Hence, increased preoccupation with freedom has been attended by a host of attacks upon what might be termed the philosophy of the constituting subject. A movement is observable in the nineteenth and twentieth centuries, then, not only toward questions of freedom, but also away from an understanding of freedom as a *property* of the subject and more as a *practice* or a *relationship* (something one does rather than has). Once thought to designate the status of a small social and political elite, distinguishing them from the bulk of humanity who did not enjoy such standing (e.g., women, slaves, foreigners), the language of freedom was for many centuries necessarily stratified and nonreciprocal. Largely as a result of the upheavals of the nineteenth century, it is now possible, even commonsensical, for us to think of freedom as entailing a certain reciprocity and egalitarianism. To invoke perhaps the most famous and historically powerful iteration of this, unlike our predecessors, we can speak of freedom as an "association, in which the free development of each is the condition for the free development of all."[2] Increasingly, then, the freedom we talk about is a situation brought about through an ongoing practical relationship with the world and others. It is not something to be found, but rather something to be created and maintained with others.[3]

Along with this shift in the political idiom of freedom has come a parallel transformation in metaphysical conceptions. One of the main ways in which this was most manifest in the twentieth century was through a turn to intersubjectivity. Instead of locating questions of freedom in the search for transcendental properties of the subject (i.e., consciousness, the categories of intuition, and the like), philosophers of intersubjectivity have sought to ground emancipatory praxis in the discursively mediated interaction between subjects. Such theories offer the insight that the identity and constitution of the subject is not determined a priori but rather is formed through intersubjective reciprocity between agents, an insight often traced back to Hegel. As such, the move to intersubjectivity can be read as a contribution to both of the two general trajectories set out: it ties the question of truth to the question of freedom, but does so in a manner that circumvents problems associated with a philosophy of consciousness.

A recent, influential contribution to this line of inquiry is the discourse ethics of Jürgen Habermas. Undoubtedly, Habermas's oeuvre represents one of the most ambitious and systematic attempts to overcome the philosophy of the constituting subject through recourse to a theory of communicative rationality that locates the transcendental condition for critique, not in consciousness, but in intersubjective discursive activity.[4] However, underlying much of the discussion to follow is a concern that, despite Habermas's important insights, no theory of intersubjective communicative rationality can bypass the disclosing function of the pre-reflective activities by which a "world" of intelligible entities (including the very "subjects" who may engage in a discourse ethics) come into view in the first place. In other words, the field of possible subjects with which one may engage is not, in the first instance, discovered discursively-intersubjectively but rather practically-holistically (i.e., practice is not reducible to language).[5]

While theories of intersubjectivity have garnered a great deal of attention with respect to their considerable contributions to post-Kantian practical philosophy, there is another alternative. The possibility that an ontological inquiry might provide another route beyond the philosophy of the constituting subject (and even an alternative to the philosophy of intersubjectivity) has been widely noted. Even as trenchant a critic of Heidegger as Habermas has praised the way in which Heidegger's "postmetaphysical historicizing" advances the "overcoming of the philosophy of subjectivity. . . . From today's standpoint, Heidegger's new beginning still presents probably the most profound turning point in German philosophy since Hegel."[6] However, despite the wide recognition that Heidegger's work has gained in terms of challenging the philosophy of subjectivity, the implications of this remain underdeveloped for practical philosophy. Hence, the questions posed here: To what extent might the movement of freedom in post-Kantian political philosophy be recast in *ontological* terms? What difference might this make to the range of practical vocabularies available to us, currently preoccupied as they are with issues of intersubjectivity? Two thinkers who are indispensable for such an inquiry are Martin Heidegger and Michel Foucault.

The choice to draw upon Heidegger in recasting freedom in ontological terms is rather straightforward. Heidegger is known not only for his insistence on ontology as the central preoccupation of philosophy, but also on the centrality of freedom to this form of analysis. Despite this insistence, and in contradistinction to the wealth of literature on freedom and transcendental subjectivity, or freedom and intersubjectivity, Heidegger's ontological thesis has not been fully explored in relation to the question of freedom. To date, no monograph devotes itself singularly to addressing the question: what did Heidegger understand by the term "freedom"? Or, more generally: what are the implications for thinking about questions of freedom after Heidegger's formulation of ontology? In fact, secondary literature on Heidegger and freedom is relatively hard to come by in either philosophy generally or political theory more specifically.[7] This lack of sustained reflection is surprising and requires rectification.

Drawing on the work of Michel Foucault to investigate this topic is a considerably less obvious move. Although Foucault did speak of his work as a "historical ontology" and of freedom as a kind of "ontological ground," nowhere in his writings does he devote himself to a sustained, straightforward discussion of what ontology means to him. And yet, a thinker's silence on a topic does not entail its absence as a structuring field. Animating the project of reading Foucault ontologically then is a conviction that—despite his occasional protestations—he cannot avoid such questions altogether. As Johanna Oksala puts this point, "If Foucault's thought does not contribute anything to ontological questioning, then neither does it ultimately contribute anything significant to political philosophy."[8] Since virtually the entire second half of this book is devoted to demonstrating the centrality of ontological considerations to Foucault's analysis of freedom, I will not rehearse the point here. Instead, I will merely direct readers to the bulk of the text as a defense of the importance of putting these two into direct conversation concerning this topic.

What is clear is that Heidegger and Foucault stand out as two of the most important and influential thinkers of the twentieth century. Each has spawned volumes of secondary literature and sparked fierce, polarizing debates, particularly as regards the relationship between philosophy and politics. And yet, to date there exists almost no work that presents a systematic and comprehensive engagement of the two in relation to one another. This book seeks to address this lacuna, but only indirectly. A different tack would focus on textual traces and personal connections. This kind of inquiry would no doubt place emphasis on Foucault's declaration at the end of his life that Heidegger was, for him, "the essential philosopher," one who determined his "entire philosophical development" (*FL*, 470; *DE2*, 1521–22). Taking up this (by no means self-evident) declaration as a textual and biographical problem is a legitimate and worthwhile project no doubt. However, this is not my primary interest or concern here. Instead, in a more general and tangential way, this book demonstrates that it is both interesting and important to read Heidegger and Foucault alongside and in relation to one another, particularly if we are to understand properly the shape of twentieth century continental thought. These two thinkers form the poles between which are stretched a great arc traversing twentieth-century European philosophy, beginning with fundamental ontology and ending in genealogical critique and an ethics of the "care of the self." One aim here is to convince that these two poles are, in fact, connected. For even if we are not entirely convinced by the answers these two specific thinkers offer, the questions they wrestled with remain unavoidable.

Despite this conceptual focus, however, in the pursuit of such theoretical questions, one cannot help but comment on the biographical details of how Foucault engaged with Heidegger. I return briefly to this question below (1.2) in order to situate the discussion that follows within the context of this secondary, exegetical problem. Before proceeding to this, however, a more detailed sketch of the theoretical problematic is required.

1.1. ONTOLOGY AND SITUATED FREEDOM

In the study that follows I attempt to trace how Heidegger and Foucault develop their respective analyses of freedom in relation to questions of ontology. Engaging with these two thinkers, I argue, allows us to develop an analysis of freedom understood not in terms of a property of the subject, nor as an intersubjective activity, but as a mode of Being-in-the-world. More specifically, I argue that this kind of relationship and stylized mode of being seeks to disclose the mutual interrelatedness of (1) the acquisition of knowledge; (2) the appearance of a domain of entities about which knowledge claims can be made; and (3) the ethical transformation of the subject of knowledge. One discloses this interrelatedness through a working out of the possibilities projected within the worldly activities of disclosure that make a horizon of intelligibility possible and thus are the field on which self-recognition and subject-formation takes place. To be in a "free" relationship to this field or clearing is not, for Heidegger and Foucault, to detach oneself from it through an act of cognitive reflection. Rather, it is to cultivate a certain ethical attitude of awareness within the activities of disclosure that constitute the ontological ground of the field itself. It is, in a word, to take *care* of the field and, through this, of oneself.

Of course, the notion that the ethical transformation of the self in and through its worldly activities is linked to the acquisition of knowledge about the world did not begin with Heidegger and Foucault. Nor is it unique to them. In fact, as both authors suggest, their formulation of the question in this manner has antecedents in the nineteenth century. Hegel, Stirner, Schopenhauer, and Nietzsche in particular might all be read with an eye to elucidating these connections. Given this longer heritage I have, at times, employed Charles Taylor's terminology of "situated freedom" to describe the formation developed here.[9] I borrow the term from Taylor not only because it evokes a historical link back to Hegel (through Nietzsche and Schopenhauer in particular), but also because for Taylor, *situated freedom* denoted a position between the largely negative notion of freedom as self-dependence and the positive notions of freedom centered around the expression of one's "true" self. As elaborated upon later in this work, the move to an ontological analysis of selfhood-in-action is an attempt to displace the aspiration to both autonomy and expressivism evoked by the prevailing language of positive versus negative liberty. Instead, in Taylor's words, "What is common to all the varied notions of situated freedom is that they see free activity as grounded in the *acceptance* of our defining situation. The struggle to be free ... is powered by an affirmation of this defining situation as ours."[10] The notion of acceptance points to a second theme: finitude. For Heidegger and Foucault, the acceptance of finitude—in the sense of acknowledging one's factical limitations in a particular worldly condition and the fact that absolute knowledge of self and world is not, even in principle, possible—does not entail the *end* of freedom, but rather its *beginning*, insofar as this acknowledgment provides the starting point for an ethical transformation of one's *mode* or *style* of being within these conditions. In concluding chapters, I will describe and defend this transformation as a *spiritual* one.

The reference above to autonomy and expressivism speaks to the need to articulate what we mean by situated freedom in relation to its historical alternatives. To better arrange the field on which this discussion takes place, it is helpful therefore to sketch some alternative discourses of freedom against which Heidegger and Foucault are working.

At the outset of this chapter, I mentioned that the discussion of freedom in Heidegger and Foucault is very much set against a larger backdrop of the philosophy of the constituting subject. This philosophical backdrop owes much to Descartes and Kant in particular, about whom we will have more to say in later chapters. For now, however, it is important to note the interrelationship between a certain conception of transcendental subjectivity and a corresponding understanding of freedom as autonomy, developed most fully and most influentially by Kant. In the brief outline that follows, I draw most extensively upon Kant, not because he is the exclusive contributor to the philosophical traditions I am attempting to sketch, but because Kant remains the single most important figure in relation to whom Heidegger and Foucault position their respective work on freedom.

The formulation of freedom as "autonomy" of the subject, against which a theory of situated freedom is developed, owes most to Kant. Kant's problematic of freedom might be outlined through a two-stage set of questions. The questions and their ramifications are: (1) How can a creature which is subject to finite conditions (i.e., of space and time) guarantee the universality of its claims to knowledge? Does not our finitude—being subject to empirical laws of physics, causality, time, and so on—serve to limit our capacity to generate truly universal claims such that knowledge itself is threatened? (2) Does not this undermining of our reason in its knowing capacity further undermine the possibility of free agency, given that such agency rests on the possibility of rational determination? If the rational determination of our will cannot be demonstrated to be generated by a knowable set of universal conditions, then isn't our agency reduced to mere responsiveness to instinct or sensuous inclinations (i.e., to finite conditions)?

Kant's unique and ingenious response to this problematic—the "Copernican turn"—is to transcendentalize finitude. To "transcendentalize finitude" is to redefine the (empirical) limits of human understanding (the "limits of representation") as transcendental conditions, knowable by the subject. If our limitations of knowing can themselves not only be known, but be shown to be transcendental conditions for knowledge (as universal and necessary organizing categories for our faculties, i.e., time and space), then, as Béatrice Han-Pile reminds us, the *"a priori study of our (limited) faculties becomes the starting point for construing the necessary form of our knowledge, thus outlining the conditions of possibility of truth itself."*[11] The famed "Copernican turn" consisted, then, in overcoming human finitude by making it the necessary, transcendental condition for knowledge as such. Han-Pile writes,

> The empirical forms of our finitude (such as the passivity of our sensibility, the partiality of our will to sensible inclinations, and so forth) are not overcome in the obvious sense that they would be denied, or miraculously bypassed by the shift to a more advanced state of the human race. Kant's more subtle argument is that although it has to be acknowledged as empirically unsurpassable, human finitude should be redefined a priori and therefore understood *positively*, i.e., as what generates the scope of our possible knowledge and ultimately (because it outlines the possibility of rational determination itself) as the cornerstone of our freedom.[12]

It is this mention of "the cornerstone of our freedom" that draws the link to the discussion at hand so vividly. The philosophy of the transcendental and constituting subject, in this case finding its expression in Kant's analytic of finitude, gives the philosophical backing for an understanding of freedom centered on autonomy. Since it is the necessary form of our knowledge, generated by the mind, which creates the possibility of rational determination, this form of knowledge (this mind) stands in a transcendental relation to the field of action. The subject does not merely *reflect* reality in the mind passively (as with Locke's *tabula rasa*) but rather actively organizes and orders reality in such a way as to make rational determination possible. The second stage in this analysis is to connect this transcendental function of the mind to positive freedom. Thus, in this model freedom is equated, not only with the transcendental subject (the free will which chooses), but also with the active removal of those external impediments to full self-determination. Whether these be societal obstacles "outside" the empirical subject, or nonrational features of the self (e.g., the passions), external determination of the will can represent only an impediment to the self-constituting and self-legislating subject. The idea of removing obstacles to self-determination is Kant's way of linking what are referred to now as "negative" and "positive" liberty. *Transcendental* freedom for Kant refers to the absolute spontaneity of the will and derives from the capacity for rational determination. This transcendental freedom is defined negatively, but it is the basis on which he can further advocate autonomy as a form of positive freedom that seeks the *conditions* in which the appropriate moral motivation can be created so as to guide rational determination of the will (acting from duty alone). In between these two notions of freedom, Kant posits the purposiveness of nature as a means of reconciling the two.[13]

Now, it is clear that both Heidegger and Foucault at least claim to be working against such a model of freedom as autonomous rational willing. What remains to be seen is whether, despite their protestations, they merely commit themselves to an amended version of the philosophy of the constituting subject—perhaps not in the name of autonomous rational will but, instead, self-determination through self-creation. My reading of the two will attempt to demonstrate their critical potential as alternatives to the prevailing (Kantian) tradition by demonstrating that the work of both is animated by an understanding of selfhood as ontologically grounded in pre-reflective practices with independent (i.e., nonassigned) ethical import (relations of "Care"). To commit oneself to an understanding of freedom as autonomy from such embodied relations would be nonsensical under this reading as it is the relations and practices themselves that provide the historical conditions of possibility for the exercise of agency.

Another important theoretical language against which this ontology of finitude and freedom is situated is what I will refer to here as *teleological* freedom. Again I will rely upon the formulation put forward by

Kant, not because his is the exclusive or definitive formulation of the language of purposiveness, but because his particular formulation was subsequently so influential on others (Hegel and Marx in particular), and because both Heidegger and Foucault make specific reference to it.

By "teleological freedom," I am referring to the recourse to a purposiveness in history as a means of reconciling the transcendental freedom of pure spontaneity with the positive freedom of a social condition in which self-determination can be realized. A teleological or developmental model in this sense is organized around three basic premises: (1) a claim regarding the fundamental structures of consciousness (or, in the post–linguistic turn era, of the structure of communication) that determine the horizon of the possible content of knowledge; (2) the generalizing claim that these deep structures are a universal property of the human species; and (3) that these structures of consciousness have an internal developmental logic. This model of freedom finds its expression in the developmental anthropologies throughout the eighteenth and nineteenth centuries, including, most robustly, in Hegel and Marx, but it also has retained credence in the twentieth century, particularly through Habermas's theory of societal evolution.[14]

In the Kantian picture, it is an a priori possibility that the division between the noumenal and phenomenal accounts of causality and freedom be resolved through the unilinear progress of history in which humanity can come to reshape the empirical world through moral action to better correspond with the demands of *abstract freedom* exercised in the noumenal realm (i.e., with reason). Thus, a natural teleology of freedom is required to fully realize the abstract freedom of the noumenal self.

It is important to note that the attribution of teleological ends to nature and human activities is not an empirically verifiable truth. Teleology is a form of reflective judgment in which particular objects are judged without subsuming them under a determinate concept of the understanding.[15] Reflective judgments do not, for Kant, generate explanations that could be proved (or disproved); they produce only maxims for reflection. This does not mean, however, that the positing of a natural teleology is unjustified, since it is precisely when we are faced with radically contingent, unexpected objects of observation that we are authorized to consider that the "very contingency of the thing's form is a basis for regarding the product as if it had come about through a causality that only reason can have."[16] Such contingent objects are the effects of an unknown causality, which Kant calls "purposiveness." Free will's efficacy in the empirical world is precisely such a contingent "eruption" that justifies recourse to purposiveness. Thus, as *The Critique of Judgment* is at pains to demonstrate, even it if is impossible to generate empirically verifiable knowledge claims about purposiveness, this does not signify a failure of judgment, but rather demonstrates its central role.

Thus, Kant posits a reflective judgment about a third kind of causality which can bridge the mechanical causality of the empirical world with the "special causality" of abstract freedom as experienced in the moral, noumenal realm. Only if mankind is itself the telos of nature—that is, that it is nature's design to produce self-legislating beings—can empirical, linear time be reconciled with abstract freedom. This telos then is world-historical progress guided by Providence. If it were not for a natural teleology that confirms humanity's ability to force the empirical world to conform to its moral commands, we would be at the mercy of "aimless random process, and the dismal reign of chance."[17] In such circumstances, the duty to obey self-legislated moral commands would lose its compulsory force and we would be doomed to the repetition of Sisyphean deeds.[18] Thus, for freedom to exist at all, we must posit—as a reflective judgment—a divine "moral author" who has set into motion a natural teleology of progress in which humans are working toward a kingdom of ends:[19] "a happiness of rational beings that harmoniously accompanies their compliance with moral laws."[20] The kingdom of ends holds out the eternal possibility that the abstract freedom of the noumenal realm may be realized even in the flow of mechanical, linear time.

Once we have posited the principle of natural teleology, we have an interpretive key to understanding the contingencies of history. Specifically, natural teleology becomes a *regulative ideal* that organizes and structures our experience of human history. This means, therefore, we can interpret world events such as revolutions, wars, and acts of seemingly purposeless violence as unintentional contributions to global progress toward universal enlightenment. This does not mean that such acts are morally right—far from it. But it does mean that they are in accordance with nature's purpose. Without a teleological interpretive framework for world history, Kant argued, these events would appear as a meaningless collection of contingent facts—a pile of empirical data with no significant relation between them.

Thus, for Kant, a concrete, positive political and moral form can be deduced from the metaphysics of freedom. For Heidegger and Foucault, however, the teleological anthropology of man, particularly when wedded to a theory of transcendental subjectivity, is precisely the frame against which their own work is situated. This critical relationship holds as true for the modified Kantianism of, say, Habermas. In this recent reformulation, it is not the underlying structures of consciousness that serve as a regulative ideal for a model of corrective societal evolution, but rather the transcendental conditions of communicative rationality that provide the basis of intersubjective discourse.[21] Nevertheless, a corrective model of teleological development toward a more and more rational society (with its corresponding understanding of freedom as an end-state to be achieved, rather than an activity to be practiced) is the animating impulse behind such work, something both Heidegger and Foucault would call into question.

Against these first two models, then—the transcendental and the teleological—we have a third: situated freedom. The remainder of this book is an attempt to provide a philosophical explication of this sense of situated freedom by drawing on Heidegger and Foucault. Even at this early juncture, it is important to note that I do not view this understanding of freedom to be an exclusively nineteenth- or twentieth-century phenomenon, nor as a final stage in some grand linear narrative—from transcendental, to teleological, and, finally, to situated freedom. The languages of transcendental and teleological freedom are still very important and influential for interpreting freedom. Likewise, the language of situated freedom can be seen in the works of other thinkers in other times. What brings together these various thinkers and modes of interpretation in a "family resemblance" is their understanding of freedom as a practical relationship to one's situation such that latent possibilities within one's worldly activities are not foreclosed. To stand in a "free" relation to the world, to oneself and one's ethical commitments, is to know that one's standpoint does not exhaust the total range of meaningful, viable, and worthwhile possibilities. The acknowledgment of the finitude of one's own position and perspective is further complicated when we unpack what it would mean to "know" such a thing as finitude. Internal to the story told by both Heidegger and Foucault is that to know something is not merely to grasp it conceptually or give a theoretical articulation of it. It is not a mode of knowing, but is, rather, more fundamentally a *mode of being*, a relation of *logos* and *bios*. The test of our comprehension of this claim is not our ability to rephrase it back in the form of theoretical claims. Rather, it is the extent to which we actually *embody* the truth of this receptivity, fragility, indeterminacy, and interconnectivity.[22] As Thomas Dumm phrases it, freedom is not "a category or zone." Rather, it is "a style of being in the world that depends on an awareness of how one cares for the world, or, to use George Kateb's phrase, how one has "an attachment to existence."[23]

Central to my thesis is that this "attachment" relationship implies a bringing together of ethical commitment, knowledge acquisition, and the disclosure of a domain of entities. As such, it can properly be referred to as an "ontological" understanding of freedom. There is considerable room for confusion here, however, since "ontology" can be given a diverse range of meanings. As Johanna Oksala notes, *ontology* commonly refers to "both the fundamental building blocks of reality and to the systematic study of them."[24] Here, I am using the term to denote a very specific *mode of analysis*, one that attempts to disclose a fundamental relationship to reality, but does so in a matter distinct from traditional metaphysics. Metaphysics is also a mode of analyzing reality, but it is a mode primarily concerned with understanding *what* constitutes reality. That is to say, as I am using the term (following Heidegger's lead), metaphysics enters into the question of Being by way of beings, that is, an analysis of those entities which count as "existing" and the property that so constitutes them as such. By contrast, ontology studies *how* reality comes to us. It forestalls the question of *what* things exist (or don't) in favor of an inquiry into the mode or manner in which the question arises to us in the first place. More specifically, in using the predicate *ontological*, I am referring to a form of analysis that attempts to grasp the basic background conditions for the horizon of intelligibility that governs our engagement with the world. In distinction to an investigation of "epistemology," ontology sees our basic understanding of the world (our *Weltanschauung*, or "worldview") as an outgrowth of more basic pre-reflective practical involvement, the sets of activities in which we are always already engaged. An ontological analysis attempts to demonstrate that a claim to know something (an epistemological claim) already contains a backgrounded understanding about what *kinds* of entities there are to know, and an ethical stance—an existential commitment—toward these entities. When we engage in an "ontological form of critical analysis," we are attempting either: (1) to be reminded of this mutual interrelatedness and the fundamental conditions that make it possible (this would be a *fundamental* ontology); or (2) to foreground the work being done by specific pre-reflective activities to animate and legitimate a particular horizon of intelligibility (this would be a *historical* ontology). Central to my argument here is that there is a necessary interconnection between these two types of analyses, one that links the kind of work represented by, for instance, *Being and Time* (on the one hand) and *The Hermeneutics of the Subject* (on the other). A basic claim animating the whole of this book is that while Heidegger engages primarily with the first kind of analysis (fundamental ontology), this leads to his claim that *historicity* is one of the fundamental features of world-disclosure. This means that, rather than subordinate the historical contingency of particular activities of disclosure to some general ontological necessity which can be grasped philosophically through deduction of its transcendental necessity, this historical contingency is *itself* taken to be fundamental. In this way, finitude is "ontologized." The conclusion of this line of reasoning is that no particular historical formation can be read as the necessary or universal condition for the possibility of social life per se. In this case, it is the notion that a certain morality can be derived from necessary and universal epistemological claims (more specifically, arguments regarding the structure of truth claims) that ontology seeks to displace.

Taken up from the other side, however, a historical ontology cannot proceed without a commitment at least minimally to *historicity* as a fundamental feature of world-disclosure. I will attempt to demonstrate this in Chapter Six, at least with respect to Foucault, by rendering more explicit what I take to be some of his ontological commitments. Investigating such commitments, I argue, does not consist in constructing a transcendental "theory" of historicity, but rather merely referencing the very *immanence* of our understandings of the world to our practical activities. What I suggest throughout this work, therefore, is that a particular mode of social or political organization that purports to be more (or less) "free" cannot be derived from the theoretical elaboration of the transcendental conditions for social and political life. If not, then this commits one to a view of "freedom" as *situated* in the specific sense I am using of the term, namely, that "freedom" is a superordinate relationship to the immanence and finitude of oneself and one's understanding of the world: a form of acknowledgment, acceptance, and care. It simultaneously refers to practices which attempt to disclose the ossifying and totalizing effects of those features of our present ontology that conceal its historical finitude.[25] The antonym of freedom (understood ontologically), might be spoken of in terms of entrapment and (self)reification. Finally, in suggesting that this concealing produces effects on the level of ethical, social, and political life, I am attempting to demonstrate the critical import of this form of analysis without committing to the claim that such effects can be understood or explained through reference to a single, invariable, and necessary condition of ontological involvement (i.e., the "fallenness" of Dasein historically), nor to the idea that acknowledgment of indeterminacy and freedom on an ontological level can be translated directly into any particular politics. This is discussed in more detail in Chapter Three and returned to again in the book's conclusion, Chapter Seven.

My attempt to think freedom and finitude in relation to historical ontology moves through several phases, each constituting a chapter in this work. In the first chapter, I interrogate Heidegger's move to fundamental ontology in *Being and Time* as arising within the horizon of a set of problems deriving from (what I will call here) the "philosophy of the constituting subject," with particular reference to Descartes, Kant, and Husserl. The move to fundamental ontology is read therefore as an attempt to dissolve the problems arising from traditional epistemology and metaphysics. I describe this as a "move" to fundamental ontology because it supports my reading of *Being and Time*, not merely as a text with an argument, but also as an event of self-understanding in relation to the historical tradition that forms the field of possible thought against which and with which it is working. Fundamental ontology is offered as a "resolution" to problems of epistemology. But these problems are "ours"; they are historically and culturally contingent, yet necessary and unavoidable. Read this way, we can also see how fundamental ontology immediately implicates itself, since a claim to reveal the mutual implication of subject and object within an already existing "world" folds back upon the claimant—in this case Heidegger—as a "subject" of knowledge. Thus, fundamental ontology not only demands an explication of the transformation of the subject in relation to this new knowledge, but it must *itself* be seen as an attempt at self-transformation. Hence the linking of knowledge acquisition to the ethical-spiritual transformation of the subject in *Being and Time*.

Chapter Three further investigates fundamental ontology's self-implication by investigating the provisional theses posed in *Being and Time*: that (1) an epistemological domain is disclosed only through a specific ethical positioning of the subject of knowledge; and (2) that this positioning is disclosed to Dasein within the horizon of time; it is disclosed historically. Both claims, I argue, drive Heidegger to consider more centrally the question of freedom, since they demand an account of this "ethical positioning." It is argued here that "freedom" originally names the condition and feature of world-disclosure that permits this ever-present possibility of transformation. This ontological characterization of freedom—referred to in this book as "epistemological indeterminacy"—is expressed as indeterminacy, contingency, and nonclosure in the historical presencing of a lifeworld. Were world-disclosure to be reducible to a set of knowable axioms or structures, then fundamental ontology's claim to the temporal horizon of knowledge would be false. Hence, Heidegger argues that Being "evades" Dasein's attempt to know it fully. Chapter Three concludes by arguing for the necessity of a form of historical analysis to complement and complete fundamental ontology. In raising the question of historicity, *Being and Time* points the way to a mode of *authentic historicizing*, one that does not merely situate us *in* history, but rather discloses us *as historical*. Heidegger's late work on technology and modern science was, in part, an attempt to provide just such a historicized account and, furthermore, to resituate fundamental ontology within the historical and cultural location of the modern West. However, for this secondary analysis to be something more than a mere empirical history of the West, Heidegger would still need to demonstrate its connectedness to ontology and the relationship to Being. One way to do this, I argue, is to posit that some modifications at the ontic level affect and modify the very ontological structure of our existence. This thesis requires, then, a *historical* ontology of freedom.

In order to provide a more robust account of historical ontology, beginning in Chapter Four I turn to Michel Foucault. Although the ultimate goal here is to bring Foucault into a constructive dialogue with Heidegger, it is important not to carelessly conflate the two thinkers. As such, Chapter Four traces three lines within Foucault's work prior to 1979 that pose significant challenges to any attempt at rendering his oeuvre commensurate with Heidegger's. These three areas of inquiry include: (1) the historicizing of the phenomenology of experience; (2) the critique of hermeneutics; and (3) the interrogation of the analytics of finitude and its relation to a positing of "original man." Here we see that while Foucault may have in his late works arrived at similar or complementary analyses to that of Heidegger, he did so through a path of thinking that is entirely his own—driven by his own questions—many of which stand in significant tension to Heidegger's own concerns.

In Chapter Five, three "terminological equivocations" form the vehicle through which I attempt to track a key transition in Foucault's thought from 1979 to roughly 1982. By following Foucault's reformulations of the terms *conduct*, *experience*, and *thought*, I highlight the precise movement of his own thinking that characterizes this period of his work. Again, just as Heidegger's move to fundamental ontology was read as an activity of thought that transforms the subject, Foucault's texts are read here not merely to elucidate an argument but also to demonstrate the slow modifications in thought that guided Foucault's work in this period. Thematically, in the transition away from the model of war toward a game model, Foucault is revealed to have a primary concern for the space of freedom within his analysis. His understanding of freedom, moreover, is taken up increasingly as a mode or style of existence, rather than as a property of the subject or a strategic form of action outside of or in resistance to power.

Chapter Six further articulates the interrelationship between an ontological analysis of selfhood and care and a historical analysis of subjectivity by drawing out critical possibilities in Foucault's late work in relation to Heidegger. I investigate the "ontological presuppositions" of Foucault's analysis of spirituality and care of the self, arguing that his distinction between philosophy and spirituality (and their related forms of activity) commits him to an understanding of selfhood as ontologically grounded more basically in our practical involvement rather than mediated by conscious thought. The second half of this chapter elaborates on how the ontology of selfhood and care implicates a historical analysis of subjectivity in the West. Foucault's history of subjectivity, with particular reference to Descartes and Kant, is read alongside Heidegger in light of this challenge.

In the concluding chapter, I return to the matter of social criticism originally raised in Chapter Three. Chapter Seven examines various attempts to develop a critical social theory of reification over the course of the twentieth century, from Georg Lukács to Axel Honneth, which evince a concern for a certain instrumentalization of human activities and relationships. I note, however, that such theories typically conflate two different senses of "reification," one pertaining to a mode of self-interpretation and one referring to social relations between agents. The chapter then draws resources from our previous discussion of Heidegger and Foucault to recast these debates, clarifying the slippage between forms of reification as well as demonstrating how historical ontology can be employed as a tool for social criticism.

1.2. QUESTIONS OF INTERPRETATION AND INFLUENCE

The primary aim of this work is not to provide an authoritative reading of Heidegger and Foucault in all respects, nor of the relationship between the two at a biographical level, but rather to use each creatively to a particular purpose. I do not seek another tracing of the "Heideggerian" influences on Foucault, and even less a total synthesis of the two. Not only would such a project be presumptuous—obscuring the originality and depth of the works of each—but it would take us too far from the real target. The real aim is to elucidate certain indispensable features of these two figures' thought insofar as they relate to the themes of historicity, ontology, and freedom.

Despite a desire to proceed more thematically, it is nevertheless impossible to avoid altogether questions of interpretation, context, and influence. As such, two secondary concerns are raised in the course of pursuing the specific inquiry at hand. The first is a more general concern than that of the specific topic of freedom. It concerns the very possibility of combining ontological and historical forms of critical analysis. This general question received thoughtful treatment in the early work of Herbert Marcuse. The second concern is Foucault's personal relationship to Heidegger and his work. I will comment briefly on each of these in turn.

1.2.a. Marcuse's Gambit Reconsidered

It was the young Marcuse who first posed the question of how Heidegger's ontological analysis in *Being and Time* might be wedded to historical analysis and social criticism. Marcuse's early work in the 1920s and 1930s developed these questions by bringing Heidegger together in conversation with Marxism, an effort which ultimately failed (by Marcuse's own admission) but which nevertheless strikes at the heart of many of the same issues engaged in this book. While Marcuse's answer may seem problematic from the present vantage point, the *question* he first posed—of how to combine ontological and sociohistorical modes of critical analysis—remains animate and important. In Chapter Three I discuss Marcuse's contributions to this problematic in more detail, arguing that ultimately the Heideggerian notion of historicity could not be reconciled with a dialectic of historical materialism since the latter cannot accept the radical contingency and indeterminacy posited by the former. Here I will merely signal that it is Foucault's work (particularly his late writings) which offers the most promising route toward the kind of synthesis Marcuse sought.[26] The possibility that Foucault might be an important, even indispensable resource for fleshing out the social and historical implications of Heideggerian ontology, and that Foucault might be employed to pick up where Marcuse left off, may seem a provocative suggestion, if not also unconventional and counterintuitive. The idea is, in fact, suggested by passing remarks made by Marcuse in an interview late in this life. Here, Marcuse mentions that for some time he (and other students of his generation) found in Heidegger "a new beginning, the first radical attempt to put philosophy on really concrete foundations—philosophy concerned with human existence, the human condition, and not merely with abstract ideas and principles."[27] However, eventually Marcuse came to feel that Heidegger's concrete analysis of actual human existence was, in fact, a false one. He felt that because Heidegger's primary concepts of analysis (such as Dasein) were never given specific historical and social content, they were too abstract. While admitting ignorance of Heidegger's later work on technology and the age of the "world-picture," Marcuse concludes that, "if there is an ontology which, in spite of its stress on historicity, neglects history, throws out history, and returns to static transcendental concepts, I would say this philosophy cannot provide a conceptual basis for social and political theory."[28] So the challenge posed here pertains to articulating historicity in relation to concrete history (the ontological and the ontic). In response to this general formulation of the challenge, the interviewer (Fredrick Olafson) asks Marcuse of the potential for just such a rapprochement between these different forms of analysis. The interviewer suggests, "Isn't it important for a social theory to show how an individual situates himself in a certain society, in a certain condition, in a certain tradition? Isn't it important that there be a characterization of that situation that is not just given at the level of relatively impersonal forces and tendencies, but that shows how the individual ties into those forces and tendencies?"[29] To this, Marcuse replies:

> There most certainly is a need for such an analysis, but that is precisely where the concrete conditions of history come in. . . . That is very difficult. It would open up a completely new topic. The entire dimension that has been neglected in Marxian theory, for example, how social institutions reproduce themselves in the individuals, and how the individuals, by virtue of their reproducing their own society act on it. There is room for what may be called an existential analysis, but only within this framework.[30]

A more complete theoretical treatment of these matters is forthcoming in Chapter Three. However, here I would merely highlight that Marcuse's formulation of a possible social and historical analysis that would link up with ontology could be mistaken for a description of Foucault's own work. For, as outlined in more detail in Chapter Six, central to Foucault's late work is the notion that processes of socialization cannot be reduced to an either/or struggle between governors and governed, between sovereign and subject. Rather, to paraphrase Marcuse from above, social institutions are reproduced *in* individuals (through processes of subjectification), but it is *in virtue of* this function that subjects also act upon their social conditions. Social change, then, is not accounted for merely by examining the moments of "tactical resistance" whereby the sovereign subject stands out, apart from and against practices of power on him or her and, in so doing, claims sovereign power as his or her own. Rather, an analysis of such change must proceed at the level of how it is that subjects modify their social conditions while simultaneously reproducing them. This simultaneity, I argue, leads Foucault to study the *modes* of being (the study of which he conceives of as a history of ethics, distinguishable from a history of moral codes) and the practices that cultivate these modes. This links up with an ontological form of analysis because the necessary simultaneity of the reconstitution/ modification is connected to an understanding of selfhood in which "selves" are actualized in fields of practical involvement, rather than transcendental to the field of action and meaning. In other words, the study of humans in their concrete history can become a means by which we disclose ourselves to ourselves as essentially historical, and thus not determined by ahistorical, metaphysical reifications of our own design.

1.2.b. Interpreting Foucault's Heideggerianism

The second "subplot" animating much of the discussion to follow is more specific and it concerns the extent and nature of Heidegger's influence on Foucault. Since exploring this influence in a direct manner is not the primary focus of this study, references to it in the body of the book are relatively scarce. Where I have argued for a convergence of their concerns, I have largely done so without reference to whether this convergence is direct and intentional or merely coincidental. I have spent less time focusing on determining when Foucault read Heidegger, on how the former was influenced by the latter, or on how we ought to track this influence. Instead, I have tried to interpret the two as independent thinkers in their own right, with areas of concern that bring them into conversation over questions of freedom, finitude, historicity, and ontology.

That said, questions of influence cannot be avoided altogether. In particular, where it has bolstered my reading of Foucault in the direction of questions of ontology I have used evidence of Heidegger's influence as a kind of secondary support. In this final section of the introductory chapter, I will attempt now to situate the arguments that follow in the context of Foucault's supposed "Heideggerianism." This involves an overview of Foucault's own statements on Heidegger as well as brief commentary on some of the literature that has focused more specifically on the question of influence. It also involves glossing over the plethora of work that attempts to bring Heidegger and Foucault together in a constructive dialogue over specific areas of concern without explicit concern for questions of influence. This literature simply proceeds to compare and contrast the two on topics such as ethics, truth, critique, nihilism, art, *technē*, spatial organization and control, and epistemology (without concern for tracing direct causal linkages as a means of explaining any perceived convergence of thought between the two philosophers).[31]

The question of Foucault's relationship and indebtedness to Heidegger has been a source of speculation since the former's death. Such investigations are fueled by the fact that Foucault's remarks on Heidegger are rare and, at times, puzzling. This has produced a small but growing body of literature speculating on influence, but very little consensus. The literature ranges along a full spectrum of possibilities: from those who think that Foucault was "essentially" Heideggerian, to those who view their respective bodies of work as necessarily mutually exclusive. I will deal with each of these positions in turn after a quick periodization of Foucault's own comments. This section is intended to be only a cursory sketch that might serve as a map for navigating through the literature. It is not an exhaustive study.

Foucault first came to be influenced by Heidegger through the latter's influence on psychoanalysis in France.[32] Heidegger's work, particularly *Being and Time*, made an important impact on a small group of psychoanalytic thinkers and practitioners in Germany, whose work was eventually called *Daseinsanalysis*. This group included Medard Boss (who was for a time Heidegger's own analyst), Ludwig Binswanger (whose *Traum und Existenz* contained a preface by Foucault when translated into French), as well as Viktor Frankl and Karl Jaspers. It seems clear that at least during the 1950s and early 1960s Foucault was heavily influenced by Heidegger via *Daseinsanalysis*, introduced to France by Jean Beaufret. Even then, Foucault seemed to look to Heidegger as an alternative to the heavy influence of Sartre in post–World War II French philosophy (an irony, given that Sartre himself helped to popularize Heidegger in this period).[33] For instance, in comparing his own work to that of R. D. Laing, Foucault said that "[Laing] was a Sartean, I a Heideggerian."[34]

By the mid-1960s however, direct references to Heidegger drop off in Foucault's work. This silence continues throughout the genealogical works of the 1970s as well, when Nietzsche appears more prominently. Where Heidegger is mentioned it is more often than not by way of contrast to Foucault's own work. For instance, in 1966 Foucault wrote: "We can envisage, moreover, two kinds of philosopher: the kind who opens up new avenues of thought, such as Heidegger, and the kind who in a sense plays the role of an archaeologist, studying the space in which thought unfolds, as well as the conditions of that thought, its mode of constitution."[35] We might question whether Foucault is correct to identity Heidegger as someone who is less preoccupied with the "conditions of thought" than he. Regardless, given that Foucault was immersed in writing "archeological" works at this time, it stands to reason that he took himself to be less a "Heideggerian" than at a previous stage.

By the end of the 1970s and beginning of the 1980s, traces of Heidegger begin to reappear. Since it is a general theme of the work presented here that Foucault's late writings converge in some respects with Heidegger, the details of this reappearing influence are worked out in the body of the text. Here, however, it is worth pointing to several important markers of Foucault's own understanding of this influence. In 1980, Foucault signaled that in some ways his studies of the modes of subjectification might be read as complementary to Heidegger's own analysis of *technē* and the modes of objectification:

> For Heidegger, it was through an increasing obsession with *technē* as the only way to arrive at an understanding of objects, that the West lost touch with Being. Let's turn the question around and ask which techniques and practices form the Western concept of the subject, giving it its characteristic split of truth and error, freedom and constraint. I think that it is here that we will find the real possibility of constructing a history of what we have done and, at the same time, a diagnosis of what we are.[36]

In 1982, a positive relation between the two was drawn not with respect to *technē* but rather with regard to the question of truth. During the Collège de France lectures *L'herméneutique du sujet*, Foucault responded to a question from the audience saying that "only two" people in the twentieth century had sufficiently posed the question of the relationship between the subject and truth, the question: "What is the subject of truth, what is the subject who speaks the truth?" Those two were Heidegger and Lacan. He then went on to state: "It is more from the side of Heidegger and starting from Heidegger that I have tried to reflect on all this" (*Herm.*, 189; translation modified).[37]

In 1983, Foucault confirmed this connection. In commenting on work by Hubert Dreyfus and Paul Rabinow (especially *Michel Foucault: Beyond Structuralism and Hermeneutics*),[38] Foucault praised the authors for saying that "Heidegger was influential" upon his work. This claim, Foucault said, was "quite true, but no one in France [had] ever perceived it."[39]

Finally, and most famously, in the last formal interview Foucault gave before he died, he stated,

> Heidegger has always been for me the essential philosopher. I began by reading Hegel, then Marx, and I set out to read Heidegger in 1951 or 1952; then in 1952 or 1953, I no longer remember, I read Nietzsche. I still have the notes I took while reading Heidegger—I have tons of them!—and they are far more important than the ones I took on Hegel or Marx. My entire philosophical development was determined by my reading of Heidegger. I nevertheless recognize that Nietzsche prevailed over him [l'a emporté]. I don't know Heidegger well enough: I practically don't know *Being and Time* nor the things recently published. My knowledge of Nietzsche is much greater. Nevertheless, these were my two fundamental experiences. It is probable that if I had not read Heidegger, I would not have read Nietzsche. I had tried to read Nietzsche in the fifties but Nietzsche alone said nothing to me. Whereas Nietzsche and Heidegger—that was a philosophical shock! But I've never written anything on Heidegger and only a very short article on Nietzsche. I think it's important to have a small number of authors with whom one thinks, with whom one works, but on whom one doesn't write. Perhaps someday I'll write about them, but at that point they will no longer be instruments of thought for me. (*FL*, 470; *DE2*, 1522)[40]

Although this passage has been quoted often enough, what has been less noted is the question to which it is a response: "In what you describe you have found a meeting point between an experience of freedom and truth. There is at least one philosopher for whom the relationship between freedom and truth was the point of departure for Western thought: it is Heidegger who from this point founds the possibility of an ahistorical discourse. If you had Hegel and Marx in your line of sight before, don't you now have Heidegger?" (*FL*, 470; *DE2*, 1521–22). So, while it seems fairly clear that Heidegger figured more prominently (or at least more explicitly) in Foucault's very early and very late work, more or less dropping out altogether as an explicitly point of reference during the middle period, it is still not clear why this shift took place or what it means.

1.2.c. Sources of Influence

This opens up another minor controversy in Foucauldian scholarship. The debate focuses not only on the extent to which Heidegger influenced Foucault, but also *how, when,* and *why* this influence came about. As already noted above, most scholars of the topic agree that Heidegger likely first came to Foucault's attention through the *Daseinsanalysis* group. This fits best with Foucault's own periodization of his reading. What has been left less explored is how this influence via psychoanalysis was inflected and altered by Foucault's interaction with other intellectual communities at the same time.

Since Foucault himself suggested that Heidegger influenced him largely by changing his reading of Nietzsche, we are led to think that the Nietzsche lectures may have been a more central text for Foucault than *Being and Time*. This is also supported by an examination of the influence of Pierre Klossowski on Foucault, something which has remained relatively quiet in the literature on Heidegger's influence. In 1969 Klossowski published *Nietzsche et le cercle vicieux*,[41] a collection of writings decades in the making with which Foucault was already deeply familiar and by which he was highly influenced.[42] In 1971 it was Klossowski who translated Heidegger's four-volume study of Nietzsche, which some argue led to an even greater "revival of French interest in Nietzsche ... above all on Michel Foucault."[43] This certainly suggests a high level of influence mediated by Klossowski and, in particular, his reading of Nietzsche. This reading is bolstered to some extent by the 1970–71 lectures Foucault gave at the Collège de France, which contain extensive discussions of *alētheia*, which has been interpreted as a hidden dialogue with Heidegger.[44] Yet the periodization of this does not seem to fit. For if Heidegger came to influence Foucault through Klossowski's translation of the Nietzsche lectures, then the height of Heidegger's influence should have been in the late 1960s, through the 1970s, precisely the time when references to Heidegger began to drop off in Foucault's own work.

A route of influence that begins earlier and has also been relatively unexplored is through Louis Althusser. It might seem unlikely that a structuralist-Marxist such as Althusser would have found much in Heidegger to recommend his young students. There is, however, at least one feature of Heidegger's work that was undoubtedly important to Althusser and which, through him, may have influenced Foucault. This was Heidegger's antihumanism and his critique of Sartre's existentialism. Althusser himself brings together these threads in commenting on the intellectual climate of the time. He writes that Heidegger's *Letter to Jean Beaufret on Humanism* "influenced my arguments concerning *theoretical* antihumanism in Marx." As a result of this influence, Althusser was "confronted by what was being read in France, in other words, Sartre, Merleau-Ponty, Bachelard, and much later on Foucault, and above all Cavaillès and Canguilhem."[45] Althusser's remarks suggest a line of influence relatively unexplored in the scholarship. While an emphasis on influence via *Daseinsanalysis* points to *Being and Time* as a primary text for Foucault, and an emphasis on Heidegger's reading of Nietzsche as primary suggests the importance of the Nietzsche lectures, Althusser's suggestion that it was the centrality of "theoretical antihumanism" in the French reception of Heidegger that carried the most weight points to "The Letter on Humanism" and perhaps "The Age of the World Picture" as central.[46]

To say, then, that there is disagreement among scholars on the extent and nature of Heidegger's influence on Foucault, indeed even the source and timing of it, would be to considerably understate the issue. Fortunately, all this need not be definitively resolved (even if that were in principle possible). For my part, I can only observe that Foucault's direct engagement with Heidegger appears to peak in his earliest writings and then again in his latest writings and that, even in these moments, his was always a creative, nondogmatic, distinctly *Foucauldian* engagement. Any further comments on influence are reserved for the body of this book.

TWO

POTENTIALITY AND AUTHENTICITY

HEIDEGGER'S PREPARATORY EXISTENTIAL ANALYTIC IN *BEING AND TIME*

THE PURPOSE OF THIS CHAPTER is to reconstruct the preparatory analytic of freedom articulated in *Being and Time*. I chose the terms *reconstruct* and *preparatory analytic* advisedly. First, those familiar with Heidegger may immediately raise the objection that *Being and Time* is not a text on practical philosophy traditionally understood, and that, even more to the point, the concept of freedom is given no extended discussion within the text. Second, to the extent that freedom is considered within the text it surely belongs to Division I, which Heidegger himself describes as only "preparatory."

Both objections are accepted. I do not take them to be the final word on the issue, however, and neither offers definitive reasons as to why a "reconstruction" of an analysis of freedom cannot be undertaken. The text, insofar as it lays out Heidegger's basic and most comprehensive statement on human subjectivity and agency, is the definitive backdrop to any other writings he might have offered on the concept of freedom specifically. Any reading of freedom in other, later texts has to run through *Being and Time* first. The fact that the text does not directly thematize the concept (at least, rarely naming it as such) does not mean that *Being and Time* is not central to understanding Heidegger on the question of freedom. Indeed, as I will argue below, freedom is theorized indirectly within the text, though it tends to be presented under the guise of authenticity [*eigentlichkeit*] and potentiality-for-being [*Seinkönnen*].

In these two terms, we see Heidegger preparing the basis of his analysis of freedom as (1) a condition of world-disclosure (potentiality); and (2) an ethical self-positioning in relation to such conditions (authenticity). Second, even though the analysis of freedom offered in *Being and Time* is preparatory in the sense that it does not aspire to a fully comprehensive or fundamental ontology, it is nevertheless essential. Such analysis may not be complete, but it is necessary. In this sense, I naturally concede that the analysis of freedom in *Being and Time* is preparatory.

The importance of Heidegger's preparatory analytic of freedom is that it provides the basic framework for understanding why potentiality is the ground of Dasein's being. If we can demonstrate that potentiality is fundamental to Dasein's constitution, not as a metaphysical "thing," but rather as an existential a priori, then several important developments for thinking about freedom follow:

1. Potentiality-for-being is foundational and, as Charles Taylor phrases it, prior to any attempt at the "ontologizing of rational procedure" (as seen in [neo]Kantian rationalism).[1]

2. Since potentiality-for-being is claimed as an existential a priori, it is not a feature of human will or cognition, and cannot be understood through a reconstruction of "pure" mind, will, or nonheterogeneous agency. It can only be accounted for through an understanding of human agency as fully "embedded" within lifeworlds that, while always structured by factical conditions, are also always open to modification over time.

3. Freedom can then be reconceptualized as an open-ended activity of ethical self-transformation through lifeworld modification, rather than submission to norm or rule governance as determined by ontologized reason.

4. The resulting conception of freedom will be nonteleological in the sense that it will not develop historically toward the predetermined telos of rational maturity (understood as a self fully submissive to the structure of reason itself). Let me unpack these ideas.

To approach a text as large, complex, and unwieldy as *Being and Time*, one must begin by limiting the scope and making conceptual distinctions for the task at hand. As stated above, I propose only a targeted (noncomprehensive) reading of *Being and Time*, aimed specifically at making explicit how preparatory work toward a theory of situated freedom is developed within the text. In the narrow Heideggerian sense of the term, I am proposing an Interpretation [*Auslegung*] of situated freedom—a theoretical account that makes explicit through a demonstration of the as-structure [*Als-Struktur*] of freedom which was always operational (in this case, within the larger project of a fundamental ontology) but remained only implicit. The conceptual distinction that I apply to the text in order to separate out the task at hand is between *experiential*, *existential*, and *ontological* levels of analysis. To understand what this means requires a brief explanation of Heidegger's phenomenology.

Part of Heidegger's project in *Being and Time* is to replace Husserl's bracketing of the experiential lifeworld [*Lebenswelt*] by foregrounding it and making it central not only thematically (as an object of study) but also methodologically (as a means of study). Thematically, Heidegger wants to demonstrate that knowledge is grounded in the experiential lifeworld and that abstract, detached, theoretical knowledge is merely derivative of the more basic and seamless kind of knowing that enables everyday life, named by Heidegger as Understanding [*Verstehen*]. The purpose of developing this account is, in part, to critique an epistemological-cognitivist picture of human subjectivity and agency, one in which humans are thought first and foremost to encounter the world through a stance of detached contemplation, mediated by conscious conceptualization. To advance such a critique, however, Heidegger would need to make this rather abstract and theoretical point by *beginning from* and *grounding it in* the everyday experiential lifeworld. This insight is the basis of Heidegger's reformulation of phenomenology. Heideggerian phenomenology means beginning from the *experiential* world. The experiential level of analysis is the description of everyday moods, states of mind, and practices. Examples from *Being and Time* are numerous and include, for instance, Being-with [*Mit-Sein*], Dread [*Angst*] and Fear [*Furcht*].

From these particular experiential modes of being and acting, Heidegger demonstrates how we can, through reflection on their meaning, reveal a new level of analysis: the *existential*. When we use an aspect of the experiential lifeworld, reflect on its *as-structure* (e.g., what is fear *as/qua* fear?), we can open up a new level of questioning—the existential—and begin to question the *as-structure* of oneself (i.e., what is Dasein *as/qua* Dasein?). To employ an example, we can observe the transition from experiential to existential in the following: I see a dog snarling at me and feel afraid (experiential). Later, I reflect on the experience and wonder: "*Why* was I afraid?" "What was the *meaning* of this fear?" "What does it *reveal* about me?" Of course, we might give a psychological explanation: my fear of dogs stems from a close encounter at some early stage in life, such that I continue to feel fear now, even when it is irrational to do so (e.g., if the dog is secured on a leash). However, Heidegger suggests that upon reflection I would note that this fear may also reveal that I have a certain concern for my own existence, and that the world *matters* to me. These characteristics of Dasein's existence that serve as the a priori conditions of possibility for the particular experiential moods (such as fear or dread) Heidegger calls "existentials." Even though existentials stand a priori to the experiential level of knowledge, we would be mistaken to see them as fixed properties of Dasein's being in the way, for example, brittleness or solidity are properties of glass. Rather, as Heidegger clearly states, "those characteristics which can be exhibited in this entity are not 'properties' present-at-hand of some entity which 'looks' so and so and is itself present-at-hand; they are in each case *possible ways for it to be, and no more than that*" (BTa §9, 67; SZ §9, 42; italics added). Generally speaking, then, personal experience can, when reflected upon, lead to insights into the existential a priori conditions which structure Dasein's concernful relations with the world and itself.

From this second level of analysis (existential), we can move to the third and most basic: the ontological. Once I have inquired into what it means for me to be, and possibly even provided some rudimentary answer to this (Heidegger's answer to the question of what it means for Dasein to be is Care, which will be explicated below), we can then possibly even move to the final, most basic question: What does it mean for *anything* to be? Or, simply, what is Being? This final level of analysis Heidegger calls "fundamental ontology," and it is the primary aim of *Being and Time* to provide an answer to this question. The first two levels of analysis (the concern of Division I) are merely preparatory in the sense that they only hint at the final question (dealt with in Division II) and do not directly answer it, though they are necessary in the sense that they demonstrate the foundational role of the experiential lifeworld to all knowledge.

I draw attention to this threefold structure of analysis in *Being and Time*, not only to help explicate the text, but also to explain and justify the narrowing of my own inquiry. Since I am concerned with explicating situated freedom and its antonym as they implicate *human lives*, I am almost exclusively concerned with the first two levels of analysis (the experiential and the existential). This also speaks to my method of narrowing the bulk of my reading to Division I, later drawing on themes from Division II (especially historicity) only insofar as they are relevant to our primary investigation.

2.1. FREEDOM BETWEEN ACTUALITY AND POTENTIALITY

Heidegger begins his analysis of the *Seinsfrage*—or, the question of the meaning of Being—with oneself, with Dasein. Since we enter into the very question of being through the level of the experiential (that is, through experiences we have with everyday life and not beginning with theoretical or abstract contemplation): "The Being of any such entity is *in each case mine*" (BTa §9, 67; SZ §9, 41). The entry point for analysis of all Dasein, and indeed for all Being, is reflection on my own personal existence. This does not mean that each should conflate their personal experience with the existential condition of all. Rather, it refers only to the initial object of inquiry, which, through careful study, can reveal a more general level of analysis. It also demonstrates that hermeneutic self-inquiry is the initial methodology of analysis. One begins an inquiry through a realization and interpretation of the meaning of one's own personal experience in the world. This integrates practical and theoretical knowledge since theoretical knowledge is itself taken to be merely a translated and refined version of everyday understanding, one which strives above all to preserve the way meaning makes itself known to us in everyday practices. Finally, in terms of content, this exposes the fact that we, as Dasein, are capable of reflecting upon our own existence. Hence, Heidegger's other famous (and famously misunderstood) claim that "The 'essence' of Dasein is its existence" (BTa §9, 67;

SZ §9, 42). Dasein, by its very definition, is one that *is* (defined in terms of its possible ways of existing) and one who has the capacity to reflect upon this existence. In later works, Heidegger highlights Dasein's capacity to stand "out" from its own various everyday modes of being by often hyphenating *Ek-istenz*, drawing attention to the etymological root of *Ekistenz* in the Latin *existere*: to stand out.

So what does the capacity to "stand out" from one's everyday experiential lifeworld and reflect upon it (thus moving to the existential level of analysis) tell us about freedom? This capacity for existential reflection opens up a new space between actuality and potentiality and it is in this space where Heidegger's conception of freedom has its grounding. We are never merely defined by what is given in our social, cultural, and historical conditions (the actual), not only because we also possess the capacity to "stand out from" and reflect upon these conditions (suggesting we are in excess of them), but also because these conditions are always already a function of ongoing interpretation (i.e., potentiality is "in" the worldly conditions themselves). Before proceeding directly to this, however, it is first necessary to trace the line of Heidegger's argument in order to demonstrate how he attempts to ground the claims with respect to freedom. I will do this by briefly looking at the first existential analytic, "worldliness" or "worldhood" [*Weltlichkeit*] (SZ §§14–24), before proceeding to Being-in as such (SZ §§–28-38) and, in particular, Understanding [*Verstehen*] (SZ §§31–32).

2.2. EXISTENTIAL ANALYTIC I: "WORLDHOOD" (§§9–24)

The first and most general of the existentials discussed in *Being and Time* is that of Being-in-the-world [*In-der-Welt-sein*]. In this section of the text, Heidegger sets himself two tasks. First, he must determine what it means to Be-in-the-world. As we shall see later, in the discussion of the second existential, for Heidegger an analysis of the *meaning* of something always refers to it as an object of Interpretation [*Auslegung*], or detached theoretical consideration that attempts to link the as-structure of an object of inquiry (that is, what the thing is *as that thing*, and not *as* something else: in relation to its determinative, defining characteristic within the given scope of the inquiry) to its fore-structure (that is, the background field of practices and knowledge required to make such an object appear *as* an object of inquiry at all). In the special sense that Heidegger uses the term, then, he needs in this first section to expose the ontological *meaning* of Being-in-the-world.

Second, Heidegger needs to demonstrate that this mode of being is an existential a priori. This means that he would need to demonstrate that no inquiry could begin at all if it were not for the already existing mode of being known as Being-in-the-world. If Being-in-the-world can be demonstrated to be the presupposition of knowledge, then it will be grounded as an existential a priori.

In order to get at what he means by Being-in-the-world, and how he grounds this as an existential a priori, Heidegger suggests dissecting the two parts of the phrase and studying them independently. He begins with "Being-in" as an existential of Dasein. To understand Being-in, Heidegger distinguishes between two senses of the preposition *in*. On the one hand, *in* denotes location and spatial relationship—Heidegger's examples include phrases like "the water is 'in' the glass," or "the garment is 'in' the closet" (*SZ* §12, 54). However, the preposition *in*—like other prepositions such as *at* and *on*—may also refer to a state of engagement or a mode of being, as in the sentences "He is hard *at* work" or "She is *in* love." Heidegger highlights this second sense by noting the etymological connection between *in* and *innan-*, meaning "to reside" or *habitare*, "to dwell" (*BTa* §12, 80; *SZ* §12, 54). It is this second sense of the term *in* (related to engagement, habitation, or dwelling with) that Heidegger demonstrates "Being-in, on the other hand, is a state of Dasein's Being; it is an existential" (*BTa* §12, 79; *SZ* §12, 54). We are *existentially involved* in the world. And, we will see, the emphasis Heidegger places on our necessarily involvement (our "Being-in") leads to his later understanding of "freedom" as a particular mode or manner of involvement, engagement, or Being-in-the-world, rather than a detached standing or status to be achieved over against such worldly conditions.

The "World" in Heidegger's existential sense does not merely refer to our physical surroundings or environment. Such a natural scientific mode of seeing the world as a set of physical parts, Heidegger argues, "must presuppose and constantly employ," the structure of the "World" as existential (*BTa* §12, 84; *SZ* §12, 58). The world, therefore, refers to the totality of meaningful relations that one always finds oneself within. My environment [*Umwelt*] is a relational field in which things and humans come before my awareness, change me, and are changed by me. It is the minimal condition for the very possibility of Dasein (that is, a being that questions its own existence), since one cannot *not* have a "world" in this sense because anything that is rendered intelligible at all must already exist within some field of meaning. As such, "world" is not meant to be taken as an ontic category—as a "thing" that "exists." Rather, it is an existential a priori of Dasein's mode of being. Dasein, by its very constitution is always *in* (engaged, busy, and concerned with) a *world* (totality of meaningful relations with other beings). The a priori mode of being that permits anything at all to matter to us, or to be rendered intelligible, is this Being-in-the-world.[2]

Within this world, Dasein encounters other beings in two basic ways: ready-to-hand and present-at-hand (*SZ* §§15–16).[3] Ready-to-hand [*Zuhanden*] is the primary mode of relating to other beings, in both chronology and importance. Dasein simply moves through the world encountering other beings within a seamless relational field. Other beings are "equipment" [*Zeug*], not in the pejorative sense of an object to be used, but rather as functional beings whose existence for us is linked intimately to their use and their relationship to other beings—including Dasein itself. This explains why "taken strictly, there 'is' no such thing as *an* equipment" (*BTa* §15, 97; *SZ* §15, 68), why one always encounters a "relational totality of equipment"—*ein Zeugganzes*. It is only in certain special cases, such as malfunction, temporary breakdown, or unavailability of equipment, that something is encountered as present-at-hand [*Vorhanden*]: "If knowing is to be possible as a way of determining the nature of the present-at-hand by observing it, then there must first be a *deficiency* in our having-to-do with the world concernfully" (*BTa* §13, 88; *SZ* §13, 61). In this case, other beings are encountered more as a series of detached objects. This is the mode in which a mechanic would approach a broken-down car, or a medical scientist might look at skin cells. It is important to note even at this early juncture that Heidegger is not normatively privileging the mode of ready-to-hand. It is not "wrong" to encounter things as present-at-hand. In fact, it is an important way of relating to other beings and obviously opens up new possibilities for knowledge (as, for example, in the natural sciences). What is wrong is to think that the mode of present-at-hand is primary (as is explicit in Descartes (*SZ* §§18–24) and, as Heidegger will later argue, implicit in Kant), or to think that one can *only* encounter the world as present-at-hand. Heidegger is reminding us in this section that even when we relate to X as present-at-hand, there is a whole field of other beings which we are simultaneously relating to as ready-to-hand and it is only because we are relating to these other things as ready-to-hand that viewing X as present-at-hand is even possible.

Finally, Heidegger extends the logic of the existential analytic to include spatiality [*Raumlichkeit*] (*SZ* §§22–24). If our primary mode of relating to the world is ready-to-hand, then spatiality of Dasein's being is also a priori established. It is only because we exist within a spatial field which we unconsciously know and seamlessly negotiate that we can relate to things as near to us and available qua equipment.

In all these existentials (ready-to-hand, present-at-hand, spatiality), Heidegger has attempted to demonstrate that epistemological theories that attempt to reconstruct the conditions for knowledge from the standpoint of a worldless, noumenal self will necessarily miss the crucial element of embodiment's foundational place in knowledge and subject formation. These theoretical models occlude the mutual relatedness of the acquisition of knowledge, on the one hand, and the positioning or ethical involvement of the subject of knowledge, on the other hand. They miss how the supposedly detached, objectifying stance of theoretical cognition is not, in an important sense, truly "detached" at all. It is a stance or mode of involvement as embedded in the world as any other, though it may not "know" itself as such and is thus self-concealing in some relevant manner. This means that the theories of freedom which I have described in Chapter One as "transcendental" and "teleological" will not be sufficient. After all, it is one thing to say that a subject must be able to "appropriate" norms and rules of conduct (to accept or refuse them as an act of "free will"), as though they are external objects. It is quite a different matter to say that the already existing ethical relations between entities establishes the ontological field in which a subject can emerge at all. In the first instance, the norms are there, at an exterior distance, and the task is to find a way of appropriating or refusing them, establishing a practical relationship to them.

The epistemological frame is presupposed in this encounter, one in which a subject encounters moral norms and must find his way within them. In Heidegger's analysis, however, we are *Da-sein*, located-being, which means that there is an ontological relationship between oneself and one's world, not merely an epistemic one. What is required is a theory of situated freedom, in which the existential commitment, or ethical involvement of the subject of knowledge is foregrounded and interpreted in its relation to selfhood and, in particular, agency.

2.3. SELFHOOD (§§25–27), BEING-IN (§§28–39), AND UNDERSTANDING (§§31–32)

To this point, Heidegger has sought to establish that Dasein exists always already within a world of meaning, that it relates to this world in two basic ways—ready-to-hand (primary) and present-at-hand (secondary)—that its being is embodied spatially and that it is capable of asking the question of the meaning of this existence. Now we must demonstrate more specifically what kind of world Dasein finds itself in and how, if at all, it can modify this world. This requires working through Heidegger's concept of "Understanding" [*Verstehen*]. Despite the relative brevity of the section on Understanding, it is clearly of central importance to Heidegger's work generally and, in particular, to any attempt to reconstruct an analysis of human freedom. It is here that Heidegger begins to develop a theory of selfhood. Furthermore, and perhaps most importantly for the question of freedom, it is here that Heidegger makes the distinction between the mode of the actual and the mode of the possible. Since in the context of the question of freedom the two parts of this analytic (selfhood and understanding) are so intimately related, I deal with them together.

Understanding is so important to an analysis of freedom because it grounds Dasein's potentiality-for-being [*Seinkönnen*]: the capacity to be something other than what is given to one in the present. In order to appreciate the radical nature of potentiality, we must approach it from the actual first. Heidegger introduces the mode of the actual through the term *Befindlichkeit* (SZ §29). This term is notoriously difficult to translate,[4] but the most literal translation is "state or condition in which one finds oneself." Since this is too long and cumbersome a phrase, I shall employ "disposition" here, though it is important not to think of this in terms of a cognitive or psychological state. Quite the opposite. Heidegger makes clear that we do not "have" a disposition; it "has" us. Therefore, it is only through a "disclosive submission" [erschließende Angewiesenheit] or acknowledgment that *"we can encounter something that matters to us"* (BTa §29, 177; SZ §29, 137–38).[5] There are three main features or inner capacities latent within disposition that can be revealed to us: the capacity to disclose (1) Being-in-the-world; (2) "thrownness," and; (3) circumspective concern [*umsichtig besorgende*], defined as the ability to become affected [*Betroffenwerdens*] by the world because it *matters* to Dasein (SZ §29, 137).

We have already sketched out "Being-in-the-world" and observed it as a mode of being in which other beings exist in a relational totality that matters for Dasein. Since the fact that beings "matter" for Dasein demonstrates that Dasein already has a relation to them, it also demonstrates that Dasein is always already in a Mood [*Stimmung*], not in the sense of a psychological state or a feeling,[6] but in the sense of a general condition that draws together all the beings within a field of intelligibility and meaning. The notion of a Mood purposefully links, for Heidegger, three components of a fundamental ontology normally seen as analytically distinct in the epistemological tradition: (1) the acquisition of knowledge; (2) the ethical-positioning of the subject of knowledge; and (3) the disclosure of a domain of objects about which knowledge claims can obtain. In this sense, therefore, "I" do not have a mood. Rather, "I," together in a relation with other beings proximal to me, *find myself* in a mood: "An entity of the character of Dasein is its 'there' in such a way that, whether explicitly or not, it finds itself [sich befindet] in its thrownness. In this condition of being found [Befindlichkeit] Dasein is always brought before itself, and has always already found itself, *not* through a coming before itself in *perception*, but rather as a finding itself [sich befinden] as being in a mood [gestimmtes]" (SZ §29, 135).[7] Since being in a mood is the presupposition for awareness of oneself and the world, it is the means by which one comes to perceptive awareness and thus is "primordial ... *prior to* all cognition and volition, and *beyond* their range of disclosure" (BTa §29, 175; SZ §29, 136). This is why Dasein can never be fully free of moods [*stimmungsfrei*] (SZ §29, 136). One of the characteristics of our actual disposition, then, is this "being within a mood," which is the means by which we are "brought before ourselves," whether explicitly or not.

The second major characteristic of our disposition is "thrownness" [*Geworfenheit*]. For Heidegger, *thrownness* "is meant to suggest the *facticity of its being delivered over*" (*BTa* §29, 174; *SZ* §29, 135); it is the characteristic of our disposition "in which facticity lets itself be seen phenomenally" (*BTa* §38, 223; *SZ* §38, 179). So, thrownness is that characteristic of our disposition that permits Facticity [*Faktizität*] to come to awareness. What is "facticity," as differentiated from factuality? Heidegger explains facticity in two important sections:

> Dasein understands its ownmost Being in the sense of a certain "factual Being-present-at-hand." And yet the "factuality" of the fact [Tatsache] of one's own Dasein is at bottom quite different ontologically from the factual occurrence of some kind of mineral, for example. Whenever Dasein is, it is as a Fact; and the factuality of such a Fact is what we shall call Dasein's "*facticity*." This is a definite way of Being [Seinsbestimmtheit], and it has a complicated structure which cannot even be grasped *as a problem* until Dasein's basic existential states have been worked out. The concept of "facticity" implies that an entity "within-the-world" has Being-in-the-world in such a way that it can understand itself as bound up in its "destiny" with the Being of those entities which it encounters within its own world. (*BTa* §12, 82; *SZ* §12, 56)

And:

> *Facticity is not the factuality of the factum brutum of something present-at-hand, but a characteristic of Dasein's Being—one which has been taken up into existence, even if proximally it has been thrust aside.* (*BTa* §29, 174; *SZ* §29, 135; italics in original)

In other words, we are physical, empirically thrown, creatures that find ourselves in circumscribed circumstances. However, we can (in fact, we *must*) continually interpretively engage with these circumstances, which always involves working out the range of possibilities projected in them. Thus we are "bound up with" our specific factual world (our "destiny"), but not determined by it. If our disposition did not have this characteristic, then facticity could not be seen phenomenally and thus could not be rendered intelligible or the object of study. Since we can know at least the fact of our facticity, we know that our condition has such a feature.

In summary, then, the mode of the actual—the disposition, state, or condition in which Dasein always already finds itself [*Befindlichkeit*]—is characterized by: (1) existence within a relational totality of beings that matter (a world), which is (2) shown to us through the mood we are always already in, and (3) conditioned by a facticity that can be shown phenomenally to Dasein's awareness.

2.4. MODE OF THE POSSIBLE

Where Heidegger's existential analytic in *Being and Time* becomes most interesting for a study on freedom is in the move beyond actuality into the realm of potentiality. To this point, we have attempted to demonstrate the main characteristics of the realm of the actual (Being-in-the-world, mood, thrownness, and facticity). However, rather than define Dasein merely by what it *is* in its determinate facticity, Heidegger insightfully demonstrates that Dasein's meaning also consists in what it *can be*. One of the unique characteristics of human being is that we need not rest content with things merely as they are, but rather also have the capacity to alter our present and live differently. However, paradoxically, we do so from within circumscribed, factical horizons which we must "come to terms with" in order to relate to authentically. The first step in this consists in the coming to awareness of our potentiality-for-being [*Seinkönnen*]. The question that Heidegger must confront then is what it means precisely to "come to awareness" of this potentiality. My reading of this tradition is that a "coming to awareness," or a "realization" of something such as potentiality consists not in a theoretical or conceptual grasp of the theme in the abstract. Rather, it is to *be* in this manner, such that potentiality is made manifest through a working out of possibilities latent within worldly activities in which one is engaged.

Grounding an analysis of possibilities or potentiality within the existential analytic would require that Heidegger demonstrate potentiality to be internally related to the basic conditions for knowledge itself. In other words, the challenge is to begin from everyday questioning of our world and arrive at a full demonstration of how possibilities for living differently are already presupposed within such a questioning. How is it possible to ground potentiality this way?

Heidegger argues that for one's being to arrive as a theme of inquiry (that is, to move from experiential to existential levels of analysis) one must already have a preconceptual understanding of the possibility of not-being. I cannot question my own existence except through recognition of the possibility of my nonexistence, that is, the recognition that my existence is not necessary, not logically required; it is not the only possible way for things to be. Just as we moved from the experiential to the existential, we can extend the argument from the existential level to the level of fundamental ontology and state that, likewise, to inquire into the significance of Being means recognizing the possibility of non-Being (or nothingness). It is to ask the question: Why is there something rather than nothing? Within this question is an implicit understanding of the internal relation between actuality and potentiality, or at least that knowledge of actuality is conditional upon knowledge of potentiality. Thus, to even grasp the question of one's own existence (or of Being itself) as a question, one must already be aware of possibilities that diverge from the mode of the actual. Hence Heidegger's claim regarding the internal relation between understanding and potentiality-for-being: "*Understanding is the existential Being of Dasein's own potentiality for Being; and it is so in such a way that this Being discloses in itself what its Being is capable of*" (BTa §31, 184; SZ §31, 144; italics in the original).

Heidegger grounds this priority of potentiality through a demonstration of the operation of understanding itself. The surprisingly short section of *Being and Time* devoted to Understanding [*Verstehen*] (§§31–32) is, therefore, of great importance to our analysis here. As Michael Gelven argues, Understanding is a crucial category within the structure of *Being and Time* for three reasons: (1) it provides an account, within the existential analytic, of how it is possible that Dasein is aware of its own possibilities; (2) it provides the basis for Heidegger's theory of interpretation, which is particularly important as Heidegger clearly considers the whole of *Being and Time* to be an *Interpretation* of the *Seinsfrage*; and (3) it provides the basis for Heidegger's theory of freedom, further elaborated elsewhere.[8]

2.5. UNDERSTANDING AND PROJECTION

Understanding [*Verstehen*] has three basic characteristics: as-structure, fore-structure, and meaning. A detailed analysis of each is not necessary here, though we must briefly sketch each in order to understanding the relation between understanding and projection, in turn demonstrating how Heidegger attempts to ground the priority of potentiality within the structure of understanding itself.

The As-structure [*Als-Struktur*] of a thing refers to the "for-the-sake-of-which" [*Um-zu*], defined in its assignment, reference, or relation [*Verweistung*] (*SZ* §15, 68) to other things (in this case, Dasein itself) that makes a thing appear *as* said thing to Dasein's everyday understanding. It is the purpose or utility of a thing within the relational world of meaning that makes up our everyday realm of coping activity. The purpose, or "in-order-to" of a thing is always already present within its constitution as an object of inquiry for Dasein because it could not appear *as* said thing except within what Heidegger calls *ein Zeugganzes* (*SZ* §15, 68)—rendered here as "totality or general field of things." This relates to Heidegger's earlier point that our understanding of the world is based in the mode of ready-to-hand. One does not encounter objects in their bare isolation and then add a meaning to them. Rather, "objects" (studied in the mode of present-at-hand) are always first "things" (functional and experienced as ready-to-hand). Interpretation [*Auslegung*] merely makes explicit the meaning of the thing which was already grasped by Understanding through the working out of possibilities already latent within everyday use of things as equipment: "This development of the understanding we call 'interpretation'. . . . In interpretation, understanding does not become something different. It becomes itself. Such interpretation is grounded existentially in understanding; the latter does not arise from the former. Nor is interpretation the acquiring of information about what is understood; it is rather the working-out of possibilities projected in understanding" (*BTa* §32, 188–89; *SZ* §32, 148).

The second characteristic of Understanding is fore-structure [*Vor-Struktur*]. If Interpretation merely makes explicit the already possessed understanding of a thing, then the aspects of knowledge which prefigure the interpretation can be referred to as the fore-structure. The fore-structure of understanding has three parts: (1) fore-having [*Vorhabe*];

(2) fore-seeing [*Vorsicht*]; and (3) fore-grasping [*Vorgriff*] (*SZ* §32, 150). Fore-having refers to the "totality of involvement" [*Bewandtnisganzheit*] that serves as the background to conscious thought. It is the preconceptual, embodied practices of relating to things and other selves that make functioning within a realm of meaning possible; the totality of the habitualized patterns of thinking and acting that make everyday coping possible. Importantly, such habitualized practices are noncognitive. That is to say, they do not consist in an explicitly or implicitly held theory or picture of the world in order for them to function and, as such, "need not be grasped explicitly by a thematic interpretation" (*BTa* §32, 191; *SZ* §32, 150) in order to "give" them meaning or make them functional. Rather, such practices are held together by nothing more than repeated activity, pointing to the immanence of our understandings of the world to our practical activities.

Fore-seeing refers to the knowledge or reflective standpoint one has when the thing in question is explicitly thought as a thing. When something occurs to detach the thing in question from its functional relation to the world of equipment (as in cases of breakdown), a basic knowledge of the thing and its relation to other things is mobilized. This knowledge need not be made explicit in the sense of theorization or articulation. Rather, it refers only to a basic cognitive awareness of the thing *as* said thing which allows one to recognize, for example, an instance of breakdown. If my car doesn't start in the morning, I might instinctively look under the hood. This demonstrates a basic knowledge of what a car is and how it works, but it does not require any explicit thinking about the purpose or as-structure of a car (i.e., I need not ask: what *are* cars?).

The third aspect of the fore-structure of understanding is fore-grasping. This is the explicitly thought level of analysis. It refers to the detached standpoint of the observer who is attempting to analyze a thing in relation to its purpose or as-structure. It functions in terms of a specific conception (a quasi hypothesis) by which the as-structure is made explicit. Thinking again of the broken-down car, it is the point at which I stand back from my car, thinking about what might be wrong with it, that prevents it from functioning as a car (thus, for example, a car that doesn't start might make a great art installation, but it does not function qua car).

The third aspect of Understanding (along with as-structure and fore-structure) is meaning [*Bedeutsamkeit*]. Meaning refers to the awareness of the as-structure of a thing. To understand the meaning of a thing, we must grasp it in terms of its function and utility within the relational totality of equipment that Dasein engages with during everyday coping. It is to understand the thing *as* that thing (*SZ* §32, 151). Since Dasein alone can think about and make explicit the as-structure of a thing, only Dasein can comprehend meaning (by the same token, only Dasein can be meaningless). No theoretically held position can have meaning, therefore, except as a making explicit of an already existing functional relationality of things as they are employed (ready-to-hand) by Dasein. Propositional meaning (the meaning of a statement or proposition) is, therefore, derivative of experiential, precognitive meaning embedded within a form of life. One does not "add" meaning to a thing in its isolation; rather, one encounters it already existing within a field of involvement: "In interpreting, we do not, so to speak, throw a 'signification' over some naked thing which is present-at-hand, we do not stick a value on it; but when something within-the-world is encountered as such, the thing in question already has an involvement which is disclosed in our understanding of the world, and this involvement is one which gets laid out by the interpretation" (*BTa* §32, 190–91; *SZ* §32, 150).⁹ Meaning, therefore, is a mode of being—"ein Existential des Daseins" (*SZ* §32, 151)—and thus must be analyzed at the level of ontology, not merely that of epistemology. The importance of this insight (particularly as a break with neo-Kantian rationalism) will become central to our argument about freedom in the sections to follow.¹⁰

How does the structure of Understanding ground the priority of potentiality? Heidegger addresses this question specifically in a dense, important passage, worth quoting at length:

> Warum dringt das Verstehen nach allen wesenhaften Dimensionen des in ihm Ershließbaren immer in die Möglichkeiten? Weil das Verstehen an ihm selbst die existenziale Struktur hat, die wir den *Entwurf* nennen. Es entwirft das Sein des Daseins auf sein Worumwillen ebenso ursprünglich wie auf die Bedeutsamkeit als die Weltlichkeit seiner jeweiligen Welt. Der Entwurfcharakter des Verstehens knostituiert das In-der-Welt-sein hinsichtlich der Erschlossenheit seines Da als Da eines Seinkönnens. *Der Entwurf is die*

> *existenziale Seinsverfassung des Spielraums des faktischen Seinkönnens. Und als geworfenes ist das Dasein in die Seinsart des Entwerfens geworfen. Das Entwerfen hat nichts zu tun mit einem Sichverhalten zu einem ausgedacten Plan, gemäß dem das Dasein sein Sein einrichtet, sondern als Dasein hat es sich je schon entworfen und ist, solange es ist, entwerfend. Dasein versteht sich immer schon und immer noch, solange es ist, aus Möglichkeiten. Der Entwurfcharakter des Verstehens besagt ferner, daß dieses das, woraufhin es entwirft, die Möglichkeiten, selbst nicht thematisch erfaßt. Solches Erfassen benimmt dem Entworfenen gerade seinen Möglichkeitscharakter, zieht es herab zu einem gegebenen, gemeinten Bestand, während der Entwurf im Werfen die Möglichkeit als Möglichkeit sich vorwirft und als solche sein läßt. Das Verstehen ist, als Entwerfen, die Seinsart des Daseins, in der es seine Möglichkeiten als Möglichkeiten ist.* (SZ §31, 145; italics added)

In this case, I will offer my own translation in text so as to facilitate the particular interpretation I am advancing:

> Why does Understanding always press forward into possibilities, whatever the essential dimensions of that which can be disclosed in it? It is because Understanding has *in itself* the existential structure of what we call *Projection*. It [Understanding] projects Dasein's Being upon its "for-the-sake-of-which" [*Worumwillen*] and, equiprimordially, upon its Meaning as the worldhood of its current world. The projection-character of Understanding constitutes the Being-in-the-world with regard to the disclosedness of its "there" as a "therein-potentiality-for-being." *Projection is the existential condition of being by which factical potentiality-for-being has its "maneuver room."* And as thrown is Dasein thrown into the kind of being that is projection. Projection has nothing to do with comporting oneself toward a plan that has been thought out, according to which Dasein would arrange its Being, but, rather, *as* Dasein, it has already projected itself and, as long as it *is*, it is projecting. Dasein always understands itself and always will understand itself, as long as it *is*, in terms of possibilities. Furthermore, the projection-character of Understanding is such that the Understanding does not grasp thematically that upon which it projects—that is to say, possibilities. Grasping it in such a

manner would take away from what is projected its very character as a possibility, and would reduce it to the given contents which we have in mind; whereas projection, in throwing, throws before itself the possibility as possibility, and lets it *be* as such. As projecting, understanding is the kind of Being of Dasein in which it *is* its possibilities as possibilities.[11]

How can we take this difficult passage and understand it through the question of freedom as potentiality for being, grounded in the very structure of Understanding? First, Heidegger is arguing that it is only through the projection of possibilities that the as-structure of a thing can be made explicit and thus, meaning can be revealed. Projection [*Entwerfen*] refers to the fact that one's everyday coping is always organized by a "for-the-sake-of-which" [*Worumwillen*] that makes particular plans possible within this realm. When one interrogates the meaning of a thing, Projection makes explicit the "for-the-sake-of-which" that organizes the realm which rendered the thing intelligible in the first place. It is important to note here that the "for-the-sake-of-which" that organizes a realm of practices, equipment, or language is not *given* by Dasein. Rather, Dasein always *finds* itself within this world, which already has a comportment toward certain practices and languages of meaning. This is why Heidegger cautions us against thinking of projection as a "plan" that Dasein might have which points to the future. Rather, the relationship is the other way around: projection "has" Dasein. What Dasein can do, however, is make this structure explicit and, in so doing, unveil *meaning*. That is why Heidegger can say that Understanding only comes about and the world only has meaning because of Dasein's capacity to project possibilities without falling into a decisionistic theory of meaning whereby humans simply "place" meaning onto things in the world. The world exists prior, complete with a structure of *Worumwillen*. Dasein, through the inherent projecting function of understanding, brings this meaning to light. To be a self-interpreting creature is to find oneself in a meaningful world, where that meaning has a future orientation, collectively sustained and modified by a community of meaning-interpreting others, without any *one* person deciding on assigning this meaning or giving it a "plan."

If Understanding (the embodied knowledge that makes coping in the actual functional) is grounded in potentiality-for-Being, then the two are always internally related. That is, our present lifeworld of meaning and practices already presupposes possible alternative modes; if it did not, such a world would have no meaning at all. These "possible alternatives" contained within the mode of the actual, Heidegger calls *Spielraum*, our "leeway," "room to maneuver," or "space of play" (*SZ* §31, 145).

Spielraum is, at least insofar as we are concerned with reconstructing an analysis of freedom in *Being and Time*, a central concept that so far has received little or no attention from commentators.[12] The concept is central to the development of a theory of situated freedom in the sense that I have been using the term, because, as Hubert Dreyfus has noted, it

> introduces the idea of a space of possibilities that constrains Dasein's range of possible actions without in any way determining what Dasein does.... The range of possibilities that Dasein "knows" without reflection, sets up the *room for maneuver* in the current situation. This is the commonsense background of circumspection.... Thus the existential possibilities open in any *specific* situation can be viewed as a subset of the *general* possibilities making up significance. They reveal what in a specific situation it makes sense to do.[13]

We can see within this concept of "room to maneuver" an important insight into thinking about freedom that cannot be accounted for under theories that attempt to reconstruct meaning and action from the standpoint of disembodied minds. *Spielraum* is simultaneously both the field of governance over meaningful action and thought *and* the range of possibilities within which Dasein can meaningfully do otherwise. Thus, it both enables *and* constrains meaningful action. What I have referred to previously as a theory of freedom taken up from the standpoint of the constituting subject will, I suggest, be unable to account for the meaningful range of possibilities, nor the capacity to modify this range slowly over time, since meaning cannot be reconstructed from the position of the autonomous, willing subject. Meaning is a feature of relations between entities within a world, according to Heidegger, not a function of Dasein's intention or of mere physical conditions:

> The Being-possible which Dasein is existentially in every case, is to be sharply distinguished both from empty logical possibility and from the contingency of something present-at-hand, so far as with

the present-at-hand this or that can "come to pass." As a modal category of presence-at-hand, possibility signifies what is *not yet* actual and what is *not at any time* necessary. It characterizes the *merely* possible. Ontologically it is on a lower level than actuality and necessity. On the other hand, possibility as an *existentiale* is the most primordial and ultimate positive way in which Dasein is characterized ontologically. As with existentiality in general, we can, in the first instance, only prepare for the problem of possibility. The phenomenal basis for seeing it at all is provided by the understanding as a disclosive potentiality-for-Being.

Possibility, as an *existentiale*, does not signify a free-floating potentiality-for-Being in the sense of the "liberty of indifference" (*libertas indifferentiae*). (BTa §31, 183; SZ §31, 143–44)

Thus, we can see that what can possibly appear to Dasein *as* a choice is determined neither by merely logical or physical possibility, but rather by the *Spielraum* of a given lifeworld—the range of the *existentially* possible.[14] Dasein's possibilities are governed by the existentially meaningful room to maneuver, or *Spielraum*, which, while open-ended and modifiable, is nevertheless limited in scope.

This means that an investigation is required into how something is made a "meaningful" possibility. The fact that the mode of the actual exists in relation to a realm of potentialities means that the question of the *meaning* of the actual is related to an inquiry into the potential. Stated in ordinary language, to truly know the meaning of X, I must first recognize that X is merely one way for things to be. Only then can I ask: of all the possible ways for things to be, what does it mean that the actual is defined by this one, particular mode called X? If I can even ask this question, I have already raised the background understanding from implicit to explicit themes of knowledge of (a) finitude and (b) potentiality.

Finitude [*Endlichkeit*] refers to the recognition of the possibility of our own not-being. When we come to awareness of the fact that we will not always be (that we will pass away in death), only then can we fully grasp the significance of the present mode of being. Thus, awareness of potentiality is internally related to the revelation of our finitude. In positing finitude as a constitutive structure of Dasein's Being-in-the-world, Heidegger ontologizes finitude in a manner not entirely dissimilar to

Kant. From this, however, he draws different conclusions for practical philosophy. Finitude is the condition of possibility for the awareness of temporality, and this realization is the basis of freedom:

> Anticipation, however, unlike inauthentic Being-towards-death, does not evade the fact that death is not to be outstripped; instead, anticipation frees itself *for* accepting this. When, by anticipation, one becomes free *for* one's own death, one is liberated from one's lostness in those possibilities which may accidentally thrust themselves upon one; and one is liberated in such a way that for the first time one can authentically understand . . . and choose not to be outstripped. (*BTa* §53, 308; *SZ* §53, 264)[15]

Authentic being, then, is defined by awareness of the fact that we are not fully determined by the mode of the actual. Rather, Dasein is grounded more primordially in the realm of the potential, though not because the actual is normatively inferior or ontologically less real (in fact, in a strict metaphysical sense, of course, the actual is more *real* than the potential). Rather, Dasein is grounded more primordially in the potential because *awareness of the characteristics and meaning of the actual are conditioned upon a priori awareness of possibilities for being otherwise*. This awareness, as I have emphasized elsewhere, is more dependent on a specific ethical positioning of the subject in relation to the world than an exercise of pure reason in its historical invariability. The ethical positioning of oneself within a given set of factical conditions and activities is, for Heidegger, the condition for realizing the latent potentiality within such conditions. Hence his linking of *becoming* with an ethical engagement in the world—what Heidegger will explicitly refer to as "freedom."

The meaning of our existence, of our lives, does not lie only in what we *are*, but also consists in what we *can be*, or what we *could have been*. Furthermore, true judgment of the value of what we are can only come about through analysis in relation to what we *might have been*. To define oneself merely through the realm of the actual is to comprehend oneself merely as an *object*, akin to all other objects (such as rocks or trees). This would be to see oneself as a static "fact," rather than a "factical being" (referred to above; see *SZ* §12, 56)—something conditioned by facts but also by an understanding of them and, through this, a capacity to think and act beyond them. Interpreting oneself exclusively as present-at-hand (as an actual entity) is basically to see oneself object-like and therefore as *other*, as not one's own—*un-eigen-tlich*.[16] This is why Heidegger defines this mode of analysis (overdetermination by the actual) using the term *uneigentlich*, most often translated as "authentic." It is through the "authentic/inauthentic" distinction that we finally arrive at a more explicit theorizing of freedom.

2.6. FREEDOM AND THE AUTHENTIC/INAUTHENTIC DISTINCTION

If it is true that Dasein is defined not merely by its actuality, but also by its potentiality, that Dasein always has an understanding of this potentiality (even if implicitly), and that potentiality is always free and primordial in relation to actuality, how does the problem of freedom arise at all? Doesn't it appear as though freedom is so structurally necessary to the basic comportment of Dasein that it cannot be otherwise (i.e., Dasein can *only* exist as a free being), and that therefore, following Heidegger's own logic, the question of freedom cannot even arise, since, at least in this particular case, there is no potentiality (i.e., no alternative mode of being). If this is true, the critic might object, freedom is (1) emptied of all content; (2) mere assertion of the will of Dasein; and/or (3) impossible to account for even as a problem for Dasein's reflection. In order to understand Heidegger's response to such objections, we must look at how he constructs the relationship between authentic and inauthentic being. My argument will be that in his early work (up to and including *Being and Time*), Heidegger understood inauthentic being to be a state of nonfreedom even within the necessary understanding of potentiality that grounds freedom for Dasein. Before proceeding onto this argument, however, it is necessary to understand what Heidegger means by "authenticity."

Despite the fact that potentiality is embedded within the very structure of Dasein's Understanding, Heidegger does not think that we understand or exercise this potentiality in many, or even most, cases. Rather, Dasein is "entrapped" within its own unawareness of potentiality such that possibilities are foreclosed. Central to Heidegger's analysis of freedom, then, is the insight that having possibilities and awareness of possibilities are internally related. Dasein always "has" possibilities other than the mode of the actual. However, the tendency to shy away from this truth and deny one's potentiality means that Dasein "falls away" from its true (potential) self and becomes enmeshed within the mode of the actual. This is inauthentic being.

In order to clarify what is meant by the internal relation between knowing and having possibilities, perhaps an example is in order. We might think of Wittgenstein's example from *Culture and Value*. There, Wittgenstein writes: "A man is *imprisoned* in a room if the door is unlocked, opens inwards; but it doesn't occur to him to *pull*, rather than push against it."[17] In the idiom I am employing here, we might clarify by saying that the man is not imprisoned (actually), but rather is entrapped (through a nonawareness of the potentiality for being otherwise). Thus, in Heidegger's parlance, the man's mode of being while in the room was inauthentic but not false. In other words, it is not enough to be in fact free. You must also be *aware* of this condition in order to possess any possibilities beyond what you would have if in fact you were detained.

The next question that must be confronted is: How does this "falling away" from awareness of possibilities occur? How does Dasein become *inauthentic* in its relation to itself and others?

Authenticity [*Eigentlichkeit*] is a controversial and much misunderstood term within Heidegger's philosophical vocabulary. Certainly, *eigentlich* can be translated as "authentic." However, recalling the etymological connection between *eigen* (own) and *eigentlich*, we can see that Heidegger really means to draw our attention to this mode of analysis as essentially self-awareness and its antonym [*uneigentlichkeit*] as essentially self-estranging. That is, the mode of analysis that defines selfhood only by the actual is a condition of "not-one's own-ness" [*un- eigen- tlich*] as an object away from oneself. Part of the reason this term has been hard to understand in terms of its relation to Heidegger's general philosophical project is its ambiguous use. On the one hand, "authentic" refers to a more pure, genuine, original, or true status. This is the sense of authentic that is employed when one inquires into the "authenticity" of a painting, for example. The inquiry is an attempt to find out if the painting is the original or a forgery. The other sense of the term, although related, is not quite the same. Another way in which we might employ *authentic* is with respect to ownership or personal connection. In this case, authenticity refers not to a return to an original condition, but rather to an acceptance or "ownership" over one's choices, the fact that a particular vocation, for example, is self-determined and that this is unique to oneself (i.e., related to me as a unique person, different from others). This usage does not reference a "good" or "bad" self, but rather different modes of self-relation, or perhaps more precisely, self-appropriation. This draws the meaning of *eigentlich* closer to "properly," in the sense in which I might say that something is "properly mine."

The first set of distinctions (genuine / not genuine) translate as *echt* and *unecht* in German. This is quite different from the second set: *eigentlich* and *uneigentlich*. The second sense of the term (as "made-one's-own") refers to the relationship to the form of life, not the form of life itself. Thus, no particular mode of being can in itself be *authentic* or *inauthentic*. Rather, we can only have an *authentic* or *inauthentic* relationship to the mode of being in which we find ourselves. An authentic relationship to this mode of being would be one in which we recognize it as existing within a range of possibilities—a situation wherein we realize that this particular mode of being could be otherwise and therefore, if we continue to live it, we have *chosen* to live this way; it was not necessary or obligatory.

Heidegger's use of *authenticity* remains almost without exception within the second register. Several textual clues demonstrate this. First, Heidegger explicitly connects *eigentlich* to *eigen*, meaning "own," "personal," "peculiar," or "unique." When the terms *authentic* and *inauthentic* are first introduced, he cautions against reading them in their colloquial senses and reminds the reader specifically that "these expressions have been chosen terminologically in a strict sense" (*BTa* §9, 68; *SZ* §9, 43). Often, when the terms are deployed, Heidegger goes to lengths to remind us of the connections between *eigentlich*, *zueigen*, and *eigen*, such as when he states that Dasein is "essentially something that can be *authentic*—that is, something of its own" (*BTa* §9, 68; *SZ* §9, 42).[18] This means that while Heidegger is using the term *authentic*, he is employing it not in its everyday use, but more in the technical sense, meaning "done on one's own" (from the Greek *autos* for self).[19]

The second set of textual supports for this reading comes from Heidegger's use of the concept of "false authenticity," and from his argument: "This means that even in that to which such a mood pays no attention, Dasein is unveiled in its Being-delivered-over to the 'there.' In the evasion itself the 'there' *is* something disclosed" (*BTa* §29, 174; *SZ* §29, 135). The very fact that Heidegger acknowledges the possibility of *false authenticity*, or of an unveiling *through* evasion, demonstrates that the authentic/inauthentic distinction is not meant to be conflated with moral evaluations of "right/wrong," "good/bad," or "true/false" modes of living. Heidegger writes that authenticity, as well as inauthenticity, "*can* be either genuine or not genuine" (*BTa* §31, 186; *SZ* §31, 146).

It is important to note that, despite the obvious normative weight of the terms within everyday language, *authentic* and *inauthentic* are not moral terms within Heidegger's system. That is to say, while "authentic being" may turn out to be normatively privileged (as many commentators argue), it is not normatively privileged simply *because* it is authentic. The authenticity of a mode of being is related only to whether Dasein has acknowledged that that particular mode of being exists within a range of possibilities, that as Dasein we have possibilities. I can let the factual conditions of my world—my relations with other things and other subjects—determine who I am, thus submitting myself to the realm of the actual. Or, I can acknowledge that, as Dasein (a being who can question the meaning of its own existence), I always have possibilities, thus it is *I* who determines my existence. Authentic being is a being "made as one's own," while inauthentic being is a being in which I do not acknowledge my possibilities and define myself only through the impersonal relation to all other Dasein—"the They" [*Das Mann*]. Many interpreters of Heidegger have uncritically equated "the They" to the social body, arguing that Heidegger is advocating a break from social bonds in some kind of radical existential break from others and our obligations to them. Such commentators have even argued that this basically antisocial attitude accounts (at least in part) for his participation in the Nazi Party and defense (implicit or explicit) of the *Führerprinzip* during his tenure as rector of the University of Freiburg in the academic year of 1933–34. There is no doubt that Heidegger himself drew a connection between the concept of *Das Mann* in *Being and Time* and the rejection of democratic principles by the National Socialist party. However, what is not clear is whether the concept of "the They," originally situated within its context of 1927, can actually be conflated with the *demos*, or whether there is a *necessary* connection between it and *any* particular politics (fascist or otherwise).

When read within its original context, "the They" clearly does not mean "the social body" itself, nor does accepting its role as a concept within Heidegger's system entail accepting any radically antisocial (or antidemocratic) ethics. "The They" refers to a characteristic of the self—not an objective body of people or set of social relations. It should always be remembered that *Das Mann* is an impersonal pronoun, not to be equated with a large social body. Rather, in this specific context, *Das Mann* refers to the characteristic within Dasein to depersonalize itself—to see oneself as essentially determined by things which are not "one's own" (i.e., by our factical conditions). Certainly, other Dasein are a part of the factical conditions into which we can depersonalize ourselves—defining ourselves merely by what others say or do. However, this externalization of the basic meaning of our selfhood is possible not because other people press themselves upon us, or because social relations are necessarily oppressive. Rather, it is possible only because within Dasein is the capacity to externalize the meaning of oneself, to depersonalize it and allow it to be determined by something (or someone) else. Thus, the difference between authentic and inauthentic being is not that authentic being is detached from others while inauthentic is engaged. Rather, it is a difference of how Dasein relates to others— the mode or manner of comportment with which Dasein engages its world—whether one loses sight of the fact that possibilities are never exhausted by the range presented to us in a given Lifeworld.[20]

In fact, far from stating that consideration of others is necessarily self-destructive, Heidegger attempts to demonstrate that it is an existential. Consideration for others is established, for Heidegger, as an existential since he argues that any particular mode of relating (loving, hating, sharing, etc.) requires a priori the basic *capacity* to consider others as something different from a mere object, that is, as another Dasein. The a priori capacity to consider others as other instances of Dasein comes before any particular consideration of specific people; it makes such consideration possible. This *a priori* Heidegger refers to as "Being-with" [*Mit-Sein*].

As mentioned above, Heidegger's hermeneutic phenomenology begins from the experiential level. That is, he first attempts to define the experiences of humans as they reveal themselves to the inquirer. After this has been done, we can use the experience to open up a new level of inquiry—the existential—by asking what conditions would have to exist in order to make the experience possible at all. Employing this transcendental analysis allows Heidegger in this case to ground the a priori of Being-with as the potential to relate to other Dasein in a manner different from our relations to things. Since things and equipment are defined in terms of their as-structure—the "for-the-sake-of-which"—this naturally opens up the question *for whom* the equipment exists. Acknowledging the existence of others is necessary to complete the structure of Understanding because other Dasein are that *for which* equipment is defined. Since other Dasein are defined via an existential analytic (i.e., in relation to the question of my own existence), we can demonstrate that placing them within a separate category of relations is necessary. Thus, we can show that other Dasein do not exist in the world for me in the same way that equipment does. The possibility of acknowledging this exists within the structure of each Dasein's experience, is thus a priori, and demonstrates that authentic Dasein could not (by definition) mean a Dasein wholly indifferent to others. Meaningful relatedness to others is an a priori possibility that makes actual respect for others possible, but it also makes possible forgetfulness of this special relation and the losing of oneself to others—in other words, non-self-aware-being, or inauthenticity [*Uneigentlichkeit*]. Potentiality stands prior to the authentic/inauthentic distinction therefore; it is an existential while the authentic/inauthentic distinction merely refers to a particular stance toward this existential: "We have defined the idea of existence as a potentiality-for-Being—a potentiality which understands, and for which its own Being is an issue. But this *potentiality-for-Being*, as one which is in each case *mine*, is free either for authenticity or for inauthenticity or for a mode in which neither of these has been differentiated" (*BTa*, §45, 275; *SZ* §45, 232). The primary feature of authenticity then is self-awareness of possibilities within a set of relations to other beings. Authenticity does not, however, relate to potentiality-for-being as an existential of Dasein. What is clear is that potentiality is *always* a background condition for any possible understanding (referred to, and discussed in more detail in Chapter Three, as the "ontological ground" of freedom).

2.7. CRITIQUE OF AUTHENTICITY

We can see then that despite Heidegger's attempt to carefully limit the use of the authentic/inauthentic distinction, and to emphasize its relationship to *eigen*, the terminology nevertheless contains significant ambiguities so as to make it problematic. The use of authenticity as a concept within Heidegger's preparatory analytic of freedom has definite limitations.

First, despite various attempts to detach the concept from notions of originary purity, Heidegger himself frequently displays nostalgia for some primordial, original form of human being that has been corrupted or perverted over time, something for which he has been rightly criticized. This classic thesis of alienation and decline, however, relies upon positing a philosophical anthropology in which a more "true" version of humanity existed at some period in time—a claim which would be overdetermined within Heidegger's general system since it cannot be grounded by the existential analytic and is not necessary to sustain the other insights.

Second, Heidegger's use of the authentic/inauthentic distinction leaves a great deal of ambiguity regarding the historical status of freedom. To clarify what I mean, we might ask Heidegger: does Dasein in all places, at all times, exhibit the same degree of inauthentic being? If so, then the degree to which Dasein is inauthentic is invariable, which would support the thesis that inauthenticity refers more to a characteristic of selfhood (i.e., determination by social relations) rather than a quality of relations that can be altered over time. However, it is clear that Heidegger thinks inauthentic being has become more common under conditions of modernity. This would imply that Dasein can become more or less authentic over historical time, meaning that inauthenticity is a condition which, while one might never totally escape it, can be transformed. What is required then is more than the rather abstract claim, derived though it may be from a fundamental ontology, that Dasein has a tendency to fall into modes of inauthenticity with corresponding ossifying effects. Additional to this would be a historical analysis of the modes of "making inauthentic," the modes by which Dasein is overdetermined by its actuality and occludes its potentiality-for-being, as well as a historical analysis of the modes of attunement which make realization of potentiality possible.

In the next chapter, we will deal with how Heidegger attempted to alter his account of freedom qua authenticity in his middle writings, as well as one attempt to translate his account of freedom into a historically and sociologically localized critique of modern capitalism, namely, the existential-Marxism found in the early writings of Herbert Marcuse.

THREE

THE FIELD OF FREEDOM

HEIDEGGER FROM FUNDAMENTAL TO HISTORICAL ONTOLOGY

> There is no freedom without a field.
>
> Maurice Merleau-Ponty

ALTHOUGH HEIDEGGER CLAIMED the work presented in essays from his middle period—such as "On the Essence of Ground,"[1] "On the Essence of Human Freedom: An Introduction to Philosophy,"[2] "On the Essence of Truth,"[3] "Schelling: On the Essence of Human Freedom,"[4] and "The Metaphysical Foundations of Logic"[5]—was a continuation of and commensurate with the project undertaken in *Being and Time*, surely one central theme must have come as a surprise to readers. Particularly unusual is Heidegger's claim in these works that the problem of Being is ultimately a problem of freedom (*GA*, 31: 300), or the even more sweeping assertion that philosophy itself is only realized in search of freedom.[6] After all, the term is only sporadically mentioned in *Being and Time*, and, to the extent that freedom has historically tended to connote a capacity of the will for spontaneous causality, it seems almost entirely antithetical to the ontological analysis of the *Seinsfrage*.[7]

The unusual place of freedom in Heidegger's middle period may account (at least in part) for the wildly divergent and contradictory interpretations of what he truly meant by the term. As Fred Dallmayr has pointed out, "No theoretical aspect of [Heidegger's] work has occasioned more controversy and heated debate than his attitude toward freedom."[8] On one end of the interpretive spectrum, Heidegger has been "reproached for having carried the modern concept of freedom to an absurd point and thus for having promoted a blind and arbitrary decisionism," a reading facilitated by the early Sartre's appropriation of the existential analytic in *Being and Time*. On the other side, however, Heidegger is also often "claimed to endorse a complete dismantling or eradication of human freedom and willing, and thus to sanction a deterministic fatalism."[9] This objection has been advanced, for instance, by Habermas.[10] There are even a few commentators, such as Leo Strauss, who have raised *both* accusations.[11]

My primary aim in reading Heidegger's middle works is not, however, to establish a definitive reading that could resolve all such conflicts of interpretation. Rather, it is to demonstrate that at the very least Heidegger makes an important, even indispensible contribution to thinking about freedom because he focuses the issue properly. Specifically, Heidegger was correct in suggesting that in thinking about the question of freedom we cannot avoid thinking *ontologically*. In claiming this, there is great potential for confusion, however, for "ontology' is not an uncontestable term of reference with clear parameters for use. At the very least, as Johanna Oksala notes, "ontology" commonly refers to "both the fundamental building blocks of reality and to the systematic study of them."[12] For present purposes, I follow Heidegger's narrow use. Ontology here does not refer to an essentialized structure of reality, that is, as a rough synonym for metaphysics more generally. Instead, ontology refers to a particular form of analysis, one that affirms the idea that knowledge claims about the world are also interpretations of what sorts of entities there are to be known, and, simultaneously, a certain ethical positioning of the subject of knowledge in relation to the world so interpreted. In saying that Heidegger focuses the issue properly, then, I mean that a thesis on freedom always contains within it an implicitly or explicitly held understanding of the fundamental framework or field of conditions within which meaningful actions may be actualized, an understanding of the kinds of entities that exist and act within this field, and the range of possibilities within which they operate.

The reading offered proceeds in five steps. First, I will track how Heidegger recast the previous discussion (Chapter Two) in terms of freedom. Second, I parse Heidegger's use of the predicate *free*, demonstrating its polysemic use during this period of his work. The third section of the chapter analyzes how Heidegger's changing understanding of freedom away from authenticity and resoluteness toward a relationship to the field of one's practical involvement required an opening up of the historical conditions for such a relationship. In the fourth part, we return back to *Being and Time* in order to explicate the concept of "historicity" in Division II of that text, and employ it as a bridge to the social and political concerns raised by Heidegger's interpreters and interlocutors. The chapter concludes with a more detailed elaboration of this transition from fundamental to historical ontology with particular reference to Herbert Marcuse's writings of the 1920s and 1930s, exploring the tensions and contradictions of an "ontologized" social criticism.

3.1. THE FIELD OF FREEDOM

Among his contributions, Heidegger offers the most sustained and systematic elaboration since Marx of the notion that our primary experience of the world is not mediated by consciousness but is instead a practical relation. This means for him that our theoretical worldviews, as well as the forms of subjectivity that comprise our sense of selfhood, are actually the outgrowth of a more basic mode of technological-practical involvement in the world, or what he called the "modes of revealing." As articulated in *Being and Time*, Heidegger attempted to demonstrate that although we come to an understanding of ourselves and our world through a practical relation, the conditions of this practical relation is not merely ours to choose in an abstract, decisionistic sense. Rather, the modes of revealing come *to* us, are disclosed to us pre-reflectively. The particular space in which we find ourselves, with its particular conditions and limitations, is what Heidegger called a "clearing" or a "determinate field."[13]

Throughout his writings Heidegger tried to outline several distinctive features of how it is we come to find ourselves within such a clearing. These distinctive features he referred to, at least in *Being and Time*, as "existentials," two of which include "thrownness" and "Being-in." In this early work, Heidegger did not specifically name "freedom" as an existential. However, after *Being and Time* (particularly in the middle essays cited at the outset) he came to the conclusion that freedom must be included as one of the fundamental conditions of world-disclosure.

In fact, it was in these works that Heidegger used the term *freedom* to describe one of the *most important* existential conditions of world-disclosure. Hence, we find claims such as, "*Freedom is ground of ground....* As *this* ground, however, freedom is the *abyss of ground* [Ab-grund] in Dasein. Not that our individual, free comportment is groundless; rather, in its essence as transcendence, freedom places Dasein, as potentiality for being, in possibilities that gape open before its finite choice, i.e., within its destiny" (*P*, 134; *GA*, 9: 173–74). The concern here with the need to think ontologically takes this opening up to the question of freedom as an existential condition of world-disclosure as its starting point. But what work is being done by the predicate *free* when Heidegger speaks of *das Freie der Lichtung*? The "freedom of the clearing" begins, I argue, from a defense of something like "epistemological indeterminacy."[14] This is to say that the world of practical involvement cannot be reduced to a determinant "perspective" or "system of thought" knowable once and for all. It is to acknowledge the finitude of our understandings of the world, not as an obstacle to the freedom of the discrete subject, but as a condition of such freedom. Heidegger gives, I think, two main reasons for this.

3.1.a. Background Understanding

The first way in which Heidegger wants to base a claim to freedom as "epistemological indeterminacy" is through a claim about the condition or ground of intelligibility and veracity. This involves making a claim about the relationship between our knowledge claims and background understanding. From *Being and Time* through to his later writings, Heidegger argued that investigation of the meaning of something within a world, a particular lifeworld or horizon of disclosure, is only possible because it is set against a larger backdrop of Understanding [*Verstehen*]. That which can be consciously reflected upon, thematized and articulated is premised upon a background world which cannot in any general holistic manner be made the object of inquiry itself. As Stephen Mulhall puts it, "The world itself is not a possible object of knowledge—because it is not an object at all, not an entity or set of entities. It is that within which entities appear, a field or horizon ontologically grounded in a totality of assignment-relations; it is the conditions for any intra-worldly relation, and so it is not analysable in terms of any such relation."[15] Thus, whenever we attempt to think the general conditions for world-disclosure, we actually begin by thinking about particular beings, activities and practices *within* a world.[16] When we do this, we engage in interpretation. Attempting to think about the meaning of specific features of our lifeworld can lead us to question the general context in which the question arises at all—this is the *Seinsfrage*, or the question of the meaning of Being. When we move to this level of analysis we can see that both the object and the subject of any particular inquiry are mutually constituted by a larger backgrounded field of meaning which cannot, even in principle, be made fully explicit. As numerous commentators have noted, this makes Heidegger a major figure in the long philosophical project to overcome traditional epistemology.[17]

After *Being and Time*, Heidegger shifted his focus away from questions of intelligibility and meaning toward questions of truth and freedom. His insight here amounts to a kind of incompleteness theorem, and may be summarized thus: the intelligibility and veracity of our articulations about the world can never be established by demonstrating a direct correspondence between the articulation and the "world-as-such" since "a world" only appears through an already existing field of intelligibility which includes the basic language of articulation by which the subject comes to the world and itself. Thus, prior to the kind of truth that exists in the correspondence between the subject's articulated knowledge claims and the objective world is the event of self-manifestation by phenomenon. Correspondence is but verification after this truth-event.

Heidegger attempted to flesh out these claims in a series of essays that preoccupied him throughout his middle period. The move away from thinking about the ground of meaning and intelligibility (as preoccupied *Being and Time*) toward the ground of veracity naturally led him to think more about the "governance" of the lifeworld and thus about human freedom. Here again, he pointed to the necessity of a background field, or lifeworld, against which the relation between propositions and things makes sense. There is nothing inherently true (or untrue) about a correlation between a word and a thing: the meaning and truth (or untruth) of the statement must reside more fundamentally in the relational world which grounds and makes possible both (the statement, by providing a language of meaning, and the thing by rendering it intelligible as a thing). He writes, "This appearing of the thing in traversing a field of opposedness takes place within an open region, the openness of which is not first created by the presenting but rather is only entered into and taken over as a domain of relatedness. The relation of the presentative statement to the thing is the accomplishment of that *bearing* that originarily and always comes to prevail as a comportment" (P, 141; GA, 9: 184). Thus, the opening [*Offenen*] and the comportment [*Verhalten*] that permit a thing to appear as such, and a statement to correlate (or not) to this thing (what Heidegger calls the "traversing of the oppositional" [*Durchmessen eines Entgegen*]), is determined first by the "relational field" [*Bezugsbereich*] in which Dasein always already finds itself. Since this relational field (and its related opening and comportment) is prior and foundational to any truth as correspondence, it is in fact the ground of truth. This, which Heidegger names *ontological truth* (GA, 9: 131), stands prior to what might be called "propositional truth": the correspondence of a proposition with a referent thing. In this sense then, even "propositional untruth" is reliant upon "ontological truth." Even a lie or a mistake still presumes the process by which the thing in question came to be rendered intelligible, to be an object for thought. The upshot of this claim is that both (a) meaning and (b) truth presuppose a "world" which cannot be reduced to a determinate set of transcendental conditions. Rather, our understandings of the world and self stand in an immanent relationship to the forms of practical involvement that disclose the world to us in the first place. "The world" as the totality of this involvement will thus always "evade" our attempts to formalize it as interpreted or thematized knowledge claims. Hence, Heidegger's first use of the term *freedom* to name this evasion, this indeterminacy.

3.1.b. *Spielraum*

The second aspect of freedom and epistemological indeterminacy is the irreducible "play-space" [*Spielraum*] that characterizes any particular actual clearing. To understand how this feature of ontological freedom is distinct from the first, it is important to point out that background understanding and projection are best understood as features of world-disclosure, while "play-space" is a feature of any particular clearing.

In order to highlight the difference between world-disclosure and a particular clearing, we might note that the latter is a specific, localized, and historical "world," "realm of intelligibility," or "horizon of disclosure." World-disclosure, by contrast, is that which makes this horizon possible. The clearing is "that which is present" while world-disclosure is "that which presences" [*das Anwesende*]. World-disclosure, then, refers also to those basic modes of practical involvement which remain backgrounded to us, which lie beyond our purview.

A clearing is revealed through the event of disclosive truth given by the sets of pre-reflexive activities by which Dasein discloses its world. Dasein is thus always already within some clearing in this process of revealing. However, no particular clearing allows for boundless, absolute knowledge. Not everything can be a meaningful way to think and act in any particular moment. Not everything can appear as a possible truth—far from it. The clearing, while disclosing some features of our world, will necessarily close off others. This closure is the finitude of the present, the finitude of Dasein's world. Heidegger writes: "Projection of the ontological constitution of beings *that simultaneously marks out a determinate field* (nature, history) as the region for possible objectification through scientific knowledge" (*P*, 104; *GA*, 9: 132; italics added).[18] The simultaneous (note that Heidegger specifically states these characteristics to occur "zugleich") and equiprimordial constitution of pre-ontological understanding (the field of knowledge and action) in projection *and* determinate limitation is key to developing an understanding of agency as *situated*. Heidegger is pointing out that the event of truth which renders the lifeworld intelligible always already occurs within a "determinate field" [*bestimmtes Feld*] that "marks out" [*abstecken*], "solidifies" [*verfestigen*], and "circumscribes" [*umgrenzen*] the "fundamental concepts" [*Grundbegriffe*] of the "relevant study" [*betreffenden Wissenschaft*].[19] Elsewhere, he writes that the event of disclosure is also simultaneously a "binding" [*Bindung*] and "obligation" [*Verbindlichkeit*].[20] In other words, no concept or line of inquiry can come before us that is not already within a determinate field of knowledge circumscribed by the form of life or factical conditions of our present ontological condition.[21]

However, *within* this circumscribed realm of intelligibility, there is always some "play-room" [*Spielraum*]. The event of disclosure reveals a range of possible meaningful modes of being for Dasein (ways of thinking, acting, living). Since it sets out the range, the event is characterized by closure and finitude. However, this does not mean that the event determines what particular modes of being will be actualized by Dasein in any specific historical moment. Dasein always has some "play-room" within the lifeworld to adopt this or that meaningful choice and actualize it. Heidegger writes: "Every accounting for things must move within *a sphere of what is possible*. . . . In accordance with its essence, such grounding always necessarily provides *a given range of what is possible*. . . . The reflection of *this* origin of the essence of ground in the grounding that pertains to finite freedom shows itself in the '*potius quam*' found in these formulations of the principle of reason (P, 133; GA, 9: 173; italics in original). To clarify the issue through a crude example, we might think of the lifeworld as offering up a set of possible routes of action and thought, only one of which will be actually taken up. Since the situation presents only *this* set of routes, determines that these are the potential routes, and even differentially distributes them as *meaningful* options (that is, governs that not all of them will appear as equally possible or meaningful), it clearly governs the range of possibilities and "binds" our choices to some degree. However, within this range, we have a measure of agency in interpreting and choosing which route to take up. This is what it means to "chose oneself."[22] The route which is actualized is a subset of the total possible options. The gap between the one actual and the total possible is what Heidegger calls "play-room." We can see, therefore, that whatever actualized modes of being Dasein enacts will only be a subset within the range of the total possible, even while acknowledging that the range is not exhaustive of *all* possibilities (and is thus finite). In this sense, the lifeworld can always be said to have some measure of freedom built into its constitution. This is the final aspect of freedom as "epistemological indeterminacy."

.   .   .

In stepping back to summarize and assess this first sense of freedom, we might note that Heidegger has employed a theoretical move in relation to finitude parallel to the one made by Kant. Just as Kant sought to redefine the finite limits of human knowledge positively, making them the transcendental conditions of knowledge per se, the condition of rational determination and thus the condition of freedom, so too does Heidegger seek to redefine finitude positively. For Heidegger, the finite nature of our understanding—what I have called here "epistemological indeterminacy"—does not threaten the conditions of freedom but rather guarantees them. The notion that freedom makes the space between determinate limitations and possibilities is a key insight of Heidegger's. It has, moreover, been highly influential on other theorists of freedom in the continental tradition, particularly Merleau-Ponty and Foucault. As Merleau-Ponty put it in *The Phenomenology of Perception*:

> Unless there are cycles of behaviour, open situations requiring a certain completion and capable of constituting a *background* to either a confirmatory or transformatory decision, we never experience freedom. Choice of an intelligible sort is excluded, not only because there is no time anterior to time, but because choice presupposes a prior commitment and because the idea of an initial choice involves a contradiction. If freedom is to have *room* in which to move, if it is to be desirable as freedom, there must be something to hold it away from its objectives; it must have a *field*, which means that there must be for it special possibilities or realities which tend to cling to being. ... Our freedom is not to be sought in a spurious discussion on the conflict between a style of life which we have no wish to reappraise and circumstances suggestive of another: the real choice is that between our whole character and our manner of being in the world.[23]

What Merleau-Ponty (and, as we will see in the second half of this book, Foucault) gestures to here is that freedom defined in terms of a "field" is primary to freedom as self-mastery, or autonomous choosing. Every act of choice is only comprehensible, indeed is only possible, because it enters into a sphere of what is possible.[24] Since the field and its relative openness is primary to the choosing subject, Heidegger famously concludes that "freedom is not mere absence of constraint with respect to what we can or cannot do. Nor is it on the other hand mere readiness for what is required and necessary (and so somehow a being). Prior to all this ('negative' and 'positive' freedom), freedom is engagement in the disclosure of beings as such" (P, 145; GA, 9: 189). This field must be a determinant field, in the sense of providing finite, limited, concrete possibilities which are not all equally available. Moreover, actualization of choice within this field alters the range of possibilities. The field of possibilities is thus disclosed *to* the agent, but also through them and their activities. The world is thus engaged in, not as a determinant "thing" over against the subject, but rather as a cluster of probabilities and possibilities that permit us to think and act in a multiplicity of ways. The "epistemological indeterminancy" that is entailed by engaging in a world-as-field-of-potentiality is, for Heidegger, the guarantee of the openness of the world, and it is something we should be thankful for rather than lament.

3.2. OPENNESS

Even if one grants Heidegger's claim that world-disclosure cannot be known through a set of determinant structures, it does not necessarily follow from this that we need accede to the language of "freedom." The most obvious objection that springs to mind might be phrased thus: the inability of human consciousness to grasp the determinant rules or structures of world-disclosure—to make the ground of our activities and inquiries fully self-transparent—does not mean that Being itself is indeterminate (much less free); it only means that we cannot know it totally.

To counter such an objection, Heidegger might point to the separation implicit within this claim between Being as it is rendered intelligible and Being *as such*. This distinction (between the thing-in-itself and thing-under-description) is at the heart of the whole epistemological tradition and is precisely the distinction he thinks cannot be sustained. It cannot be sustained because, for Heidegger, both are constituted by this larger field or context of meaning. The epistemological approach, one in which a problematic of subject-object arises, fails to see the productive and reciprocal relationship between Dasein, the object of inquiry, and the general field of inquiry itself. Epistemological approaches ignore how the inquiry itself—the "seeing" of the thing—is part of the process of constituting something as a thing (the disclosure) and, as such, they miss how the decontextual interpretation is never getting at the "thing-in-itself" (a concept that Heidegger is attempting to displace altogether).

Together, the two main features of world-disclosure mentioned above (background understanding and *Spielraum*) ground the first sense of freedom as "epistemological indeterminacy." This is properly called an *ontological* feature of freedom because this is not something that Dasein *has* or does not *have*. Rather, it is a feature of the disclosure by which things appear to Dasein within an intelligible totality—a feature of that by which a "world" is presented to and through Dasein. Hence Heidegger's repeated association of ontological truth with ontological freedom: "The essence of truth reveals itself as freedom" (*P*, 147; *GA*, 9: 192).

It should be clear by this point that ontological freedom *prefigures* human subjectivity and agency. As Heidegger states, it is "the ground of the possibility of Dasein" (*EHF*, 94; *GA*, 31: 134). This reversal of the relationship between selfhood and (ontological) freedom requires a conceptual reordering in terms of how we think about freedom and agency as such:

> With respect to the schema, we must effect a *complete repositioning of freedom*, so that what now emerges is that *the problem of freedom is not built into the leading and fundamental problems of philosophy, but, on the contrary, the leading question of metaphysics is grounded in the question concerning the essence of freedom.*
>
> But if our essential questioning must take *this* direction, if the fundamental problem of philosophy must be viewed from this perspective, then it is irrelevant whether Kant was correct to interpret freedom within the framework of causality. Even if he was not correct in this, still, according to the new thesis, causality, movement, and being as such, are grounded in freedom. *Freedom is not some particular thing* among and alongside other things, but is *superordinate and governing in relation to the whole . . . freedom must itself, in its essence, be more primordial than man.* Man is only an *administrator* of freedom, i.e. he can only let-be the freedom which is accorded to him, in such a way that, through man, the whole contingency of freedom becomes visible.
>
> Human freedom now no longer means freedom as a property of man, but *man as a possibility of freedom*. Human freedom is the freedom that breaks through in man and takes him up unto itself, thus making man possible. (*EHF*, 94; *GA*, 31: 134–35; italics in original)

In the passage above, note that Heidegger is still speaking of freedom in the ontological sense. We are still concerned here with the conditions of world-disclosure, particularly with demonstrating that such conditions are necessarily indeterminate and primary to human activities of knowing and interpreting. We are not yet speaking of a feature of human agency in a direct sense.

To move us from freedom as "epistemological indeterminacy" to a form of (ontic) human freedom, it might be helpful to again set out a possible objection to the picture given above. A critic might say the following: Your notion of ontological freedom is purely descriptive of the constitution of realms of intelligibility and actualization of meaningful choice. As such, it cannot properly be called "freedom" since there is, by your own admission, no way that Being can *not* be free. If this "freedom" merely refers to a feature of the constitution of a field of practical involvement (a clearing) then this field, by definition, *must* be free. If this is so, "freedom" loses any specific normative character (we could just as well say that world-disclosure was determined by this particular form of indeterminacy), and/or we lose any critical purchase for evaluating different ways of thinking and acting in relation to the world. In other words, there can be no cause for concern as world-disclosure must, regardless of us, be free in the ontological sense given above. This objection is an important one to dissect since it appears, in various guises, in criticism of Heidegger's work.

To take on this objection, we might begin by asking: What would happen if we did not *know* that world-disclosure was free in the senses given above? Or, more to the point (as it shifts the question away from knowledge and toward general embodiment or comportment), what if our form of life was structured such as to deny ontological freedom? How might we comport ourselves toward the world in this case?

Crudely put, Heidegger wants to argue that there are two basic modes of comporting ourselves with respect to ontological freedom: one that acknowledges it and one that does not. In this way, he introduces, not two different structures of reality on the ontological level, but a superordinate distinction between two modes of relating to that reality. The form of comportment that acknowledges the indeterminacy of Being (ontological freedom) is what he calls "letting-be" [*Seinlassen*], an "open comportment" [*offenständigen Verhalten*], or at times "releasement" [*Gelassenheit*]. The other mode—that which denies ontological freedom—is that which closes off the possibilities latent within a field of practical involvement. In "On the Essence of Truth" Heidegger writes,

> However, because truth is in essence freedom, historical human beings can, in letting beings be, also *not* let beings be the beings that they are and as they are. Then beings are covered up and distorted. Semblance comes to power. In it the nonessence of truth comes to the fore. However, because ek-sistent freedom as the essence of truth is not a property of human beings; because on the contrary humans ek-sist and so become capable of history only as the property of this freedom; the nonessence of truth cannot first arise subsequently from mere human incapacity and negligence. Rather, untruth must derive from the essence of truth. Only because truth and untruth are, *in essence, not* irrelevant to one another, but rather belong together, is it possible for a true proposition to enter into pointed opposition to the corresponding untrue proposition. (P, 146; GA, 9: 191)

It is also important to keep in mind that these two modes are both instances of Care [*Sorge*], not in the moral and intentionalist sense carried with the English term, but in the sense of a general mode of comportment, embedded with relations that *matter*, embodied in a form of life. Thus, neither are they something we "think" or "do"—they are forms of life we *are* (hence Heidegger's claim above that "ek-sistent freedom . . . is not a property of human beings . . . on the contrary humans ek-sist and so become capable of history only as the property of this freedom").

Now, on first blush, the mode of comportment that acknowledges finitude and indeterminacy as the ground of freedom seems defined negatively and appears to be rather passive. Neither "letting-be" nor "releasement" appear to be things we can enact. They are defined rather by what we *don't* do—that is, don't control, don't order, don't enframe, and so on. This is another common concern with Heidegger's work: that it leads us to a passive quietism, a mere nonordering that is the positive offshoot of us standing in awe of Being as such. This appears to critics as antihumanist (which it may be, if we take a rather specific sense of the term), conservative, or even reactionary. And, undoubtedly, there are points in Heidegger's career when he advances such an interpretation. Nevertheless, he didn't only say such things and, to the extent that he did, it was not logically required. Rather than think of "letting-be" as primarily a passive mode of comportment, Heidegger repeatedly insisted that "to let-be is to engage oneself [*Sicheinlassen*] with beings." He even claims that this mode of comportment will be "exposing," "suspending," or "off-putting" [*aus-setzend*] for us:

> However, the phrase required not—to let beings be—does not refer to neglect and indifference but rather the opposite. To let be is to engage oneself with beings. On the other hand, to be sure, this is not to be understood only as the mere management, preservation, tending, and planning of the beings in each case encountered or sought out. To let be—that is, to let beings be as the beings that they are—means to engage oneself with the open region and its openness into which every being comes to stand, bringing that openness, as it were, along with itself. . . . To engage oneself with the disclosedness of beings is not to lose oneself in them; rather, such engagement withdraws in the face of beings in order that they might reveal themselves with respect to what and how they are, and in order that presentative correspondence might take its standard from them. As this letting-be it exposes itself to beings as such and transposes all comportment into the open region. Letting-be, i.e., freedom, is intrinsically exposing, ek-sistent. (*P*, 144; *GA*, 9: 188–89)

But more detail is needed here for these statements to stand out in their specific meaning. How precisely can "letting-be" also be an "engagement" with Being? In order to see how "letting-be" can be an engagement we have to understand better the alternative. What is the mode of comportment that does not acknowledge ontological freedom, that does not "let beings be"?

In Heidegger's terminology, an engagement that is freeing is one that loosens one's relation to oneself such that our involvement within a world with its own, preexisting ethical significance and latent potentiality is revealed to us. This engagement will be a mode of comportment that *embodies a respect for its own contingency* and, in this limited sense, will be more basic or primordial than one that doesn't. As Richard Rorty states in his reading of Heidegger, "An understanding of Being is more primordial than another if it makes it easier to grasp its own contingency."[25] William Connolly also confirms this reading, praising those "element[s] of connectedness, receptivity, interdependence, and belonging" which can be derived from this sense of freedom as indeterminacy, contingency, and finitude. Connolly argues we learn from Heidegger that "one stands in a more free relation to one's own ideals when one affirms that the world might never be exhausted by a single perspective or a constellation of contending perspectives. The world is always richer than the systems of thought through which we comprehend and organize it."[26] I would rephrase this formulation slightly to argue that it is not merely one's "ideals" that we stand in a more free relation to, but rather more basically and more fundamentally, our *selves* and our *world*. That is to say, it is not a conceptual frame held together by ideas and ideals, but a practical one, held in our activities and practices.

But what does this mean in practice? It means at least that a "free relation" to the world—to the field of practical involvement in which we find ourselves—involves some form of activity (an engagement) that works "on" or "against" the particular metaphysical entrapments of the present. This means in practice being attuned to the contingency and indeterminacy of world-disclosure, which, in turn, means accepting that "we" (our selfhood) are beholden to this contingency—that we are contingent beings who are "held" by ontological freedom: "But if ek-sistent Da-sein, which lets beings be, sets the human being free for his 'freedom' by first offering to his choice something possible (a being) and by imposing on him something necessary (a being), human caprice does not then have freedom at its disposal. The human being does not 'possess' freedom as a property. At best, the converse holds: freedom, ek-sistent, disclosive Da-sein, possesses the human being" (P, 145; GA, 9: 190). While this formulation does not appear on first reading to relate directly to the freedom normally thought of as a feature of human life (and has even been misconstrued as the antithesis to human freedom), Heidegger clearly does not support such a reading. Rather, he is attempting here (as throughout much of his middle writings) to demonstrate the internal relation between the potentiality latent within worldly activities themselves (the freedom of Being) and the freedom of particular humans in their particular worlds (the freedom of beings).

In other words, Heidegger draws our attention to the fact that we are free only because we belong to a world that discloses a range of possibilities that are accessible to us. However, tapping this potential requires first that we give up the aspiration to total sovereignty, to a fully transparent world in which the external world conforms perfectly to my internal desires, which, Heidegger would argue, in principle is not even possible. Thus, while the existence of such worldly possibilities is a condition of freedom, so too is our openness to them: "The openness of the world *shows itself* in our respective openness."[27] There is a mutual interrelatedness to our ethical (self)positioning and the possibilities for transformation within the worldly activities that comprise our world of practical involvement. This openness to the possibilities of the world requires a constant attentiveness to our immanence, a positioning of oneself that cultivates sensitivity and receptivity to what is offered. This openness is what Heidegger calls "disclosedness" [*Erschlossenheit*]. Heidegger himself makes this move from contingency and indeterminacy in world-disclosure to situated human freedom more explicit in "On the Essence of Truth":

> But here it becomes evident also that freedom is the ground of the inner possibility of correctness only because it receives its own essence from the more originary essence of uniquely essential truth. Freedom was initially determined as freedom for what is opened up in an open region. How is this essence of freedom to be thought? That which is opened up, that to which a presentative statement as correct corresponds, are beings opened up in an open comportment. Freedom for what is opened up in an open region lets beings be the beings they are. Freedom now reveals itself as letting beings be. (P, 144; GA, 9: 187–88)

One way of fleshing out in more detail what this open comportment might mean is through examining its antonym.

3.3. METAPHYSICS AND (SELF)CONCEALMENT

Since Heidegger's ontological thesis regarding freedom begins from a positive redescription of our finitude, he argues that, paradoxically, modes of practical involvement in the world which take as their point of departure the possibility of absolute knowledge and full self-transparency are actually more occluded to themselves and serve to conceal the conditions under which freedom is realized. Heidegger can formulate "letting-be" as an "engagement" with the world because he sees this engagement as one that works against this tendency to (self)concealment.

Throughout his career, Heidegger attempted to articulate the various ways in which a mode of revealing might come to conceal its own practical involvement in a world, to conceal the fact that rather than merely "reflect" reality, modes of revealing are engagements with reality on a practical level, thus implicating the acquisition of knowledge about the world with an ethical relationship in the world. That this concealing/revealing is a central preoccupation of Heidegger's entire oeuvre can hardly be doubted. What did change, however, was his analysis of the various ways this concealing/revealing was manifest, as well as his account of how and why it occurred.

As we saw in the previous chapter, *Being and Time* presented the problem of (self)concealment in ontological terms. In other words, Dasein has a tendency to conceal its own practical involvement in a world (and thus, of the potentiality for transformation within such a world) because this concealing tendency is part of its very being. Dasein is constitutionally predisposed to flee from its own finite worldliness. In Division II of *Being and Time*, Heidegger argued that the horizon of death permitted the grasping of one's own finitude, thus providing an opportunity for Dasein to recall its worldliness, not to evade its condition, and thus (if only momentarily or inconsistently) to comport itself authentically. Inauthenticity, fallenness, and entanglement—the antonyms of a "free" and authentic mode of being-in-the-world—were analyzed only at this level of ontology and, thus, were presented without reference to social or historical variation in their manifestation. Put succinctly, if Dasein tends toward self-concealment as a feature of its very being, and by extension, as a feature of world-disclosure as such, then the analysis of this concealing need not take into account the differential social, cultural, and historical contexts in which Dasein finds itself.

For much of his career Heidegger did not see himself as working against any particular, historical case of inauthenticity, fallenness, or entanglement, but rather against the general tendency in Western thought toward thinking of knowledge as primarily a function of detached contemplation—as mediated by consciousness—rather than derivative of modes of practical involvement. Thus, his original project was described as a "phenomenological destruction" of epistemology and metaphysics themselves (or, even more grandly, of "the history of Being in the West"). In *Being and Time*, showing that consciously reflected upon articulations of reality (Interpretation) presuppose a background which is not itself verifiable, Heidegger had attempted to demonstrate that Understanding is grounded only in a historically situated form of life.[28] This means that the whole manner of questioning in which metaphysics attempts to grasp the structure of reality independent of a temporally situated form of life is (a) mistaken and (b) *itself a form of life that entangles our mode of comportment in the present.*

Metaphysics is, for Heidegger, the paradigmatic case of our self-concealment, arising out of *Seinsvergessenheit*. As the latter term connotes, in a metaphysics of the present, we "forget Being." But stated at this level of abstraction, the two words "forget Being" don't mean much.[29] This is why I've tried to show that, for Heidegger, "world-disclosure" is characterized by a certain "freedom" with respect to our forms of knowledge—an epistemological indeterminacy. What metaphysics causes us to "forget" is this indeterminacy, which in turn is partially derived from the fact that it is our capacity for aspectival modification that makes world-disclosure indeterminate and transformable in the first place. We are entrapped in our own forgetfulness of ontological freedom insofar as the presupposition that Being is a "thing" which can be known independent of our descriptions and articulations of it serves to orientate our actions, telling us what counts as "true" or "false" ways of relating to the world.

Of course, merely naming the problem of metaphysics is not to overcome it. In fact, Heidegger is ambiguous about whether "metaphysics" is something that can, even in principle, be "overcome":

> Our talk of the end of metaphysics does not mean to suggest that in the future men will no longer "live" who think metaphysically and undertake "systems of metaphysics." Even less do we intend to say that in the future mankind will no longer "live" on the basis of metaphysics. . . . It means the historical moment in which the essential possibilities of metaphysics are exhausted. The last of these

possibilities must be that form of metaphysics in which its essence is reversed. (N4, 148; GA, 6.2: 178–79)

What Heidegger suggests here is that the very "nearness" of the metaphysical picture is what blinds us to its working. While Julian Young's language of "absolutization" is perhaps somewhat misleading,[30] his formulation of the problematic is nevertheless insightful:

> What [metaphysics] misses is not the being of beings, not being, but rather the fact that there are just these universal traits which have categorial status for us is dependent on the selection made from the smorgasbord of attributes possessed by reality itself which is made by the linguistic practices, the forms of life, in which we live, and move, and have our being. And missing that, missing, *not* our horizon of disclosure but rather its *horizonal character*—the perspectival character of our basic perspective on things—it elevates its account of the being of beings into *the* (one and only) categorial account of reality itself. . . . Through misunderstanding what it has discovered in discovering the being of beings, it elevates (what is in fact) a particular disclosure to tyrannical status, a status which allows the possibility of no other reality-revealing horizon. I shall refer to this phenomenon as "absolutization." As Heidegger uses the term, the error that is metaphysics may be defined as the absolutization of some (of any) horizon of disclosure.[31]

Such metaphysical interpretations, as Heidegger puts it, put us into an *unfree* relation to the world and to ourselves, not because they are "wrong" (noncorrespondence to reality *as such*), but rather because they are totalizing. As he put it in "The Question Concerning Technology": "Where this ordering holds sway, it drives out every other possibility of revealing. . . . [It] conceals disclosure itself" (BW, 332–33; GA, 7: 28). Hence the tragic irony that Heidegger attempted to warn against in his late writings: the more we pursue our "freedom" in the name of mastery over the world, the more we conceal that it is indeed the world, the field of practical involvement, that discloses us, the less free we stand in relation to this field and through it to ourselves. Hence late Heidegger's identification of the technological pursuit of mastery over the world with a certain pathology of Western modernity. This mode of revealing that had come to prevail in Western modernity was, for

Heidegger, problematic not only for specific, historical reasons (what he might refer to as "ontic" problems) but also because it is particularly hard to grasp *as a problem*. This is the mode of revealing that conceals itself *as a mode of revealing*; thus, as Leslie Paul Thiele puts it, "betray[ing] a resentful unwillingness to acknowledge and affirm the limitations and contingencies that constitute Being-in-the-world."[32]

For Heidegger, traditional philosophy is of little use in working through this condition. Philosophy, in the traditional sense, must be contrasted therefore, with a more basic "thinking" (P, 242; GA, 9: 317). This distinction requires, of course, that Heidegger employs a rather restricted (some say polemical) use of the term *philosophy*, something he increasingly resorted to, beginning with the "Letter on Humanism." Philosophy here refers to the history of Western thought that places primacy on metaphysics: "Philosophy, even when it becomes 'critical' through Descartes and Kant, always follows the course of metaphysical representation" (P, 252; GA, 9: 331). Heidegger calls philosophy "a technique for explaining from highest causes" (P, 242; GA, 9: 317), saying that it leads to the twin problems of "the dominance of subjectivity" (P, 242; GA, 9: 317) (the tendency to see objective reality as reducible to personal "values"),[33] and the "unconditional objectification of everything" (P, 242; GA, 9: 317).[34]

The tight relationship between Western philosophy and metaphysics is, according to Heidegger, the root of the current problematic of "humanism." Thus, we have now a three-part intersection of terms or concepts consisting of philosophy, metaphysics, and humanism.[35] As we have already seen in numerous other writings, and again restated here, Heidegger thinks that metaphysics is the attempt made within Western philosophy to understand Being (world-disclosure) through beings (the specific "things" that we encounter in the present). He states his case thus:

> Metaphysics does indeed represent beings in their being, and so it also thinks the being of beings. But it does not think being as such, does not think the difference between being and beings. . . . Metaphysics does not ask about the truth of being itself. Nor does it therefore ask in what way the essence of the human being belongs to the truth of being. Metaphysics has not only failed up to now to ask this question, the question is inaccessible to metaphysics as such. (P, 246; GA, 9: 322)

Humanism then, according to Heidegger, is a form of metaphysics: "Every humanism is either grounded in a metaphysics or is itself made to be the ground of one" (P, 245; GA, 9: 321). It examines humanity in search of some universal and permanent essence that can be known independent of the particular historical and practical worlds in which humans always find themselves. This claim would seem to be refuted by the turn taken in Kant, whereby the "essence" of the human is defined as freedom, not substance. However, as Heidegger is quick to point out, post-Kantian humanism posits a rationality, an *animal rationale* (P, 245; GA, 9: 322), that ultimately determines the telos of human development much as had earlier substantive theories of human nature. This preoccupation with rational determination is the root of modern Western humanity's self-understanding, and, since it names our capacity for reflection upon the world, of freedom. Humanism, and its metaphysics of *logos*, is the key, we are told, to unlocking freedom: "But if one understands humanism in general as a concern that the human being become free for his humanity and find his worth in it, then humanism differs according to one's conception of the 'freedom' and 'nature' of the human being" (P, 245; GA, 9: 321). In opposing the conflation of rationalism and freedom which Heidegger identifies in humanism, he is careful, however, not to be read as opposing all humanism or, even more strongly stated, as being against the *human*. The particular metaphysical form of humanism inherited from the Enlightenment does not, Heidegger reminds us, hold the monopoly on thinking about humanity itself. It is on this basis that Heidegger interprets his earlier work, particularly *Being and Time*, as being against the metaphysics of humanism, but not advocating an antihuman philosophy. If *Being and Time* is "against humanism," then

> this opposition does not mean that such thinking aligns itself against the humane and advocates the inhuman, that it promotes the inhumane and deprecates the dignity of the human being. Humanism is opposed because it does not set the *humanitas* of the human being high enough. Of course the essential worth of the human being does not consist in his being the substance of beings, as the "Subject" among them, so that as the tyrant of being he may deign to release the beingness of beings into an all too loudly glorified "objectivity". . . . It ought to be somewhat clearer now that opposition to

"humanism" in no way implies a defense of the inhuman but rather opens other vistas. (*P*, 251–52; *GA*, 9, 330; and *P*, 264–65; *GA*, 9: 348)

We can, then, draw four key features from Heidegger's critique of metaphysical humanism. First, he wants to disassociate the particular form of metaphysical humanism (presumably descending from Kant) from having a monopoly over thinking about humanity. Placing oneself against this metaphysical humanism is not, for instance, to advocate the inhumane. Second, metaphysical humanism must be normatively evaluated in terms of its role in placing humanity as the "tyrant of being." Since metaphysical humanism places our utmost humanity in the reconstruction of a disengaged "Subject" who stands over against the "object" of the world, it claims we are most ourselves when we are least embedded within our worlds. Heidegger wants to argue that this makes us into tyrants, driven by a desire to confirm our autonomous subjectivity by objectifying the world and marshalling it according to our will. Against this "tyrant of being," Heidegger juxtaposes the "shepherd of being."[36] A shepherd of being is one who is lives with, guides, and cultivates, but is ultimately reliant upon and is respectful to the world. Third, we can see here that Heidegger's ultimate goal in criticizing metaphysical humanism is to "open new vistas" [*andere Ausblicke öffnet*]. Thus, while his task here is critical, it is ultimately aimed at making space for new, alternative possibilities, those foreclosed by the totalizing nature of metaphysical humanism. Finally, what all this suggests is that to take up a problem like "metaphysics" is really to work against specific instances of entrapment—of the tendency to grasp problems related to the structure of reality as though disassociated from the form of life and modes of practical involvement which provide the conditions of possibility for their intelligibility and veracity. The goal here is not to find some single "solution," to overstep metaphysics in a grand gesture. This would be to take up our world only as a "problem" which needed to be solved. More modestly and carefully, we might say that metaphysics does not represent a problem we can solve, but a particular relationship, or a way of taking up problems. The manner in which we engage in our practical, particular problems is an outgrowth of the understanding of Being in the West called metaphysics, to be sure. But just as certain is that this understanding is sustained and thus transformed by slight modifications in the manner of our practical activities as much as it is "overcome" through grasping it conceptually. In the remainder of this chapter, I shall unpack why this activity must be historically mediated.

3.4. FROM FUNDAMENTAL TO HISTORICAL ONTOLOGY

> The necessary correlate of the phenomenological reduction is the becoming-historical of philosophy.
>
> **Herbert Marcuse**

Up to this point, we have focused attention on the form of analysis Heidegger calls fundamental ontology. However, as is hopefully more apparent by now, in the turn to questions of human freedom made after *Being and Time*, Heidegger was forced by the logic of his own position to consider the problem of articulating superordinate criteria that could distinguish between different modes of relating to fundamental ontology. In this section, I shall argue that such modes are necessarily historically mediated. It is one thing to state that Dasein is the kind of being that conceals its own involvement in a world (an ontological thesis); it is yet another thing to move beyond this and demonstrate *how* and *why* this concealing occurs in its particular historical manifestations (a historical inquiry). Later work on the "history of Being in the West" was meant to provide a more contextual analysis of this sort, resituating fundamental ontology within the historical and geographical location of the modern West. However, for this secondary analysis to be something more than a mere empirical history of the West, Heidegger still needed to demonstrate its connection to ontology and the understanding of Being. One way to do this, as Béatrice Han-Pile has suggested, would be for Heidegger to posit that there are some modifications "at the ontic level that are so considerable that they act on the very ontological structure of our existence and modify it."[37] These modifications, moreover, would not be modifications on the level of consciousness, but would unfold, rather, on the level of practical involvement. Hence the corresponding form of historical analysis would proceed through an analysis of the *basic practices* that make up the prevailing modes of revealing in a given epoch—not grounded in ideas, but in praxis. The challenge, then, put forward by Heidegger's ontological analysis of freedom, is to think through the question of historical change, but to do so through reference to these basic practices and not via an idealist conceptual history nor rationalist teleology. Thus, even for those who find Heidegger's ontological analysis of freedom compelling, the need for a corresponding historical form of critical analysis becomes increasingly apparent.

In the remainder of this chapter, we explain why this must be a historical repositioning and further unpack the problem of historicity in Heidegger's early writings as a means of preparing the discussion to come (specifically an engagement with Foucault). This requires, first, examining the place of historicity and "authentic historicizing" in *Being and Time*; and, second, relating this back to the more general question of social and political theory, that is, whether the first matter is of any use to social criticism. In this, I draw upon not only Heidegger's own writings on the matter, but also those of one of his more famous students to take up similar questions in the immediate wake of *Being and Time*: Herbert Marcuse (1898–1979).

3.5. HISTORICITY AND AUTHENTIC HISTORICIZING

One of the primary tasks of Division II of *Being and Time* is to arrive at the question of temporality and relate it back to the existential analytic sketched in the first half of the text. Heidegger has already provided a general outline of various dimensions of Care, the different elements that come to view when we view the structure of Care from the vantage point of such matters as Understanding, Angst, Spatiality, and so on. The task remains, however, of demonstrating how these different aspects hold together, that is, of disclosing *"the totality of the articulated structural whole of care, in the unity of its articulation as we have unfolded it"* (*BTa* §65, 371; SZ §65, 324; italics in original). The question of this unity is, in the technical sense of the term as Heidegger employs it, the question of the *meaning* of Care, and it is a central claim of the text as a whole that the meaning of Care—what makes it intelligible as articulated structural whole—is Temporality (*BTa* §65, 374; SZ §65, 327). Chapter IV of Division II (§67–71), in particular, is devoted to expounding upon this claim, followed by a demonstration of its explanatory value through a return to many of the main categories of Division I, reread now in light of the structure of temporality they imply and/or inhabit (e.g., Understanding, Anxiety, Falling, Discourse, etc.).

It is only in Chapter V of Division II that Heidegger turns directly to the question of historicity. In opening this chapter, Heidegger anticipates the possible objection that he has presented matters as though there is "no possibility of a more radical approach to the existential analytic" (*BTa* §72, 424; SZ §72, 372) than the one given by the previous analysis of the temporal structure of Care, with an emphasis on futurity and, in particular, on being-toward-death as the key to unlocking an authentic relationship to Dasein's essential temporality. Heidegger anticipates the objection that this previous analysis is "one-sided" insofar as it has bypassed the question of birth, or "Being-towards-the-beginning" (*BTa* §72, 425; SZ §72, 373). This possible objection is raised only instrumentally, however, for Heidegger is not directly interested in the question of natality for its own sake (as Hannah Arendt was years later).[38] Rather, it merely serves as a vehicle for bringing to light the "temporally stretched" character of Dasein—the notion that what we experience as a life is a connected whole stretched between beginning and end (related to what is later named as "self-constancy" [*Selbst-ständigkeit*]). The main point that Heidegger wishes to make in this section is that we do not, in fact, understand and experience this connectedness as a mere sequence of punctuated experiences *in time*, but rather as itself a meaningfully organized temporality. We do not first and foremost find ourselves "in" time, but rather find ourselves as temporal: "Dasein does not fill up a track or stretch 'of life'—one which is somehow present-at-hand—with the phases of its momentary actualities. It stretches *itself* along in such a way that its own Being is constituted in advance as a stretching-along. The 'between' which relates to birth and death already lies *in the Being* of Dasein" (*BTa* §72, 426; SZ §72, 374). Heidegger calls this specific temporally stretched character of Dasein its "historizing" or "happening" [*Geschehen*].

If it is the case that the fundamental existentials of Dasein can be disclosed in both authentic and inauthentic ways, then it stands to reason that Dasein's historizing can also be disclosed in these two basic modes as well. Heidegger has already suggested to us that the mode of relating to the temporality of our existence as a series of punctuated "now-moments" (that is, as present-at-hand "in time") is inauthentic. He then proceeds to explicitly name the authentic mode, stating: "To lay bare the *structure of historizing*, and the existential-temporal character of its possibility, signifies that one has achieved an *ontological* understanding of *historicity* [*Geschichtlichkeit*]" (*BTa* §72, 427; SZ §72, 375).[39] At this step in the argument, it is not altogether clear why we are making the leap to historicity and, from there, to historiography, since this seems to involve not only a transposition of the question of Dasein's temporality in the experience of its own (individualized) life to the question of collective history, but also a move from fundamental ontology to a specific ontic science. Other than giving some provisional assurances that the connection between the two levels of analysis can be found in the problem of Dasein's "self-constancy" [*Selbst-ständigkeit*], Heidegger does not provide much yet to make explicit the linkages. We can anticipate, however, that the answer will be that authentic historicizing will be defined in terms of its role in laying bare the "temporally stretched" structure of Dasein. Put another way, we can only study ourselves historically (in an ontic sense) at all because we are always already temporal in this ontological and phenomenological sense. An "authentic historicizing" or "authentic happening" will be the kind of ontic relating that discloses this basic structure more readily to us.

Authentic historizing must, for Heidegger, therefore avoid a naïve empirical positivism, one that would view historical facts as analogous to brute empirical data, observable in a neutral and objective manner by a disconnected and dispassionate historian. "History" in this case would be merely the arrangement of this data in its original, simple facticity, without any active interpretive or creative intervention on the part of the historian. We are unlikely today to be seduced by such a hermeneutically impoverished picture of historiography, but the conflation of an empirical, naturalistic view of history and the idea of historicity contained within social sciences was a major concern at the time of writing *Being and Time*. It was, for instance, central to the historical-hermeneutic turn made by such predecessors as Wilhelm Dilthey and Count Yorck.[40] Nevertheless, in our ordinary, everyday sense of something as belonging to the past, we can find traces of this impoverished vision. We speak, after all, of something as "historical" as if the quality of being so is that the object belongs to a previous world that is gone and cannot be retrieved.

Authentic historizing, by contrast, does not merely locate humans and their equipment within time. Rather, it discloses us as temporal and historical in such a way as to release us for *our own* present, that is, for whatever is required in the current situation. For thrownness is not merely a general existential of Dasein. It is also conditioned by its specific, historical character. Dasein does not just find itself in "a world"; rather, it finds itself in a *specific* world with a specific, concrete historical inheritance. Heidegger calls this Dasein's "heritage" [*Erbe*] (*BTa* §74, 435; SZ §74, 383). The fact that we do not choose our specific inheritance (and can thus tend toward resentment of it, viewing it as an imposition) and yet cannot meaningfully exist without *some* inheritance, means we must both affirm heritage and critically wrest with it. This critical appropriation of heritage, Heidegger calls "primordial historizing," the process by which Dasein *"hands* itself *down* to itself," or grasps its fate [*Schicksal*] (*BTa* §74, 435; SZ §74, 384). Furthermore, since this heritage is the outgrowth of a historical experience of a community of people, whenever a critical appropriative relationship to it is grasped authentically, it also involves the realization of its essentially collective basis. Thus, "if fateful Dasein, as Being-in-the-world, exists essentially in Being-with Others, its historizing as a co-historizing and is determinative for it as *destiny* [*Geschick*]" (*BTa* §74, 436; SZ §74, 384). The community in which our existing fatefully is bound up and through which we grasp our destiny is what Heidegger calls our "generation."

The fact that some object appears to us as "historical," even when (perhaps especially when) it no longer appears as useful equipment within its original world and instead appears to us only as present-at-hand (e.g., the ruins of a temple) can only strike us as significant and meaningful because such objects are originally part of a world of existential significance, are employed as ready-to-hand by other creatures for whom the world can be meaningful (or not). It is only because the temple was part of a world that it can now appear meaningfully as part of our world (albeit in a different way, i.e., as a "historical object"). And this, in turn, is only possible because it was part of the temporally structured world of humans, stretched as they were between birth and death. To grasp this authentically is to relate to it in such a way as to reveal not only the temporal dimension of this other human world, but also *one's own*. To repeat, then, the final move in this argument is to say that, because authentic historizing reveals the essentially temporal structure of our own existence in a way that frees us for the kind of creative, critical appropriation of our heritage that permits us to move beyond a slavish repetition of the past, paradoxically, authentic historizing is ultimately *future-oriented*.

To be released for the future is not to assert simply and naively that anything is possible. This is the kind of falsehood we often teach children, for instance, when we offer them platitudes such as, "You can be *anything* you want to be." Such popular mantras are more than merely vacuous since they also individualize and personalize the experience of failure whenever the concrete limitations of one's own possible futures are met. If I accept such platitudes, then the realization I cannot in fact be *anything* I wish to become is likely to be experienced as a personal failure (weakness of the will, lack of effort, etc.). The alternative is a recognition that the limitation on options is (at the most generally level) existentially-ontologically required for there to be such a thing as meaningful choice at all. We should instead more properly say that to authentically "hand oneself down to oneself" means to grasp and realize one's possibilities by creatively and critically appropriating the concrete realities into which one is born and thrown, including historically mediated heritage. To do this, we have to accept the past as something beyond our ultimate control but also constitutive of our sense of self and actualization as agents, a process Heidegger also occasionally names as "repetition."

In effect, here we can see Heidegger reformulating the paradox of freedom and constraint—already highlighted above via the concept of *Spielraum*—into the language of historicity. The same structural relationship between agency and constriction we found in Heidegger's characterization of the opening of a field is played out here, except now in relation to a critical appropriation of one's inheritance. In both cases, the capacity to creatively and critically transgress an inherited field of meaning and action requires a simultaneous acceptance and acknowledgment of the resources handed down to us by this field. There can be no "wholesale" transcendence of a historically inherited field or space of opening, only a creative reappropriation that realizes latent possibilities and, in so doing, simultaneously fulfills and exceeds that field.

While we might accept this description at one level, it is also likely to leave us somewhat frustrated. For if it is the case that Dasein is constitutionally structured by this movement of simultaneous transgression/

constriction, then this tells us nothing about what *particular* elements we ought transgress in any specific case. It appears therefore agnostic as to any particular direction we might develop our inheritance, and thus effectively useless as a tool for any specific sociopolitical projects. Periodically, Heidegger acknowledges something of this limitation: "In the existential analysis we cannot, in principle, discuss what Dasein *factically* resolves in any particular case. Our investigation excludes even the existential projection of the factical possibilities of existence. Nevertheless, we must ask whence, *in general*, Dasein can draw those possibilities upon which it factically projects itself" (*BTa* §74, 434; SZ §74, 383).

We are approaching now a central, constitutive problem with ontological analysis of this sort. If we wish to avoid the reductive tendencies of an epistemological tradition—one that posits a more basic grasp of reality is to be found only when the world can be reduced to (ahistorical) propositional content (Truth as correspondence), a position which further entangles us in subject-object dualisms—then we need to preserve *some* sense of freedom in the ontological sense, that is, in the sense of an indeterminacy in the presencing of world. This indeterminacy is expressed in a variety of ways in Heidegger, but there is a core insight at the heart of all of these variations, namely, that the "actuality" of the world is revealed through "understanding," itself actually a *process* (specifically, a process of working out the possibilities projected in worldly practical relations within which we always already find ourselves), and is thus fundamentally temporal in structure. Hence, "actuality" is best thought of as a temporally structured dynamic relationship: "Being" is only possible on the basis of Care, an articulated totality of temporally stretched relations. The necessary, irreducible indeterminacy of Being is "ontological freedom."

However, "ontological freedom" imports a set of new difficulties from which Heidegger struggles to liberate himself. For one thing, the thesis risks becoming so large and all-encompassing as to run the risk of self-trivialization. As we touched upon above, if Being is necessarily "free" (where "freedom" signals this indeterminacy in the relevant sense), then this "free" situation *cannot but* be the case. Thus, the thesis risks becoming trivial in the sense that it is without consequences. It appears to make literally no difference whether we apprehend the truth of ontological freedom or not, since we have just said that it is fundamental in the sense of being always already the case (whether we know it or not). More to the point, if ontological freedom is wholly inalienable in this way, it can have no bearing upon ontic freedom—social and political realities—since any particular sociopolitical situation must equally reflect the basic structure of Care and Being-in-the-world.

We might think we can find a solution to this by simply accepting the limitations of the position. That is, we could simply concede that there are *no* sociopolitical implications to be derived from ontological investigation of this sort. Thus, lack of a social or political theory here might be a problem for someone else, but that is a wholly external critique, entirely foreign to the self-understanding of Heidegger's project. Heidegger does periodically disavow that an ethics can be deduced from fundamental ontology. However, on closer inspection, this attempt to inoculate ontological freedom against such criticism will not work. Because *on its own terms*, the thesis on ontological freedom must be nontrivial in the sense that it must represent itself as a genuine improvement upon alternative theses, an improvement with some worldly significance. Otherwise, its own critique of the epistemological-cognitivist picture is rendered vacuous or inconsequential. The critique of epistemological-cognitivism is rendered "unworldly" and merely "academic" in the pejorative sense. By the logic of Heidegger's own reasoning, this cannot be the case, however. Fundamental ontology cannot, under the weight of its own conclusions, remain only a general sketch of a structure of Being-in-the-world, only an "idea." For, insofar as it remains only a general structure without historically mediated content, it retains features of the very metaphysics it seeks to displace. It becomes an abstract concept, divorced from a world, the result of a tendency it was originally meant to criticize. As Heidegger himself once put this problem, "a regard for metaphysics still prevails even in the intending to overcome metaphysics. Therefore our task is to cease all overcoming, and leave metaphysics to itself."[41]

The solution to this has been to introduce various kinds of superordinate distinctions, some versions of which we have already discussed. For instance, ontological freedom can retain its status as fundamental in the sense of "always already the case" while, at the same time, immunizing itself against the claim to insignificance by admitting that while ontological freedom is inalienable, there is a difference between grasping this fact and concealing it. Thus, we introduce a superordinate distinction between a condition in which ontological freedom is *disclosed* and a condition in which it is *disguised* (in some nontrivial manner). This sort of superordinate criterion is, as we have already seen, the basis for the distinction between authenticity and inauthencity (Chapter Two), which is later transposed directly into the language of freedom versus nonfreedom (above, in this chapter). If such a superordinate distinction is required, then it will be historically mediated and will provide the basis for mediation between ontic and ontological levels. The challenge then is to give some concrete historical content to this basic notion, that is, to ask what *particular* socially constituted basic practices and relations exist that currently serve to conceal the more basic structure of ontological freedom. Or, inversely, what practices and relations can free us from the condition of self-concealment that currently holds us captive?

3.6. PRAXIS, RADICAL ACTION, AND NECESSITY

Immediately after the 1927 publication of *Being and Time*, close readers of the text observed this problem and began to work on a solution. As noted previously,[42] it was the young Herbert Marcuse who first took up the challenge of providing such an analysis. Marcuse affirmed Heidegger's general ontology, yet at the same time sought a social and historical-materialist complement that might unlock the key determining criteria whereby the particular, concrete superordinate criteria might be disclosed to humankind. Because Marcuse was convinced that *capitalism* was the primary obstacle to our self-realization, between 1928 and 1933, he wrote a series of works that attempted to construct a bridge between Heidegger's existential analytic of Dasein and a properly reconstructed Marxism as a means of concretizing the work of fundamental ontology. These works include essays such as "Contributions to a Phenomenology of Historical Materialism" (1928); "On Concrete Philosophy" (1929); "On the Problem of Dialectic" (part 1, 1930; part 2, 1931); "New Sources on the Foundations of Historical Materialism" (1932); and "On the Philosophical Foundation of the Concept of Labour in Economics" (1933);[43] as well as his 1930 habilitation *Hegel's Ontology and the Theory of Historicity*.[44] Since our interest in these early works is merely to recover the original animating impulse behind the attempted synthesis, and use them as an example of the sort of mediating project we envisage here, we need not reconstruct the arguments in all of their internal diversity and complexity. Without involving ourselves in a full explication of early Marcuse, then, we can see that he is grappling with a problematic that leads us into conversation with Foucault.[45] How might Heidegger's account of freedom as residing within a field of possibilities be complemented with a historical analysis that takes into account the particular factual possibilities of the present without reduction to either naïve historical positivism or rationalist determination?

. . .

We began this chapter by arguing that, among his contributions, Heidegger offers the most sustained and systematic elaboration since Marx of the notion that our primary experience of the world is not mediated by consciousness but is instead a practical relation. This overarching similarity between the two otherwise very different thinkers provides the first tool with which someone such as Marcuse can construct a bridge between them. For both Heidegger and Marx, objects are not primarily apprehended and appropriated through perception, observation and conceptual ordering (a kind of cognitive grasping), but are rather related to as "equipment" through sensuous, practical coping activities. Marcuse's way of putting this is to insist upon *praxis* as the "decisive attitude [*Haltung*] of human Dasein" (Marcuse, 33). Elsewhere, he becomes more specific. Marcuse employs the category of "labor" to express the foundational practical relationship between subject and world. Labor is for him not one activity among many, but is instead human Being-in-the-world itself: "Labour is an ontological concept, that is, a concept that grasps the being of human Dasein itself and as such" (Marcuse, 124). In this elevation of labor to an ontological concept, Marcuse is, of course, providing an unorthodox reading of both Marx and (even more so) Heidegger. For while Heidegger may have intended Care to designate a set of practical relations, nowhere does he suggest that labor in a narrow sense has any primacy here. So this is one of Marcuse's creative contributions: the notion that the phenomenology of Care must be recast in terms of the "first principle of historical materialism," namely, that its own "production and reproduction" is Dasein's "primary care" (Marcuse, 25), and that the category of labor names the activity for the actualization of this first need.[46]

Even as an ontological concept, however, labor is related to and conditioned by historicity. For while labor may be the sensuous, practical medium through which humans interact with and appropriate their world—a point derived from a general phenomenology—this is only ever experienced in specific sociohistorical contexts. For "every concrete-historical Dasein there belongs a concrete-historical 'life-space,'" wherein Dasein "creates the possibilities of his existence as possibilities of production and reproduction" (Marcuse, 27). So Marcuse wants to affirm Heidegger's ontological claims with regard to Dasein as coming to itself through a set of practical relations within the world in which it is thrown, structured by temporality and historicity, but he also wishes to concretize the point by rendering those "practical relations" as labor, conditioned by specific sociohistorical circumstances. He affirms Heidegger's rendering of temporality as "neither an a priori form of intuition [*Anschauungsform*] nor an empirical order of objects but rather a fundamental constituent of Dasein through which alone Dasein can be," calling it "decisive" (Marcuse, 13); while, at the same time, putting the concept to some practical use in theorizing Dasein's lived reality by extricating it from the relatively high level of abstraction it enjoys within fundamental ontology. As such, it is not enough merely to transpose temporality into a *general* question of historicity. We must move one more step forward, toward a confrontation with the "question of the material constitution of historicity," in other words, toward an ontic study of the *specific* experience of historicity today, an experience mediated by the specific praxis prevailing over our current form of life. Only in so doing can we accomplish the "breakthrough that Heidegger fails to achieve or even gesture toward" (Marcuse, 16).[47]

But how can analysis of the "material constitution of historicity" avoid becoming mere empirical history—that is, a litany of factical events "in" time, rather than an authentic historizing that discloses Dasein *as* temporal? How can such a material and historical analysis of particular laboring praxis be a radical extension of the path opened up by Heidegger, rather than an external imposition? How is this anything but mere ontic historiography of the kind criticized by Heidegger as concealing of Dasein?

Marcuse's answer to these questions is precisely to do as we have already suggested: to posit a transformation on the ontic level that is fundamentally transformative for existence as such. The praxis that transcends its ontic situatedness is what Marcuse calls the "radical act." Rather provocatively displacing the critique of capital as the heart of Marxism, Marcuse argues instead that the "central concern" of this tradition is "the historical possibility of the radical act—of an act that should clear the way for a new and necessary reality as it brings about the actualization of the whole person" (Marcuse, 3). The gap between ordinary praxis and radical action is not then to be found in a difference of scale. Rather, it is qualitative: "Every act is a human 'transformation of circumstances,' but not every action also transforms human *existence*" (Marcuse, 4). The truly radical act is not one that has merely incidental "world-historical" significance in the ontic sense; that is, it is a major event "in" history, viewed retrospectively. Rather, it is the moment in which the proper agents of history realize themselves as such, when the subject and object of historical motility merge in a self-conscious unity (where *self-conscious* here denotes more than "grasped theoretically," but instead means realized in and through a unique praxis).

It stands to reason, then, that traditional philosophical analysis will be inadequate for grasping such a "happening." Such a qualitative shift cannot be properly comprehended from within traditional frameworks of analysis since it fundamentally reorients the basic relations constitutive of our theoretical frameworks and, as such, it can only be experienced as a radical rupture, event, or happening. Hence the centerpiece of Marcuse's work during this period: "The truths of Marxism are not truths of knowing [*Erkennens*], but rather truths of happening [*Geschehen*]" (Marcuse, 1).[48]

In this way, a second bridge is built between Marx and Heidegger. If the first emerged out of a shared commitment to "practical relations" over cognitivist views of agency, the second is constructed by translating the phenomenological analysis of "resoluteness" in Heidegger as a "moment of decision" on par with the radical act in Marxism (Marcuse, 15).[49] Heidegger did provide some resources for such a reading, particularly whenever he frames resoluteness in terms of "the disclosive projection and determination of *what is factically possible at the time*" (*BTa* §60, 345; *SZ* §60, 298). Frustratingly, however (as we have seen), Heidegger avoids giving an account of what precisely is "factically possible at the time," nor any real criteria for determining this. In some cases, he explicitly denies the very possibility of providing such concrete content.[50] (Hence it was possible to take the notion of resoluteness as devoid of content in the direction of a decisionistic existentialism, à la Sartre.)[51] Marcuse, by contrast, sought to remedy the perceived vacuity of resoluteness by linking it to a Marxist construal of radical action that, in his view, provided more concrete content. In addition to his critique of a tendency toward abstraction, Marcuse sought moreover to distance his appropriation of resoluteness (now comprehended in terms of radical action) from the isolated *individualistic* overtones of Heidegger's formulation. As he puts it, "One must undoubtedly oppose Heidegger's attempt . . . to refer the decisive resolution back to the isolated Dasein rather than driving it toward the resoluteness of the act" (Marcuse 16). Instead, Marcuse sought to think resoluteness qua radical action as a collective happening. In this, Marcuse did not originally see himself as operating wholly *outside* of Heidegger's original formulation, but rather extending and radicalizing the already existing resources for thinking collective action and historical appropriation made available in *Being in Time* through such language as the "destiny" of a "generation." As Marcuse summarizes these points:

> Phenomenological analysis demonstrated that human Dasein is essentially historical, and it recognized praxis as Dasein's originary conduct—and therefore opened up to view once again the ways in which "theoretical reason" is grounded in concrete historical existence, not as accidental facticity, but rather as a being-bound to one another in accordance with being. Historical materialism merely provides the concrete interpretation of this state of affairs when it speaks of "social being" (concrete being-in-the-world with each other) as the bearer of historical motility and of its "mode of production" (the praxis of doing things in the environment) as the determining factor of that which happens. (Marcuse, 32–33)

The transposing of the question of radical action into sociopolitical terms (in this case, very specifically in terms of the collective overcoming of capitalism) is thus presented not as a refutation of the phenomenology of a happening, but rather as its concrete realization.

In order to better understand Marcuse's appropriation of the Marxist conception of radical action as the historical achievement of subject-object identity, it is helpful to consider momentarily its corrupted form. Following the path set out by Lukács's philosophical explication of Marx's category of reification in *History and Class Consciousness* (1923), Marcuse considers prevailing modes of productive activity and social organization under capitalism as deficient and pathological in the sense that they are fundamentally self-estranging. Under conditions of capitalism, praxis is distorted such that (1) the creative, productive capacities of humans are experienced as standing over and against subjective freedom—one's "own deed becomes an alien power opposed to him" (Marcuse, quoting Marx, 4);[52] and (2) relations between humans come to be experienced as instrumental, or objectlike—the "taking-on-oneself of the law of the thing rather than letting one's own Dasein happen" (Marcuse, 138). The former is commonly described in terms of alienation, the latter as reification.[53] In so taking on this language, Marcuse also adopts a distinction (found, for instance, in Marx's *1844 Manuscripts*) between objectification and reification. Objectification is that *necessary* externalization of human essence through laboring praxis. However, Marcuse argues, "objectification always carries within it a tendency toward reification and labour a tendency toward alienation, so that reification and alienation are not merely chance historical facts" (Marcuse, 112).[54] The structural distinction between "ordinary" objectification and its pathological forms provides Marcuse, then, with the criteria for recognizing and affirming resoluteness, in other words, "what is factually possible at the time." As he puts it: "The guidelines for action in which concrete philosophy culminates will never contain ... abstract norms, empty imperatives. They will necessarily have been drawn from the necessities of concrete existing in its historical situation and will in every case be addressed, not to an abstract universal, but to a concrete, existing subject" (Marcuse, 46). So the distinction between authentic and inauthentic praxis is related to a "concrete, existing subject" for Marcuse by way of a theory of resoluteness qua radical action.

This, in turn, is also meant to provide a kind of methodological tool for theoretical intervention. For it is the task of a properly "concrete philosophy," not merely to reflect upon such action-events, but to contribute to the overturning of alienated and reified modes of objectification. Marcuse suggests it can do so in a twofold manner. First, such work performs the "initial ground-clearing" for such action by providing a clear economic-historical analysis of the situation (Marcuse, 30–31). For Marcuse, philosophy becomes concrete when it properly integrates, and remains informed by, social theory.[55] However, this kind of work can only be "ground-clearing" since the ultimate aim of any such analysis of systems of power, in all their concrete, material facticity, must ultimately lead to, and take hold of, "the primary modes of conduct of historical Dasein." Such modes of conduct "reshape the worlds of meaning (ideologies)," but since they are derived from concrete historical circumstances, they are "not accessible to a phenomenology of historicity as the fundamental structure of Dasein" (Marcuse, 30). Thus, material-historical studies of a concrete situation are coupled with an analysis of the "primary modes of conduct" in such a way as to disclose not merely Dasein as "in" history, but also fundamentally historical in such a way as to properly release us for radical action in the present.

To recapitulate: Marcuse sought to construct a bridge between the ontological-phenomenological analysis displayed in *Being and Time* and the material-historical project of Marxism by drawing out the central Heideggerian notion of historicity and showing under what conditions it could have concrete factical content while, at the same time, avoiding a certain "ontic reductionism" (i.e., collapsing into empirical history). He does so by suggesting that some praxis (radical action) is transformative not merely of circumstances but of existence. Such action is possible when it seizes upon the "necessity" of our historical situation, a necessity that can be uncovered by concrete philosophy and subsequently transcended through praxis.

So the standard of "radicality" here is its "necessity." But from whence do we derive our understanding of necessity? It is fine to claim that the benchmark of necessity cannot be "abstract norms" or "empty imperatives," but instead must come from the "fateful happening" given over by the historical situation. It is an altogether different thing to give this a concrete form and, moreover, to explain whether its overcoming of distorted praxis is a localized or universal phenomena. We have seen that Marcuse wishes to pin the necessity of radical action upon a distinction between authentic praxis and its inauthentic deviations. Radical action moves us away from alienated and reified condition of labor, toward a praxis that enables us to grasp ourselves authentically—to truly "give ourselves to ourselves."

Here Marcuse falters, however, exposing the cracks between Heidegger and Marx, but opening up for us the question of historical ontology. Let us look closely at one particular passage where this becomes evident. In his 1928 essay "Contributions to a Phenomenology of Historical Materialism," Marcuse writes,

> Radical action is, according to its essence, *necessary*, both for the actor and for the environment in which it is performed. Through its historical occurrence it transforms necessity—transforms something that had become utterly unbearable—and posits in its place precisely the necessity that alone can sublate the unbearable. Any act that does not have this specific character of necessity is not radical and also might just as easily not take place, or might just as easily be performed by someone else. This leads to the last, decisive meaning of necessity: necessity is *immanent* to the radical act. That it must occur right now, that it must be done precisely here and precisely by this person, means that it cannot, under any circumstances, be forced on the doer [*Täter*] from outside; that the doer *must*—in the sense of an immanent *must*—commit it now because the deed [*Tat*] is given along with the doer's very existence. (Marcuse, 5)

In this passage, a tension is exposed through Marcuse's ambiguous relating of radicality to necessity. For on the one hand, he wishes to give resoluteness concrete content by suggesting that it is measurable by the standard of "radical action" which, in turn, is recognizable by its conformity to "historical necessity." On the other hand, however, necessity itself is defined in terms of, and subordinated to, radicality. An act is radical because it is necessary, but radical action *transforms necessity*; necessity is said to be *"immanent* to the radical act." Radical action and historical necessity appear to define each other in a circular manner and therefore seem only tautologically related. As such, they fail to provide "resoluteness" with any concrete content.

Marcuse thus brings us to a certain impasse. On the one hand, he seeks to employ insights from Heidegger in order to avoid a certain mechanistic determinism. Radical action is not beholden to necessity, understood within the framework of naturalistic laws of causality (as with Kant's vision of a linear, empirical reality or as with certain versions of positivist Marxism prevalent in Marcuse's own time). Rather, it is conceived of as a happening that creates "a new world by means of the transforming act" (Marcuse, 32), and is thus comprehensible as "necessary" only in the *wake* of that emergent world. Necessity is immanent to radical action. Such a formulation puts him most clearly on the Heideggerian side of this dilemma. Elsewhere, he affirms a very Heideggerian rendering of the matter:

> Dasein does not "make" history as its product, it does not live in history as if history were its more or less coincidental space or element; rather, the concrete existing of Dasein *"is"* happening [*Geschehen*] that is understood as "history" [*Geschichte*]. To regard the ontological historicity of Dasein as mere facticity or something like it would not only mean over-looking the actual life-sphere of Dasein at the very outset of the philosophical undertaking, but would also contravene the findings of phenomenology, which alone may serve to guide it. (Marcuse, 38)[56]

Casting Dasein's freedom as ontologically necessary means, however, that we find ourselves in serious tension with the Hegelian legacy appropriated by Marx. For if necessity is only intelligible in the wake of radical action, transformed as it is by this such an act, then necessity is not Absolute. This means abandoning the ideal of a teleological view of historicity, whereby the standard of necessity by which we judge radical action "runs ahead" of us, and is only fully grasped as such in the final stages of its realization. On this alternative Hegelian reading, necessity is not given *by* radical action, but stands above it as an organizing principle of the whole. In his early writings, Marcuse baulks at such a reading. He even attempts to assimilate Hegel to a Heideggerian frame, pushing against an interpretation of the former as the paradigmatic philosopher of "Absolute being": "For constituting the *totality* of be-ing in the historical being of human life forbids precisely any statement about 'absolute being' and any determination of be-ing from the standpoint of 'absolute logos.' Hegel's dialectic, which was originally based on the concept of life, could only become an absolute dialectic when this original historicity of life came to a standstill within his system" (Marcuse, 82). Thus, one route to a proper synthesis of Marx and Heidegger is to sacrifice the Hegelian conception of the Absolute upon the altar of indeterminacy and contingency (represented here as "ontological freedom"), and merely accept that the standard of necessity is only found within radical action itself, only from within the "happening" of history. Embracing this exit strategy does not come without significant costs, however. For if historical necessity is not read in relation to Absolute Being, then it cannot prevail over the multiplicity of lifeworlds. The significance of radical action is thus only relational to the specific oppositional context, that is, the constrictors of its particular factically given time and place. In this way, fundamental ontology, even when adapted and made to service a universalized phenomenology of labor, nevertheless leads to a certain relativizing tendency with regard to sociopolitical consequences. Returning to Marxism then, one would have to concede for instance that the struggle against alienation and reification is only a local one: that the movement of history is an open-ended process of radical transcendence, recovery and return that cannot, even in principle be definitively and finally overcome. This would not mean that a proletariatian revolution against capitalism is not called for—even necessary, in the specific sense with which Marcuse is employing the term—but it does demote this from any pretensions to a definitive realization of nonalienated being.[57]

. . .

As we now know, Marcuse eventually abandoned this bridging project, concluding that he had failed to convincingly mediate between the two forms of analysis.[58] After 1933—a date he repeatedly characterized as an "event" or "happening" for philosophy itself—Marcuse concluded that there was no way to authentically recover and appropriate the opening originally found in Heidegger. An ontologically framed conception of freedom was, for Marcuse, too tainted with decisionism, and historicity too susceptible to empty abstraction and thus fatalistic resignation. Thus, after this period, he increasingly turned away from Heidegger toward Hegelian-Marxism, resolving the tensions of these early writings by simply revoking his earlier reading of Hegel, affirming the idea of Absolute Being and the related Marxist vision of capitalism as a universalization of the general process of human alienation (such that its overcoming could be seen as the overcoming of alienation as such).

To explore this Hegelian alternative would be to pursue another line of inquiry altogether.[59] Instead, what concerns us centrally here is the alternative possibilities for a concretized conception of historicity that resolves the dilemma by grasping the other horn, so to speak. That is, what remains to pursue is the possibility of conceiving of radical action as a happening along the lines that Marcuse has extracted from Heidegger, but without submitting this to an Absolute standard. Instead, we would be left with a radical act whose necessity is only manifest from within the concrete, particular world out of which it emerges. Such a binding of action and necessity need not concede all language of universality, but it will have to concede that the test of its universality can be nothing other than a phenomenological one—that is, one mediated by the experiential reality of a subject within concrete community. This vision would confirm Marcuse's suspicion of fundamental ontology's tendency toward "false abstraction," but it would also diagnose a concomitant tendency in absolutist dialectics toward the conflation of particular, experientially grounded struggles of freedom with the struggle against alienation per se. In other words, what would remain would be an "ontology of actuality": a vision of emancipatory praxis wherein the meaning of emancipation would remain multiple and itself a terrain of contestation.[60] This, I shall argue, is central to the critical-historical work of Michel Foucault.

FOUR

FOUCAULT CONTRA HEIDEGGER

BEFORE PROCEEDING on to a discussion of how Foucault's late writings might help fill out the general problematic of situated freedom following from the previous chapters, it is necessary to sketch out Foucault's initial critique of Heidegger. It is not my main interest here to detail the relationship between the two thinkers in all its different facets. This has, at any rate, been done in more detail by others.[1] What *is* required, however, is a setting of the background of Foucault's critical relation to Heidegger prior to the later writings on subjectivity, ethics, and freedom. To establish this background, I propose examining three lines of critique running through Foucault's work prior to 1979, each of which implicates Heidegger. These include: (1) the historicizing of the phenomenology of "experience"; (2) the critique of hermeneutics; and (3) the interrogation of the "analytics of finitude" and its relation to a positing of "original man."

It should be stated at the outset that these lines of critique are not presented in any systematic fashion in Foucault's work nor should they necessarily be taken as direct criticisms of Heidegger per se. Direct references to Heidegger himself are quite sparse in Foucault's writings—especially after his first two works. Rather than direct citation, Foucault tends to refer rather obliquely to concepts and terminology that we can only assume are meant to be references, if not to Heidegger, at least to Heideggerian philosophy generally.[2] Finally, many of these criticisms are general enough that, while the scope of their critique might include Heidegger, they certainly are not *exclusively* aimed at him. In fact, Foucault is often speaking of whole intellectual traditions, such as existentialism, phenomenology, hermeneutics, and what he calls the "analytics of finitude." In each of these cases, we might say that Heidegger has contributed to the fields. However, it is also true that his contributions were almost always creative and idiosyncratic. Frequently, he significantly altered, even reversed, the terms of the tradition in a manner that others within it resisted (as with phenomenology). In some cases Heidegger specifically disavowed a relationship to the field of study (as with existentialism), or first embraced but later distanced himself from it (as with hermeneutics). Finally, as with Foucault's analytics of finitude, the net is cast so wide as to include nearly every philosopher since Kant. Despite all this, these lines of critique, even when not specifically aimed *at* Heidegger, all implicate him (at least in Foucault's mind: we shall see later whether fairly or not), and stand as obstacles to any attempt to bring the two thinkers together in a fruitful theoretical development.

4.1. HISTORICIZING THE PHENOMENOLOGY OF "EXPERIENCE"

The first line of inquiry and critique actually begins largely from *within* Heideggerian philosophy and only emerges as a critique through a slow process of reinterpreting and rearticulating of key concepts. The heart of this critique is that while existential phenomenology claims to begin with situated, concrete existence, it does so through recourse to "experiences" which are not themselves given a historical or social analysis. Such an existential phenomenology (most evident in *Being and Time*) relies therefore on a set of "experiences" that are at best underdeveloped theoretically and at worst merely posited naïvely. This tension emerges primary in Foucault's earliest work on madness and psychiatry,[3] because it is in these works that Foucault is most interested in such experiences as madness (*folie*), mental illness (*maladie mentale*), and unreason (*déraison*). It should also be noted that although Foucault specifically references Heidegger and Heideggerian scholars in these writings, the work here is best taken as a critical engagement with existentialism and phenomenology as it was articulated in France during the 1950s and early 1960s. Thus, while Heidegger looms large, so too do Husserl, Sartre, and Merleau-Ponty, for instance. In some cases, it is not always clear that Foucault's criticisms are meant for Heidegger specifically, or rather for some other reading of these broad philosophical traditions.[4]

Foucault's earliest work is his most explicitly Heideggerian, and it is not hard to see why. Heidegger's work to that point, introduced in France after the Second World War primarily through Sartre and Jean Beaufret, focused on demonstrating that the subject was not a metaphysical "thing," a transcendental ego, or an idealist mind. Rather, the subject was always conditioned by its being-in-a-world. Subjectivity was, Heidegger proposed, the center of a set of relations of meaning, intelligible only against a larger background of practices given to the self by its lifeworld. These practices were relational, temporal, and to some extent unknowable. The subject was, therefore, fundamentally social, historical, and occluded from itself. Such a notion of "embedded subjectivity" was of great interest and use to young Foucault. In fact, we might say that the "embedded subject" in this sense is the presupposition for his early studies of madness and unreason. As Keith Hoeller puts it, "In order to write the history of madness, one must put the patient back into a world again and write the history of madmen *and* society, patients *and* doctors. In other words, what all these critics of psychiatry have in common is the Heideggerian notion that human beings are always constituted by the concept of 'being-in-the-world,' and that 'madness' is a societal event which occurs *between* people who may in fact have conflicting values and goals."[5] In his earliest writings, Foucault explicitly saw this task as an extension of Heideggerian philosophy and consistently deployed language that evoked the phenomenological tradition. For instance, he describes his task in *The Birth of the Clinic* to examine "where 'things' and 'words' have not yet been separated, and where—at the most fundamental level of language—seeing and saying are still one. We must reexamine the original distribution of the visible and the invisible insofar as it is linked with the division between what is stated and what remains unsaid" (*BC*, xii; *NC*, vii). Later, again invoking the language of Heidegger and Merleau-Ponty, he claims that "the relation between the visible and invisible . . . is necessary to all concrete knowledge" (*BC*, xiii; *NC*, viii). The Foucauldian subject, at this point in his writings, is always a subject constituted by her being-in-the-world, whose experiences are grounded not only in the visible (consciously reflected upon Interpretations), but even more primordially, in the invisible (background Understanding). So, we can see why it is that Foucault would say later in his life that he had taken up existential analysis in a "Heideggerian way."[6]

From this base, however, Foucault began increasingly to distance himself from the language and conceptual tools of post-Heideggerian phenomenology. Even in revised drafts of *Mental Illness and Psychology*, new headings are telling. Part 1, written in 1954, is entitled "Les dimensions psychologiques de la maladie," concludes with the chapter "La maladie et l'existence," and is referred to as a "phenomenology of mental illness."[7] However, part 2 (written in 1962) is called "Folie et culture" and contains chapters on "La constitution historique de la maladie mentale" and "La folie, structure globale." In each of these new titles, note the new emphasis on cultural, social, and political dimensions of the question. In fact, the new version of part 2 begins with the following statement, already a form of autocritique in relation to the first half of the book: "The preceding analyses have fixed the coordinates by which psychologies can situate the pathological fact. But although they showed the forms of appearance of the illness, they have been unable to show its condition of appearance. It would be a mistake to believe that organic evolution, psychological history, or the situation of man in the world may reveal these conditions" (*MIP*, 60; *MMP*, 71). Thus, we can see Foucault is beginning to open cracks between the two parts of the post-Heideggerian phenomenological project. On the one hand, the subject is thoroughly *situated* in a world. On the other hand, however, claims to know this situatedness rest upon the presence of existential "experiences" whose historical and social situatedness are never themselves interrogated. These two halves of the phenomenological project at the same time point to a general movement away from the individual subject in its world toward histories of forms of experience, constituted socially. In other words, Foucault began to show not only *that* the subject was conditioned by its being-in-the-world, but more precisely *how* it was so. So while it is clear that Foucault saw his early work as a continuation of the path opened up by Heidegger, it is also clear that he quickly began to use the general insight into historicity and deploy it against Heidegger's work itself. The first point of reversal involves the status of existential "experiences."

To get at Foucault's uneasiness with the existential-phenomenological category of "experience," we might begin by asking: how does Heidegger develop his claim into the historicity of Dasein? As we saw in Chapter Two, Heidegger claims we can arrive at this insight by beginning from a phenomenology of concrete experiences, specifically ones such as dread, boredom, angst, fear, and so on. When we examine these experiences and inquire into *why* they occur, we find not merely personal psychological reasons (i.e., I have a fear of water now because I once almost drowned), but also *existential* grounds. Namely, we discover that our selfhood is only experientially accessible to us through a preexisting world that matters to us and is meaningful. As Hubert Dreyfus puts it, *Existenzialen* "reveal Dasein as *dependent upon a public system of significances* that it did *not produce*."[8] This "system of significances"—this world—is the precondition for our subjectivity. This insight into the existential ground of our experiences is the basis on which philosophers and psychologists of this time tried to develop an existential psychology based on *Daseinsanalysis*. Thinkers in this tradition included Ludwig Binswanger, Medard Boss, Viktor Frankl, and Karl Jaspers, a school with which Foucault had considerable familiarity. In fact, one of Foucault's first published works, written in 1953 while he was still a doctoral student, was "Dream, Imagination, and Existence," a preface to the French translation to Binswanger's *Traum und Existenz*, first published in 1930.[9]

The connection between experiential events such as dread or being-toward-death and the insight into our historicity is, however, incomplete when it cannot account for the conditions of the event itself. To account for the possibility of such experiences would require a *social history of forms of experience*. While this social history was secondary to the existential phenomenologists, it became clear even in the writing of works such as *The Birth of the Clinic* and *The History of Madness*, that this was the heart of the study of "embedded subjectivity." As Foucault put it in a retrospective moment in 1984: "At the time I was working on my book about the history of madness, I was divided between existential psychology and phenomenology, and my research was an attempt to discover the extent these could be defined in historical terms" (*DL*, 174). Two new lines of inquiry not accessible to existential phenomenology at the time were thus opened up by Foucault's appropriation of the categories of experience during this period: First, what makes such experiences possible? What are the historical conditions of possibility for the experience of "death," "angst," or "madness" in their current formulations? Second, by what mechanisms can we access the truth of these experiences? What are the techniques which allow us to see experiences "existentially" and what makes these techniques available? Existential phenomenology after Heidegger had promised to demonstrate that experiences of "death" and "angst" (for example) could open us up to an awareness of the ground of our selfhood and being as relational, temporal, and free. However, it had not shown *how* such experiences could come into existence in the first place—how they became possible "things" for us to experience, think about and analyze in their historical specificity. Also, it had not analyzed the techniques by which the gap between the "everyday" and the "fundamental" or "authentic" experience of the event could be traversed. Foucault's answer to these questions was to point to the specific *historical* conditions under which forms of experience are presented to the subject, and techniques of verification and analysis are made manifest through institutional practices.

One example of this that most directly speaks to Heidegger's concerns is Foucault's analysis of death in *The Birth of the Clinic*.[10] In this work Foucault attempted to analyze the social and institutional mechanisms that made possible the "introduction of death into knowledge." Foucault highlighted the fact that death was not a "primordial" condition for grasping the historicity of human existence. Rather, it too was an event with a history. In the late eighteenth century, Foucault claims, "death" was rediscovered as a theme, only to become more pronounced and significant in the nineteenth century. It was only in the nineteenth century that death took on the function that Heidegger ascribes to it: as an "experience" which raises the individual from average, everyday life and makes its authentic individuality possible. Foucault writes that it was only under these historical conditions that death became "constitutive of singularity; it is in that perception of death that the individual finds himself, escaping from a monotonous, average life; in the slow, half-subterranean, but already visible approach of death, the dull, common life becomes an individuality at last; a black border isolates it and gives it the style of its own truth" (*BC*, 211; *NC*, 176).[11] Elsewhere, in a passage that even more directly implicates Heidegger within a historical tradition, Foucault writes that this understanding of death is then reinscribed back into the *living bodies* of subjects through institutional power, making it possible for us to experience death in a new way. Only through the institutionalization of the new form of "death" could it really be *experienced* as a living event, as an *existential*:

> It was when death became the concrete *a priori* of medical experience that death could detach itself from counter-nature and become *embodied* in the *living bodies* of individuals.
>
> It will no doubt remain decisive for our culture that its first scientific discourse concerning the individual had to pass through this stage of death. . . . Generally speaking, the experience of individuality in modern culture is perhaps bound up with that of death: from Bichet's open cadavers to Freudian man, an obstinate relation to death prescribes to the universal its singular face, and lends to each individual the power of being heard forever; the individual owes to death a meaning that does not cease with him. (*NC*, 201; my translation)[12]

Thus, Foucault could implicate the "fundamental structures of experience" with the history of institutional developments in clinical medicine and psychiatry. This meant that the phenomenon of experience, which Heidegger, Sartre, and Merleau-Ponty had relied upon as secret keys (that is, hidden to the subject and in need of interpretation) to the existential fact of our social, historical, and ultimately contingent subjectivities, was taken down from its quasi-positivist status as "event" beyond or before discourse. As Foucault put it at the end of *The Birth of the Clinic*:

> That with which phenomenology was to oppose itself so tenaciously was already present in its underlying structures: the original powers of the perceived and its correlation with language in the original forms of experience, the organization of objectivity on the basis of sign values, the secretly linguistic structure of the datum, the constitutive character of corporal spatiality, the importance of finitude in the relation of man with truth, and in the foundation of this rela-

tion, all this was involved in the genesis of positivism.... So much so that contemporary thought, believing that it has escaped it since the end of the nineteenth century, has merely rediscovered, little by little, that which made it possible. (*BC*, 246; *NC*, 202–3; translation modified)

Clearly this passage stands as an indictment of phenomenology after Heidegger, indicating that it secretly relies upon a positivism—the positivism of an "experience" which is simply "given" or made present to observation before the act of interpretation—in order to ground its insights into the historicity of the subject. If the subject is grounded only its open-ended historicity—in what I have called in previous chapters *ontological freedom*—then the claim is reversed backward upon phenomenology itself and comes to be the source of an interrogation about the historical nature of our existential "experiences." We have yet to "démontrer les conditions d'apparition" (*MMP*, 71). Otherwise, such a phenomenology risks reifying uncritically the standpoint of the subject, as least when it comes to her existential experiences.

By the time of *The Order of Things*, Foucault had almost completely abandoned his early interest in existential phenomenology on precisely these grounds. In the foreword to the English edition, written in 1970, Foucault was clear:

> If there is one approach that I do reject, however, it is that (one might call it, broadly speaking, the phenomenological approach) which gives absolute priority to the observing subject, which attributes a constituent role to an act, which places its own point of view at the origin of all historicity—which, in short, leads to a transcendental consciousness. It seems to me that the historical analysis of scientific discourse should, in the last resort, be subject, not to a theory of the knowing subject, but rather to a theory of discursive practice. (*OT*, xv)

To put in in the terms employed in Chapter One, Foucault here is resisting the need to relate a theory of historical development via the philosophy of the constituting subject.

Of course, it took time for Foucault to take such a strong position. In fact, much of his own earliest work could be criticized on these terms. While Foucault's early work opened up the possibility of studying "madness" and "death" as historically singular forms of experiences always already conditioned by institutional power, it did so by implicitly relying on other "primordial experiences" that were not themselves given full account. This appears to be, for instance, the role that Unreason (*déraison*) plays in relation to mental illness (*maladie mentale*) and madness (*folie*) during this time. Unreason is a more basic, primordial form of experience that seems to precede (and, at times, evade) the institutional production of mental illness and madness. In this sense, then, Foucault's early works don't escape his own critique. Instead, they too labor under what John Caputo calls "phenomenological naivete." Caputo writes, "The goal of the early writings, which is to find an 'undifferentiated' experience of unreason, before it is differentiated into reason and madness, before the lines of reason are drawn in its virginal sands, perfectly parallels the phenomenological goal of finding a realm of pure 'prepredicative' experience, prior to its being carved up by the categories of logical grammar."[13] All this is to say, however, that Foucault was at this time working both with and against the phenomenological category of "experience" in hopes that it would open up the possibility of a concrete historical philosophy. One might argue that this reversal, this folding backwards upon itself, is precisely what Heidegger proposes as the necessary trajectory for a new phenomenology. Rather than ground phenomenology in the structures of consciousness (as with Husserl), Heidegger anticipated Foucault's objection that phenemonology historicize its own knowledge in the form of hermeneutics. As made explicit in sections 31 and 32 of *Being and Time*, but generally elaborated upon throughout his writings, Heidegger sought to embrace precisely the form of an ongoing process of disclosure and reflexive interpretation as foundational to understanding. Understanding here refers not to a state of mind or a level of analysis, but rather to the conditions of intelligibility themselves. This means that Heidegger's use of the term *hermeneutic* to describe his work in *Being and Time* is meant to evoke not a reconstruction of a specific mode of analysis (a cultural, linguistic, or historical field as distinction from the form of analysis particular to the natural sciences, as exemplified by the hermeneutics of Schleiermacher and Dilthey), but rather to demonstrate the interrelationship between understanding and ontology. As Gadamer put it in the preface to his *Truth and Method* (hereafter cited in text as *TM*), "Heidegger's temporal analytics of Dasein has, I think, shown convincingly that understanding is not just one of the various possible behaviors of the subject but the mode of being of Dasein itself . . . and hence embraces the whole of its experience of the world" (*TM*, xxx). The conclusion to be drawn from this is that the categories of experience in Heidegger were always meant to be taken as historical, even if Heidegger himself did not open them up as such. What this suggests is that a complementary form of historical analysis is required to complete the ontology Heidegger first proposed. More will be said on this a point of possible rapprochement between Heidegger and Foucault in the next chapters. What matters at this stage of the discussion is merely to point out Foucault's initial uneasiness with the quasi-positivist status of "experiences" in post-Heideggerian existential phenomenology.

4.2. CRITIQUE OF HERMENEUTICS

The leads us to the second line of critique that implicates Heidegger: Foucault's critique of hermeneutics and its relation to what he later calls confessional or pastoral power. As we saw above, Foucault employed the broad Heideggerian insight into the constitutive function of background practices vis-à-vis objects of knowledge (i.e., that in order for something to appear as a object for inquiry, it must first be disclosed by a general field of knowledge which is itself grounded in embodied practices and is not, in any general holistic manner, available to inquiry itself) in order to critically historicize supposedly ahistorical experiential categories such as "madness" and "death." We also saw that while this is, in a broad sense, a *deployment* of Heideggerian thought (the connection to which Foucault made explicit in his earliest writings), it was also a *critique and reversal* of it. Most clearly, we can see this with Foucault's discussion of death. If Foucault is correct that the contemporary experience of death began, as he says, "in the last years of the eighteenth century," then this undermines Heidegger's assertion, in Division II of *Being and Time*, that "being-toward-death" is an (ahistorical) existential. More important, however, is Foucault's critique of *how* we investigate such existentials.

For Heidegger, in order for an "everyday" experience (such as fear) to open up reflection on our existential condition generally, it requires a specific set of techniques which can raise us from the level of "everyday understanding" to "fundamental ontology." These techniques are not the epistemological techniques given by traditional philosophic models in the West (whereby foundational premises are sought that are true and necessary that can then lead to conclusions via proper inferences). Rather, Heidegger draws upon the hermeneutic tradition to suggest that a new set of *relational activities* are the techniques of knowledge appropriate for us to grasp fundamental ontology. These activities are gathered under the name *interpretation*. There are actually two different terms that Heidegger employs which both can be translated as "interpretation": *Auslegung* and *Interpretierung*. David Hoy usefully clarifies the distinction thus: "*Auslegung*, the standard translation of which is 'interpretation' with a lower-case 'i,' includes the everyday phenomena of ordinary skills like hammer, typing, or driving. *Interpretierung*, translated as 'Interpretation' with an upper-case 'I,' includes thematized, discursive articulation and theorization. *Interpretierung* is itself said to be a derived form of *Auslegung*, but Heidegger obviously does not mean to denigrate *Interpretierung* since that is what *Being and Time* is."[14] *Auslegung* refers, then, to the form of thought that is required for everyday coping within sets of practices. It is, therefore, not contrasted with Understanding (as pre-reflexive) but is rather the making explicit of the form of knowledge already within Understanding, upon which *Auslegung* is always already reliant. *Auslegung* is a specific practice by which one makes explicit the meaning of things already grasped by Understanding through the working out of possibilities already latent within everyday use of things as equipment. As Heidegger writes: "This development of the understanding we call 'interpretation.' . . . In interpretation, understanding does not become something different. It becomes itself. Such interpretation is grounded existentially in understanding; the latter does not arise from the former. Nor is interpretation the acquiring of information about what is understood; it is rather the working-out of possibilities projected in understanding" (*BTa* §32, 188–89; *SZ* §32, 148). *Interpretierung*, on the other hand, is a specific instance of *Auslegung*, one that does not try to "think" a specific activity (such as hammering, typing, or driving), but rather attempts to "think" *Auslegung* existentially, that is, in relation to its ground within a lifeworld, in relation to the condition of Being-in-the-world. It is in this sense that Heidegger offers *Being and Time* as an *Interpretation* of the everyday activity of *Auslegung*: "'Understanding' in the sense of *one* possible kind of cognizing among others (as distinguished, for instance, from 'explaining') must, like explaining, be Interpreted as an existential derivative of that primary understanding which is one of the constituents of Being of the 'there' in general" (*BTa*, §31, 182; *SZ* §31, 143). In other words, while Heidegger thinks that "interpretation" can replace the traditional model of epistemology as a technique for apprehending the structure of reality, he is unclear on the status of this claim itself. In order to account for this insight, Heidegger differentiates between two "levels" of interpretation: one is the everyday activities of relating thought to background understanding, the other is a specific activity that attempts to reconstruct the conditions for this first activity.

It is this "second-order" notion of interpretation that Foucault picks up on and submits to critique. More generally, when Foucault uses the term *hermeneutics* he is most often referring to the general philosophic tradition that (contrary to the rationalist model) grounds its claims to knowledge not in the grasping of final, certain, "clear and distinct" ideas, but rather in the ongoing activity of "interpretation" in the two senses outlined above. Thus, Foucault's critique of hermeneutics also implicates Heidegger. This critique has five main features: First, interpretation in this sense opens up a gap between the signifier and the signified which cannot be closed, or even fully explained. Second, the task of closing this gap is given over to an "interpreter" whose position of epistemic privilege masks the function of power in the interpretive act. Third, it is precisely the infinite task of closing this gap that permits the hermeneutic project to drive ever inward to the very heart, soul, inner unconscious, and so on of the signifier, demanding the infinite intensification of interpretive techniques and analytics. Fourth, the hermeneutic project thus masks its origins not in an interpretive problem but rather in the historically situated and ever-changing requirements of institutional power. Finally, such a process relies upon an implicit (if not also explicit) claim to a hidden truth about "original man"—some state of pure, authentic subjectivity wherein signifier and signified were once one (this part of the critique is dealt with below under the heading of "The Analytics of Finitude"). Each of these claims needs to be unpacked in turn.[15]

4.2.a. Excess of the Signified

Foucault's clearest and most extended treatment of the problem of signifier and signified in modern hermeneutics comes from the introduction to *The Birth of the Clinic*. There he addresses himself directly to the hermeneutic tradition (derisively referring to it as "commentary") and is worth quoting at length:

> *Commentary* questions discourse as to what it says and intended to say; it tries to uncover the deeper meaning of speech that enables it to achieve an identity with itself, supposedly nearer to its essential truth; in other words, in stating what has been said, one has to re-state what has never been said. . . . To comment is to admit by definition an excess of the signified over the signifier . . . but to comment also presupposes that this unspoken element slumbers within speech (*parole*), and that, by a superabundance proper to the signifier, one may, in questioning it, give voice to a content that was not explicitly signified. By opening up the possibility of commentary, this double plethora dooms us to an endless task that nothing can limit: there is always a certain amount of signified remaining that must be allowed to speak, while the signifier is always offered to us in an abundance that questions us, in spite of ourselves, as to what it "means" (*veut dire*). Signifier and signified thus assume a substantial autonomy that accords the treasure of a virtual signification to each of them separately; one may even exist without the other, and begin to speak of itself: commentary resides in that supposed space. . . . Commentary rests on the postulate that speech (*parole*) is an act of "translation." (*BC*, xvii–xix; *NC*, xii–xiii)

Contained within this passage are several important points. First is Foucault's claim that "commenter, c'est admettre par definition un excès du signifié sur le significant." The basic premise of hermeneutic interpretation is that meaning cannot be reduced to merely what was actually said. The signified (the meaning which is projected in language and behavior) is not reducible to the intentions of the signifier. Thus, the signified is always "in excess" of the signifier. This opens up a gap—an "espace supposé"—between that which is literally said and that which is actually *meant*. Into this gap steps the interpreter. It is the role of the hermeneutic interpreter to grasp the full significance of what was said, to bring it to a deeper, more profound or more comprehensive account, one not accessible to the signifier herself. However, as Foucault points out, this gap can never be completely closed off. Rather, the excess of meaning will always "run ahead of" the particular articulations which attempt to encapsulate them. This, as we saw in previous chapters, is precisely what Heidegger intends to say. It is one of the bases on which we can speak of an *ontological freedom*—the infinite projectedness of meaning beyond the field of the intelligible dooms us to endlessly perform within the hermeneutic circle.[16] For Foucault, however, the hermeneutic circle of interpretation is "une tâche infinie que rien ne peut limiter." Or, as he reiterated in a later essay, it is one of the main "characteristic[s] of hermeneutics [that] interpretation finds itself with the obligation to interpret itself to infinity, always to resume" (*EW*2, 277). Foucault's "archaeological period," incorporating *The Order of Things* and *The Archaeology of Knowledge*, might be read as an attempt to study language without resorting to the hermeneutic circle. Such an analysis could proceed if the gap between signifier and signified were collapsed by a structuralism that reduced the signifier (the speaking subject) to merely the bearer of semantic rules which precede and, indeed, constitute her. This form of analysis is precisely what Foucault imagines in *The Birth of the Clinic*, already anticipating his archeologies, when he writes: "Is it not possible to make a structural analysis of discourses that would evade the fate of commentary by supposing no remainder, nothing in excess of what has been said, but only the fact of its historical appearance? . . . A systematic history of discourses would then become possible" (*BC*, xix; *NC*, xiii). Of course, such an analysis runs up against its own problems. By collapsing the signifier into the signified—reducing the speaking subject to merely the "object-effect" of semantic rules governed by a hermetically sealed *épistémè*, Foucault's archeologies struggled to account for modification over time of the rules governing symbols and knowledge, but also struggled to account for their own condition of possibility (that is, the structuralism was so totalizing so as to consume the archeologist's standpoint as well). This is mentioned only peripherally here since it is not necessary to look at the critiques of Foucault's archeological works in much detail. What we are trying to signal here is only how Foucault's early work on *épistémè* as systems of knowledge with little or no room for an active speaking subject emerged in part out of a frustration with the "infinite task"—between signifier and signified, between interpretation and understanding—in post-Heideggerian hermeneutics.

4.2.b. Pastoral Power

The next aspect of Foucault's critique of hermeneutics is more explicitly political, and is the one feature of his critique that remained relatively unchanged throughout his career. This critique is pursued through a demonstration of the interrelationship between hermeneutic philosophy and what he calls confessional or pastoral power. Just as Foucault had attempted to show in his first works on madness, the "discovery" of a field of knowledge owes more to the changing demands of institutional power than it does to the uncovering of a truth that was previously hidden. Hermeneutic philosophy, Foucault argues, is equally bound up with the development of institutional and disciplinary power. The key link here is that hermeneutic philosophy can only arise through a positing of an "inner" self that is simultaneously more fundamental and more occluded than our "outer," public self. The notion that there is an inner, authentic self that requires interpretation is, according to Foucault, made possible in the first instance not by theoretical discoveries or cultural transformations, but rather by transformations in practices of governance. The specifics of this claim cannot be totally elaborated on here, but we do require a general outline.

According to Foucault, hermeneutics' relationship to pastoral power begins with transformations in Christian confessional practices, particularly in the fourth and fifth centuries.[17] It was then that various practices such as confession, renunciation, meditation, purification, and so on, no longer served as preparatory work which aimed to make the subject fit to receive truth from an external source.[18] Instead, the relationship was reversed, and the practices came to serve a disciplinary function. These practices became not "tests of the self," but rather techniques of extraction used to draw out the hidden truth which was posited to reside "within" the subject. It was only through these new interpretive practices that the subject could release the truth of itself. As a key turning point in this historical story, Foucault contrasts Marcus Aurelius with the fourth-century theologian Cassian. With Cassian and the early Christian theologians, "we will have moved on to a regime in which the subject's relationship to truth will not be governed simply by the purpose: 'how to become a subject of veridiction,' but will have become: 'how to be able to say the truth about oneself'" (*Herm.*, 362; *HS*, 345). Later on in the text, Foucault summarizes and makes more explicit the tripartite relation between this new question of truth, the hermeneutic tradition, and pastoral institutions such as the confession. He writes,

> It is, I think, an absolutely crucial moment in the history of subjectivity in the West, or in the relations between subjectivity and truth, when the task and obligation of truth-telling about oneself is inserted within the procedure indispensable for salvation, within techniques of the development and transformation of the subject by himself, and within pastoral institutions. . . . I think we should consider it a highly significant event in the relations between the subject and truth when truth-telling about oneself becomes a condition of salvation, a fundamental element in the individual's membership of a community. The day, if you like, when refusal to confess at least once a year was grounds for excommunication. (*Herm.*, 364; *HS*, 346)

With Cassian and the Christian pastoral tradition, truth is no longer grounded in tests of existence, but rather "a matter of prescribing a hermeneutic attitude towards oneself: deciphering possible concupiscence in apparently innocent thoughts" (*Herm.*, 503; *HS*, 483–84).

Of course, even if one accepts this hypothesis about transformations in early Christianity, we are still a long way from a critique of modern hermeneutics. The connection between modern hermeneutics (in which Foucault includes Heidegger) and pastoral power is made through the extension of specific fields of knowledge/power from the early Christian world to the modern hermeneutic sciences, especially psychology and psychiatry. Sexuality, as a body of knowledge, an institutional discourse, and a personal practice, is the paradigmatic case for Foucault of just such a field:

> Instead of adding up the errors, naïvetés, and moralisms that plagued the nineteenth-century discourse of truth concerning sex, we would do better to locate the procedures by which that will to knowledge regarding sex, which characterizes the modern Occident, caused the rituals of confession to function within the norms

of scientific regularity: how did this immense and traditional extortion of the sexual confession come to be constituted in scientific terms? (*HS1*, 65; *VS*, 87)

Foucault then goes on to list five of these mechanisms by which the confession came to be constituted in its current scientific form:

1. *Through a clinical codification of the inducement to speak.*
2. *Through the postulate of a general and diffuse causality.*
3. *Through the principle of latency intrinsic to sexuality.*
4. *Through the method of interpretation.*
5. *Through the medicalization of the effects of confession.* (*HS1*, 65–67; *VS*, 87–90)

On the fourth point, regarding "interpretation," Foucault adds a key element. For while confession appears to be a function purely of a confessing subject, when we highlight the role of interpretation in this act, we can see that the central role is in fact played by the confessee, not the confessor. This is because confessional practices must *pass through* the interpretative function of the listener for them to gain validity. Hence,

> The truth did not reside solely in the subject who, by confessing, would reveal it wholly formed. It was constituted in two stages: present but incomplete, blind to itself, in the one who spoke, it could only reach completion in the one who assimilated and recorded it. It was the latter's function to verify this obscure truth: the revelation of confession had to be coupled with the decipherment of what it said. The one who listened was not simply the forgiving master, the judge who condemned or acquitted; he was the master of truth. His was a hermeneutic function. . . . By no longer making the confession a test, but rather a sign, and by making sexuality something to be interpreted, the nineteenth century gave itself the possibility of causing the procedures of confession to operate within the regular formation of a scientific discourse. (*HS1*, 66–67; *VS*, 89–90)

We can see here that Foucault wants to directly link confessional power, the sciences of mental health, and interpretive hermeneutics, particularly as they converge in the nineteenth century. The thesis regarding the interrelationship between interpretive hermeneutics and pastoral power is most clearly observable in the specific case of psychology as both a field of knowledge and an institutional system of organization, discipline, and control. It takes the discussion too far afield to engage with Foucault's wide-ranging and complex critique of psychology and psychoanlaysis, but since they are for Foucault part of the hermeneutic tradition and related to pastoral power, it is at least important to note as a specific instance of the general thesis that implicates hermeneutic philosophy.

Besides merely "historicizing" the phenomenological experience of "madness" in his early works, Foucault also sought to demonstrate that the constitution of a field of knowledge was already implicated in a set of institutional demands of governance and discipline. This is not to say that the human sciences are directly *derivative* of the particular institutions in which they first appeared historically. But it is to implicate them deeply in the matrix of disciplinary technologies of truth and power that Foucault is trying to analyze. His clearest statement on this relationship comes in *Discipline and Punish*, where he makes the link between the human sciences and the prison system, or "carceral network," explicit:

> I am not saying that the human sciences emerged from the prison. But, if they have been able to be formed and to produce so many profound changes in the episteme, it is because they have been conveyed by a specific and new modality of power. . . . The carceral network constituted one of the armatures of this power/knowledge that has made the human sciences historically possible. Knowable man (soul, individuality, consciousness, conduct, whatever it is called) is the object-effect of this analytic investment, of this domination-observation. (*DP*, 305; *SP*, 356–57)

When we take this general thesis into the particular relationship of pastoral power to interpretive hermeneutics, we might say that the emergence of a field in which language was seen as a key to unlocking the hidden inner truth of the subject is made historically possible by the development of institutional power attached to mental illness and sexuality. Thus, in the case of psychology, psychiatry, and psychoanalysis in particular, Foucault sought to show that they (as fields of knowledge) owed more to strategic developments than epistemological discoveries.

For instance, in *The History of Madness*, Foucault echoes Nietzsche of the *Genealogy of Morals* (while also historicizing and grounding this in a social history), when he writes:

> The distinction between the physical and the moral only became a practical concept in the medicine of minds when the problematics of madness were displaced towards the interrogation of a responsible subject. The purely moral space that was then defined measures exactly the psychological interiority where modern men seek both their depth and their truth. . . . From then on, psychology, as a means of cure, was organized around the idea of punishment. . . . Where the mad were concerned, only the practice of punishment separated the medicine of the body and the soul. A purely psychological medicine was only made possible when madness was alienated into guilt. (*HM*, 325–26; *HF*, 411–12)

Generally speaking, then, Foucault is attempting to demonstrate that the objectifying practices of governance directly on the human body (which were discussed most explicitly in *Discipline and Punish*) are not the only means by which disciplinary power is mobilized. Rather, interpretive dialogues can themselves function as discipline through a *subjectifying* practice of power. The dialogues between psychiatrist and patient, priest and confessor, or social scientist and agent, are not merely disclosing some inner, hidden self that was not fully transparent to itself. Rather, they are productive of new forms of subjectivity more amenable to the governance of such "interpreting elites." The modern self is constantly called forth to give an account of itself, to translate the hidden "unthought"—the "psychological interiority where modern men seek both their depth and their truth"—into discourse thus making it visible and amenable to governance. In telling the "hidden truth" of ourselves, we aid the normalizing function of disciplinary power and self-imposed integration into prevailing institutional or discursive power fields. The agent learns through these dialogues to search for those hidden "inner" truths, to correct her previous self-interpretation and replace it with a new account of "who she really is," and in so doing, a new subjectivity is produced. As Dreyfus and Rabinow put it:

> At least in the West, even the most private self-examination is tied to powerful systems of external control: sciences and pseudosciences,

religious and moral doctrines. The cultural desire to know the truth about oneself prompts the telling of truth; in confession after confession to oneself and to others, this *mise en discours* has placed the individual in a network of relations of power with those who claim to be able to extract the truth of these confessions through their possession of the keys to interpretation.[19]

What Dreyfus and Rabinow point to through their use of the term *interpretation* in the passage above is a link not only between pastoral power and psychiatry, but between pastoral power and interpretive hermeneutics more generally. Thus, even if we avoid the traditional empiricist model (which attempts to "know" humans through observation and explanation, as merely one object of study among others), or the traditional rationalist one (in which knowledge is derived from deduction from true and necessary premises), the hermeneutic model (in which knowledge is acquired through interpretive dialogue between subjects) is not immune to the Foucauldian critique of the internal relationship between forms of knowledge and disciplinary power.

Whether Foucault has been fair in his characterization of these domains of knowledge and practice, or whether his claim regarding the interrelationship between them is a historically accurate picture is not something I intend to comment on. The point here is that Foucault understood hermeneutic philosophy to be a form of commentary derived from actual existing practices of governance that *constitute* a subject who takes her "inner" self to be the locus of truth about herself, something which is in need of extraction and interpretation by experts. Furthermore, from this standpoint, this general critique of hermeneutics, I submit, is applicable to Heidegger (particularly his early works) insofar as Heidegger self-consciously describes his work as a hermeneutic interpretation of Being which is "covered over" by everyday understanding.

. . .

To summarize Foucault's critique of hermeneutic philosophy (itself only one part of his general critique of Heideggerian philosophy), we can isolate and redescribe three lines of analysis. First, Foucault argues that hermeneutics posits an excess of signification beyond the signifier which cannot, even in principle, itself be analyzed. The gap between what is *said* and what is *meant* can never be closed. Thus, hermeneutics perpetuates its task of interpretation at precisely the point where it can give no account of its own object of study—the "excess" of meaning. Second, by claiming that meaning requires interpretation, hermeneutics is wedded to an intensification of interpretive techniques which drive ever "inward" attempting to extract the hidden "truth" of the subject. This hidden truth, Foucault suggests, is never merely "there," but is rather constituted by the hermeneutic techniques themselves. Finally, hermeneutics masks the historical conditions of its emergence through institutions of pastoral power. From the Christian confessional, to psychoanalytic techniques, to the "better accounts" of modern social science, hermeneutics is made possible only through a set of institutional developments explainable, not by reference to the uncovering of great "truths" about humanity, but rather to the demands of power in the development and exercise of those institutions.

4.3. ANALYTICS OF FINITUDE: THE UNTHOUGHT AND "ORIGINAL MAN"

In Foucault's breakthrough study of the 1960s, *The Order of Things*, he added two different, but interlocking criticisms of hermeneutic philosophy in general and Heidegger in particular. The first revolves around the question of the "unthought," and the second interrogates the role of the "origin."

One of preoccupations of *The Order of Things* is marking the transition from the "Classical" to the modern era in the emergence of language as a field of study. At the beginning of the seventeenth century, the relatively unproblematic resemblance of words and things (of which Foucault takes *Don Quixote* to be exemplary figure) begins to break down. Beginning with Bacon, but coming to full fruition with Descartes, unproblematic resemblance comes under attack. Indeed, assuming resemblance is itself taken to be a primary error: "At the beginning of the seventeenth century, during the period that has been termed, rightly or wrongly, the Baroque, thought ceases to move in the element of resemblance. Similitude is no longer the form of knowledge but rather the occasion of error, the danger to which one exposes oneself when one does not examine the obscure region of confusions"

(*OT*, 56; *MC*, 101). With Descartes, knowledge becomes a function of intuition and deduction—the capacity to see clearly and to arrange the parts of information together in the proper order (*OT*, 58–60; *MC*, 103–5). What is really important for Foucault, and what differentiates his account from most others of this time, is the transformation in the ground of signs and language that this permits. This modification, for Foucault (of this period in his writing), is more foundational to the general *épistémè* of the period than any particular theoretical picture generally held during the period—such as Mechanism (*OT*, 330; *MC*, 452). What is more important is that through the epistemological transformations of the period language is no longer taken to be something *within* the world. Rather, it is a system of human symbols that, if marshaled properly, can be used to organize and transmit clear thoughts *about* the world. The corollary of this claim about the foundation of the Classical *épistémè* is that the transition from it to the modern one will also be achieved not through a loosening of any particular theoretical picture (e.g., Mechanism), but rather through a general transformation in the system of signs and language that permit and organize inquiry into such "pictures." This is why Foucault will locate the end of the Classical period, and beginning of the modern, with the "return of language" (*OT*, 330; *MC*, 452). This return, Foucault argued at the time, continued right up to his present and directly implicated the rise of hermeneutic philosophy in the nineteenth century (especially via Schleiermacher and Dilthey), but also Heideggerian philosophy in the twentieth. Foucault writes, "The threshold between Classicism and modernity . . . had been definitively crossed when words ceased to intersect with representations and to provide a spontaneous grid for the knowledge of things. At the beginning of the nineteenth century, they rediscovered their ancient, enigmatic density" (*OT*, 331; *MC*, 453). He then goes on to list the new ways in which language has existed "right up to our own day," including a clear reference to hermeneutics: "If one's intent is to interpret, then words become a text to be broken down, so as to allow that other meaning hidden in them to emerge and become clearly visible" (*OT*, 331; *MC*, 454). From the transformations of the nineteenth century, particularly exemplified by Nietzsche and Mallarmé, "the unity of general grammar—discourse—was broken up [and] language appeared in a multiplicity of modes of being" (*OT*, 332;

MC, 454). These transformations are the precondition for all our current preoccupations with language as a discloser of being:

> It is quite possible that all those questions now confronting our curiosity (What is language? What is a sign? What is unspoken in the world, in our gestures, in the whole enigmatic heraldry of our behaviour, our dreams, our sicknesses—does all that speak, and if so in what language and in obedience to what grammar? Is everything significant, and, if not, what is, and for whom, and in accordance with what rules? What relation is there between language and being, and is it really to being that language is always addressed—at least, language that speaks truly? What, then, is this language that says nothing, is never silent, and is called "litterature"?)—it is quite possible that all these questions are presented today in the distance that was never crossed between Nietzsche's question and Mallarmé's reply. (*OT*, 333; *MC*, 456)

The most important transformation to come out of the positing of language as a discloser of being, Foucault argues, is that this places "man" at the center of all knowledge, but does so in a paradoxical manner. When "Classical *discourse*, in which being and representation found their common locus, is eclipsed, then, in the profound upheaval of such an archeological mutation, man appears in his ambiguous position as an object of knowledge and as a subject that knows" (*OT*, 340; *MC*, 465). This, the famous "analytic of finitude" charaterizing post-Kantian philosophy—through the nineteenth century to the present—is comprised of three "doubles" that constitute "man" in "sa position ambiguë d'objet pour un savoir et de sujet qui connaît." They are (1) the transcendental and the empirical, (2) the cognito and the unthought, and (3) the retreat and the return of the origin. The first of these is a characterization of Kant and critical rationalism and does not directly implicate Heidegger. The last two, however, do.

4.3.a. The Unthought

Foucault opens chapter 9, section 5—the "cogito" and the unthought—with a provocation to post-Kantian critique thought: "If man is indeed, in the world, the locus of an empirico-transcendental double, if he is that paradoxical figure in which the empirical contents of knowledge necessarily release, of themselves, the conditions that have made them possible, then man cannot posit himself in the immediate and sovereign transparency of a *cogito*" (*OT*, 351; *MC*, 479). Elsewhere, he elaborates on this, adding:

> The modern *cogito* (and this is why it is not so much the discovery of an evident truth as a ceaseless task constantly to be undertaken afresh) must traverse, duplicate, and reactivate in an explicit form the articulation of thought on everything within it, around it, and beneath it which is not thought, yet which is nevertheless not foreign to thought, in the sense of an irreducible, an insuperable exteriority. In this form, the *cogito* will not therefore be the sudden and illuminating discovery that all thought is thought, but the constantly renewed interrogation as to how thought can reside elsewhere than here, and yet so very close to itself; how it can *be* in the forms of non-thinking. The modern *cogito* does not reduce the whole being of things to thought without ramifying the being of thought down to the inert network of what does not think. (*OT*, 353; *MC*, 482)

This demand to address oneself to the "unthought," which is the secret, hidden, and "truer" version of the thinking subject means that, rather than seeing phenomenology as a *reversal* of the Cartesian and Kantian analytic, it is recast as only the most recent, the most "sensitive and precisely formulated acknowledgement" of the very problem. For Foucault, then, while it "may seem that phenomenology has effected a union between the Cartesian theme of the *cogito* and the transcendental motif that Kant had derived from Hume's critique" (a mantle most recently taken up by Husserl), in fact, contemporary phenomenology has only "changed its point of application" (*OT*, 354; *MC*, 483). While it is true that Husserl's version of transcendental analysis can permit a dimension of the "unthought" insofar as it attempts to show "how thought can elude itself and thus lead to a many-sided and proliferating interrogation concerning being," it remains trapped within the same problem of traversing the empirical/transcendental divide since the transcendental standpoint from which this "unthought" is viewed must be secured against its own insights (i.e., against erosion by the elusiveness of thought working upon itself) and hence posits a perfect self-transparency (the return of the Cartesian *cogito*) for which it cannot give an account (*OT*, 354; *MC*, 483–84). Immediately following this discussion, in a passage that can be read as a mode of autocritique of his own early appropriation of phenomenological categories in his studies of psychology and madness, Foucault writes that "even though [phenomenology] was first suggested by way of anti-psychologism . . . it revived the problem of the *a priori* and the transcendental motif." Making the link back to Heidegger most explicitly, this explains why for Foucault, phenomenology, "has always been led to questions, to *the* question of ontology," despite being "inaugurated by a reduction to the *cogito*." Concluding, he chastises this movement: "The phenomenological project continually resolves itself, before our eyes, into a description—empirical despite itself—of actual experience, and into an ontology of the unthought that automatically short-circuits the primacy of the 'I think'" (*OT*, 354–55; *MC*, 484).

So, to trace the logic of Foucault's critique, we might proceed as follows: Beginning at least with Kant, modern European philosophy has been preoccupied with the paradoxical role of "man" as both the product of historical forces (language, culture, economics, politics, etc.) and as the subject which investigations into those forces. If we are the product of historical forces, and this is the presupposition for our social sciences, then we must assume that knowledge of these forces is itself structured by those same forces. Our knowledge of ourselves is, therefore, dependent on our knowledge of the forces of history. So we develop the human sciences to try and "carve out" specific domains of knowledge by which we can slowly piece together the empirical evidence for *how* specifically the historical forces at play affect "man." Taken together these "forces" (linguistic, cultural, social, etc.) are the "background field" for the subject to appear. They are, however, not knowable to the subject *in* its historical context. Hence, they constitute what Foucault is calling here "the unthought." They would only be knowable to something—some subject—which could, through proper methodology, sheer force of will, or the like, stand *outside* these historical forces long enough to know them. Whatever this capacity is, it will be attributed to a transcendental subject, viewed as the condition of possibility for self-knowledge and, we shall see, for freedom, since it is on the basis of this self-knowledge that self-governed action can proceed. Foucault seems to be saying that Heidegger placed his existential phenomenology at the end of this struggle. Heidegger thought that he had overcome this problematic by making Dasein a thoroughly *historical* being. However, because the condition for Dasein's knowledge of this historicity was a mode of interpretation called hermeneutics, which permitted Dasein to transcend "everyday understanding" and achieve (albeit only momentarily) a glimpse of fundamental ontology, it still retains the transcendental-empirical bifurcation of "man." In his role as hermeneutic interpreter, "man" can interpret the "unthought" theories and beliefs of the background, make them explicit, and thereby close the gap between the empirical and the transcendental self. This makes Heidegger's project only one more step in a long sequence, from Kant to Hegel, Schopenhauer, Marx and Husserl. According to Foucault, in these thinkers,

> the inexhaustible double that presents itself to reflection as the blurred projection of what man is in his truth . . . also plays the role of a preliminary ground upon which man must collect himself and recall himself in order to attain his truth. For though this double may be close, it is alien, and the role, the true undertaking, of thought will be to bring it as close to itself as possible; the whole of modern thought is imbued with the necessity of thinking the unthought. (*OT*, 356; *MC*, 486)

The only way for modern thought to close this gap, between the transcendental and the empirical subject, is to "work backwards—or downwards": to painstakingly reconstruct the historical conditions which produced the subject in the first place, thereby stripping the layers of historical forces away to reveal the "original man" beneath it all.

4.3.b. Original Man

In the third and final "double" constituting the analytic of finitude in modern thought for Foucault, we are presented with the paradoxical role of origins, beginning with a comment on the eighteenth century. Foucault notes that during this "Classical age," European thought was overly preoccupied with a return to origins: in economics, natural history, and linguistics in particular. It was hoped that if we could locate the original state of nature behind or beneath our historically altered practices, a vision of "original" or "authentic" man would emerge that could be used as a critical tool over against existing practices. "Original man" serves, then, both as a touchstone for the true, as a regulative or corrective tool for the present, and as an interpretive key for unlocking the teleological purposiveness of history. We can observe the slow gathering of these various roles in the development and deployment of "state of nature" theories throughout the seventeenth and eighteenth centuries.[20] The multiple roles the "original man" played in work throughout the Classical age means that distinctions between empirical and normative claims are hard to impose upon it. As Foucault notes, "It was of little importance whether this origin was considered fictitious or real, whether it possessed the value of an explanatory hypothesis or a historical event: in fact, these distinctions exist only for us" (OT, 359; MC, 489). In the transition from Classical to modern thought (roughly during the early eighteenth century) this origin became an impossibility. Since the fields of study themselves (economics, natural history, and language) came to be seen as constituted by historicity, a point outside of history for their beginnings was "no longer conceivable" (OT, 359; MC, 490). This produced a kind of crisis within such sciences. The need for an ahistorical touchstone was still there—something that could serve the function of grounding the truth of the field as a proper field of study, the corrective function for ethics, and the interpretive function for history. However, since the investigators came to see themselves as *within* historicity itself, such an origin, if it did exist, could never be articulated by them. Such sciences, then, "could never, therefore, truly express their origin, even though, from the inside, their whole history is, as it were, directed towards it. It is no longer origin that gives rise to historicity; it is historicity that, in its very fabric, makes possible the necessity of an origin which must be both internal and foreign to it" (OT, 359; MC, 490). The knowing subject of such sciences of man would never be "contemporaneous with that origin which is outlined through the time of things even as it eludes the gaze" (OT, 359; MC, 490). This has the effect of opening up a gap between "modern man" and himself. "Modern man" is a knowing subject, but the conditions of this knowledge are a historical inheritance prior to, other than, and ultimately *inaccessible* to him in his original state since he always stands within their wake, affected by them. In other words, "It is always against a background of the already begun that man is able to reflect on what may serve for him as origins" (*OT*, 360; *MC*, 491). This has two consequences. First, "the origin of things is always pushed further back," and: "it signifies that man . . . is the being without origin . . . whose birth is never accessible because it never took 'place'" (*OT*, 361; *MC*, 493).

In one of the few places where Foucault references Heidegger by name, he specifically includes him in this problematic of origins. Foucault indicates that at the end of the nineteenth century and beginning of the twentieth a novel attempt to solve this problem was developed. The new task was to find the ground of time itself in the hope that if we could demonstrate how the experience of temporality conditioned experience, then time would be prior to history. If "modern man" could not have a history except *because* he always already had experiences conditioned by temporality (i.e., if temporality was an existential), then this notion of time could serve the function of a bridge back to our origins—not conceived of historically, but as "authenticity." Foucault writes, "A task is thereby set for thought: that of contesting the origin of things, but of contesting it in order to give it a foundation, by rediscovering the mode upon which the possibility of time is constituted—that origin without origin or beginning, on the basis of which everything is able to come into being" (*OT*, 362; *MC*, 493). This struggle to locate the experience of time outside and prior to history, has been "since the nineteenth century . . . the starting point of all our attempts to re-apprehend what beginning and re-beginning, the recession and the presence of the beginning, the return and the end, could be in the human sphere" (*OT*, 362–63; *MC*, 494). Foucault concludes by placing Hölderlin, Nietzsche, and Heidegger as "only" at the point of "extreme recession of the origin—in that region where the gods have turned away, where the desert is increasing, where the *technē* has established the dominion of its will; so that what we are concerned with here is neither a completion nor a curve, but rather that ceaseless rending open which frees the origin in exactly that degree to which it recedes; the extreme is therefore what is nearest" (*OT*, 364; *MC*, 496). In the context of our discussion of Heidegger, then, we can see that Foucault does not take the project of *Being and Time* to be an exception to the general problematic. Rather, it is merely an extension and modification of the larger problematic. This undermines Heidegger's whole project of a critical reconstruction of the history of Being. It also takes Heidegger's claim (particularly explicitly in Division II of *Being and Time*) to have found in our experience of temporality an originary, primordial ground for historicity and to have located it historically. In so doing, Foucault demotes Heidegger's transcendental hermeneutic ontology to a particular, localized response to the aporias of modernity.

4.4. CONCLUSIONS

The preceding chapter was devoted to an explication of Foucault's explicit and implicit criticism of Heidegger and Heideggerian philosophy. In presenting an overview of Foucault's critique of Heidegger we risk, of course, imposing too much order and structure upon Foucault's critique. It should be kept in mind, therefore, that this is a *creative, directed* reconstruction—that Foucault himself did not attempt to present any systematic evaluation of Heidegger's philosophy, and that the criticisms that did emerge in his work did so over a long period of time, through multiple stages of his own work, and are not only inconsistent but are even, at times, contradictory. In particular, we have seen in the transition from early studies of madness and psychiatry, to archeologies of knowledge, through to the genealogies of power/knowledge that Foucault moved from a relatively sympathetic position to one that was more incommensurable with Heidegger. It should also be noted that many of the criticisms outlined above were presented as criticisms of broad philosophical movements, such as existentialism, hermeneutics, and phenomenology—movements to which Heidegger was no doubt a main contributor, but which nevertheless cannot be collapsed into merely one thinker. At best, we can say that Heidegger may have been exemplary of the problems Foucault found with these traditions of thought generally. These problems may be summarized as follows: (1) Heidegger's fundamental ontology is arrived at in the first instance from a phenomenology of existential experiences (such as *Angst*) whose historical conditions of possibility are not themselves given investigation. Foucault's *historical* ontology of the singularity of our forms of experience cuts against this reliance. (2) The "existential experience" as given (above) is not complete and self-transparent. That is to say, it requires *Interpretation* in order for the subject to explore its existential significance. This produces three hermeneutic problems for Foucault:

(a) the "excess" of the signified produces an inexorable interpretive task, which (b) produces imperatives of intensification of interpretive techniques which, in turn, (c) mask the embeddedness of hermeneutics in institutions of pastoral power. (3) The imperative to raise "everyday" understanding to the level of fundamental ontology is resolved through a reconstruction of the history of Being, tracing backward to the point of total transparency and unity of the subject. This, for Foucault, firmly places Heidegger within the "analytics of finitude" characteristic of modern thought, reliant as it is upon the *cogito*/unthought distinction, as well as the retreat and return of the origin.

The case for any kind of effective or constructive dialogue between Heidegger and Foucault seems foreclosed at this point. However, I think that setting up the points of divergence between the two philosophers is important for understanding the argument in subsequent chapters.

FIVE

FOUCAULT'S "AUTOCRITIQUE"

THREE EQUIVOCATIONS OF CONDUCT, EXPERIENCE, AND THOUGHT

> Fundamental and flagrant contradictions rarely occur in second-rate writers; in the work of the great authors they lead into the very center of their work.
>
> **Hannah Arendt**

IT HAS OFTEN BEEN NOTED that in the eight year gap between the publication of volume 1 of *The History of Sexuality* (*La volonté de savoir*, 1976) and volumes 2 and 3 (*L'usage des plaisirs*; and *Le souci de soi*; 1984), an important shift occurred in Foucault's thinking. Commentators almost universally agree that this period inaugurated some form of "autocritique,"[1] as well as ushering in a new research agenda. What is less clear, however, is precisely the significance and extent of this change. Some insist that this period saw Foucault make a fundamental break with his previous work, while others insist on continuity and modification merely in emphasis. It is also worth noting that the question regarding the extent of this movement has implications for substantive issues. For instance, those who emphasize a large break are subsequently forced to choose "which Foucault" had the proper analysis: some opt for the earlier emphasis on power and tactical resistance,[2] while others prefer the emphasis on autonomy and aesthetic self-fashioning in the later works.[3]

Rather than attempt to intervene in such debates directly, my specific aim here is to help us think about freedom in relation to questions of ontology—that is, in relation to the question of how it is that a "world" of entities appears before us at all. This will involve, therefore, a selective reading of Foucault, one that attempts to draw out conclusions that Foucault himself did not make explicit, nor perhaps would have agreed to himself (just as with my reading of Heidegger in the previous chapters). It is not my primary interest to establish an authoritative reading of Foucault that will resolve exegetical problems, but rather to suggest that Foucault is an important—even indispensable—resource for thinking about freedom in ontological terms. This involves examining freedom in terms other than as reducible to a property of the subject, or by reference to the relatively abstract forces of a historical teleology (idealist or materialist). The goal is to think about freedom as both a condition and feature of that by which a "world" is disclosed to us, by which a horizon of intelligibility is made manifest and by which it nevertheless remains open to modification and change. My claim is that, in his late works, Foucault provides us with the richest vocabulary we have to date for thinking about freedom and historical ontology.

This vocabulary is not, however, without its ambiguities, difficulties, and reversals. Thus, this chapter proceeds in two parts. The first part (5.1) is organized around equivocation in Foucault's use of the terms *conduct*, *thought*, and *experience* from roughly 1977 to 1982. These three concepts, I argue, together comprise the locus of a new questioning out of which arises Foucault's final position. This final position, read in the second part of the chapter (5.2), is organized around the following question: How can one think "freedom" in relation to historical ontology? My hypothesis is that while "thought" remains a central concept in Foucault's understanding of freedom (indicating a possible return to subject-centered accounts of freedom as self-reflection), Foucault's understanding of thought is that it presupposes activities of "care" which are *themselves* the ontological ground of freedom.

My reconstruction of Foucault in relation to this question moves through three stages of his analysis. The first stage examines the principle of contingent eventalization. The second stage relies upon what he termed the principle of the irreducibility of thought. Third and finally, Foucault came to a formulation of freedom as ethical-spiritual transformation. This ethical-spiritual transformation places emphasis not on individual self-reflection but on *care* within relational activities. The reading of Foucault I offer looks to this *mode of being* within activities as the heart of freedom, which most closely realizes the Heideggerian notion of freedom as a careful engagement with the disclosure of being and provides the basis for a *history* of the practices of attunement to which Heidegger only tangentially refers. In other words, it provides an opening for the combining of Foucault's historical modes of critical inquiry with Heidegger's ontological investigations.

5.1. THREE EQUIVOCATIONS

5.1.a. The Model of War

In order to understand his "autocritique" and what I am calling here the "three equivocations," it is important first to establish that against which the autocritique is working. This earlier position might be referred to as the "war model."

Foucault described *Surveiller et punir* as a history of the "microphysics of power," which would also serve as a genealogy of the modern soul. His aim was to bring to light a perspective on the interiorized self, or soul, that would see it not as "the reactivated remnants of an ideology," but rather as "the present correlative of a certain technology of power over the body" (*DP*, 29; *SP*, 38). In other words, Foucault sought to extend his critique of historical hermeneutics (presented in the previous chapter) by demonstrating that the ideological formulations of a particular age—the ideas, concepts, and cultural manifestations— were mere effects of what he called the political technology of the body, defined by the microtechniques applied to the body on a regular and carefully regulated basis that, over time, produced new forms of subjectivity in the West. In describing the kind of power needed for such a political technology of the body—disciplinary power—Foucault writes,

> the power exercised on the body is conceived not as a property, but as a strategy . . . one should take as its model a perpetual battle rather than a contract regulating a transaction or the conquest of a territory. In short this power is exercised rather than possessed; it is not the "privilege," acquired or preserved, of the dominant class, but the overall effect of its strategic positions—an effect that is manifested and sometimes extended by the position of those who are dominated. (*DP*, 26–27; *SP*, 35)

Using this model of "perpetual battle,"[4] Foucault also sought to demonstrate that a history of the present could be written without resorting to a philosophy of the constituting subject.[5] In other words, a new form of political and social organization (such as disciplinary society) could be brought into existence without anyone in particular devising to do so. Rather, the new regime of knowledge/power could emerge as the regularized, overall *effect* of a set of strategic positions originally devised for specific, localized purposes. As he put it in a 1978 talk,

> "Discipline" isn't the expression of an "ideal type" (that of "disciplined man"); it's the generalization and interconnection of different techniques themselves designed in response to localized requirements (schooling, training troops to handle rifles).... In fact there are different strategies that are mutually opposed, composed, and superposed so as to produce permanent and solid effects that can perfectly well be understood in terms of their rationality, even though they don't conform to the initial programming: this is what gives the resulting apparatus its solidity and suppleness. (*EW3*, 231–32; *DE2*, 847)

This also meant, however, that strategic *resistance* against such localized exercises of power could feed into the overall regime. The struggle to reverse or overthrow this or that particular practice exercised against oneself could facilitate the stabilizing of an overall regime of power.[6] Resistance was internal to the constitution of a regime of knowledge/power and could not be read as merely in opposition to it. This resistance simultaneously reinforced power relations *and* undermined them, precisely because "resistance" is not a singular thing, but rather a set of conflicting and contradictory acts exercised by subjects against and in relation to the particular power practices exercised upon them. Because power relations in a given era are not "univoques," they

> define innumerable points of confrontation, focuses of instability, each of which has its own risks of conflict, of struggles, and of an at least temporary inversion of the power relations. The overthrow of these "micro-powers" does not, then obey the law of all or nothing; it is not acquired once and for all by a new control of the apparatuses nor by a new functioning or a destruction of the institutions; on the other hand, none of its localized episodes may be inscribed in history except by the effects that it induces on the entire network in which it is caught up. (*DP*, 27; *SP*, 35–36)

So, we can see that there is some room for resistance in this war model, and that through a study of this strategic battle, Foucault can account for historical change. What is less clear, however, is whether the mere fact of historical change can be spoken of in terms of "freedom." From the standpoint of traditional Western political philosophy, at least, this would appear to be a peculiar formulation of freedom, inasmuch as change here is more the *effect* of practices of power on subjects, rather than the agency of subjects against such practices. In this formulation, there appears to be no "remainder" to power relations which locates the site from which freedom makes a counterattack.[7] Rather, because power relations themselves are multifold and internally contradictory, simply by exercising them subjects create spaces for change and even strategic reversal. Foucault is quite clear that "it is not the activity of the subject of knowledge that produces a corpus of knowledge, useful or resistant to power." Rather, it is the regime of power/knowledge itself that "determines the forms and possible domains of knowledge" (*DP*, 28; *SP*, 36).

In this model of war, then, "freedom" refers neither to a state of being nor property of the constituting subject, nor does it refer to a particular kind of creative activity whereby new ways of thinking and acting are brought into being. Rather, insofar as there is any freedom within this model it is merely the contingent effects produced by the operationalization of power on bodies or perhaps the stubborn remainder of a quasi-materialist claim about bodies as "resistant material," never fully compliant to power.[8]

5.1.b. The Arts of Government, Governmentality, and Conduct

The war model, heavily influenced by Nietzsche, still conceived of power as a relatively impersonal set of forces to which one is subject (i.e., practices of governance *on* subjects). "Freedom" in this model is thus largely conceived of as a *tactical reversal* of certain specific power relations on oneself. Despite what Foucault often implied, this form of freedom is still largely reactionary. In other words, it would be hard to connect this understanding of freedom to "the engagement with beings as such," since Foucault rarely discusses it as participatory; rather, it is resistant. Furthermore, it turns out that this capacity for tactical reversal or resistance is itself another manifestation of power. As an example, we might think here of two billiard balls shot at each other. Upon collision the trajectory of both is changed in perhaps unpredictable ways. Yet it would be hard to say that the billiard balls are "free" since the movement of each is merely the product of the set of forces to which it is subject.

Even during the Collège de France lectures of 1977–78 (*Sécurité, territoire, population*), however, Foucault began to show some equivocation in his analysis of power and governmentality presented in *Discipline and Punish* and volume 1 of *The History of Sexuality*, leading to his use of the term *conduct*.[9] This equivocation, the resulting new lines of inquiry opened up by it, and the connection to Foucault's important later text, "The Subject and Power," are exemplified by his remarks on the translation of *oikonomia psuchōn*, a phrase used by early Christian ministers to describe the pastorate. The discussion of "conduct" and the *oikonomia psuchōn* follows on the heels of the first precise definition of "governmentality" that Foucault provides. He states that he means three things in using this term:

> First, by "governmentality" I understand the ensemble formed by institutions, procedures, analyses and reflections, calculations, and tactics that allow the exercise of this very specific, albeit very complex, power that has the population as its target, political economy as its major form of knowledge, and apparatuses of security as its essential technical instrument. Second, by "governmentality" I understand the tendency, the line of force, that for a long time, and throughout the West, has constantly led towards the pre-eminence over all other types of power—sovereignty, discipline, and so on—of the type of power that we can call "government" and which has led to the development of a series of specific governmental apparatuses (*appareils*) on the one hand, [and, on the other] to the development of a series of knowledges (*savoirs*). Finally, by "governmentality" I think we should understand the process, or rather, the result of the process by which the state of justice of the Middle Ages became the administrative state in the fifteenth and sixteenth centuries and was gradually "governmentalized." (*STP2*, 108; *STP*, 111–12)

We can observe the gathering together and specifying of two shifts in Foucault's thought in this passage, one theoretical, the other historical.

The theoretical shift is the precise differentiation between "the arts of government" and "governmentality." From roughly 1975 to 1977 (incorporating works from *Les anormaux*, *Il faut défendre la société*, *Surveiller et punir*, and *La volonté de savoir: Histoire de la sexualité, vol. 1*), Foucault was primarily concerned with what he called "the arts of government." As defined in *Les anormaux* in 1975, the "arts of government" were a specific set of political technologies developed in the Classical age (beginning in the eighteenth century) whereby the power of the sovereign was no longer manifest through exclusion, execution, or incarceration,[10] but rather through "the invention of positive technologies of power ... a reaction of inclusion, observation, the formation of knowledge, the multiplication of effects of power on the basis of the accumulation of observations and knowledge. We pass from a technology of power that drives out, excludes, banishes, marginalizes, and represses, to a fundamentally positive power that fashions, observes, knows, and multiplies itself on the basis of its own effects" (*A2*, 48; *A*, 44). The Classical age sees the birth of "government" in the modern sense of the term, by which Foucault means three things: (1) "a juridico-political theory of power centered on the notion of the will and its alienation, transfer, and representation in a governmental apparatus"; (2) "a State apparatus that extended into and was supported by different institutions"; and (3) "a general technique of the exercise of power that can be transferred to many different institutions and apparatuses" (*A2*, 49; *A*, 45).

Now, in the passage quoted above in which Foucault first differentiates "governmentality" from "governance," we can observe a theoretical shift away from a study of the first two aspects of "the arts of government" (the positive technologies of power and the state apparatus) toward the last ("the *general technique* of the exercise of power"). This involves making an analytic distinction between the operations of power within specific (in this case, state) institutions and the *technique* or *form of rationality* employed by such institutions. If the rationality is not reducible to its institutional embodiment in this time and place, then it can (at least in theory) be tracked in other manifestations. This theoretical distinction also permits a shift in historical emphasis. In the case of "the arts of government," Foucault studied "governmentality" only insofar as it served to put into place a specific regime of power at a specific place and time (namely Western Europe of the eighteenth century and beyond). However, in *Sécurité, territoire, population*, with his announcement of the interest in "governmentality" per se, Foucault detaches the term from the historical specificity with which it was originally devised and articulated. "Governmentality" now names a form of rationality immanent in many different fields of life (not only within the arts of government) that has its origins in a much earlier periodization (linked all the way back to early Christian pastoral power).[11]

Foucault's introduction of governmentality as an independent field of study derives from his claim that, while it was foundational to the emergence of the arts of government in the Classical age, it is also not reducible to such arts. Rather, governmentality is a "généralité singulière" that emerges prior to and independent of the modern arts of government.[12] Specifically, governmentality has its roots in what Foucault terms "pastoral power," associated with the rise of early Christianity. However, as I noted earlier, this notion of governmentality emerges only to undergo subsequent questioning almost immediately.[13] A certain equivocation, if not direct modification, of the concept of governmentality is introduced in the context of his discussion of this pastoral power or, more specifically, that known to the Greek patriarchs of the third and fourth century A.D. (Foucault specifically names Gregory Nazianzen) as "*oikonomia psuchōn*." Foucault begins by translating this phrase as *l'économie des âmes* (the economy of souls), but states right away that this "takes on a completely different dimension and a completely different field of references with the pastorate" than with the Greek notion of *oikos*. Rather than being restricted to the household or management of the family (incorporating slaves, women, and children), the economy of souls "must bear on the whole Christian community and on each Christian in particular." Thus, he concludes, because of the confused association of *oikos* to the household (whereas *oikonomia psuchōn* is more universal), perhaps "economy" is not the best translation for the phrase. He notes that since the Latin translation of the term is *regimen animarum*, this would potentially lead us to employ *régime des âmes*, connecting pastoral power back to earlier discussions of the arts of government and, more precisely, to governmentality. However, Foucault specifically opts *not* to use the terms *régime* or *gouvernement* to describe this relationship. Rather, he takes advantage of another term in French which possesses a useful ambiguity in meaning that is "quite interesting for translating this economy of souls." This term, rarely used in this context (except, Foucault claims, for some citations in Montaigne) is *conduite* (*STP2*, 192–93; *STP*, 195–96).

Whether or not Foucault is correct to use the word *conduite* in his translation of *oikonomia psuchōn*, and whether this particular kind of relationship can be accurately assigned to the activities of early Christians in this period is not something I will comment upon here. What matters for my purposes is to note that even at this early stage (four years before the publication of "The Subject and Power"), Foucault was keen to draw an analytic distinction between *gouvernement*, *gouvernementalité*, and *conduite*. He deliberately employs the term *conduite* because it contains within it a double sense not evoked by governmentality, something he sees as crucial to his analysis of this specific form of relationship. Foucault writes that the term *conduite* refers to several things at once: "Conduct is the activity of conducting (*conduire*), of conduction (*la conduction*) if you like, but it is equally *the way* in which one conducts oneself (*se conduit*), lets oneself be conducted (*se laisse conduire*), is conducted (*est conduit*), and finally, in which one behaves (*se comporter*) as an effect of a form of conduct (*une conduite*) as the action of conducting or of conduction (*conduction*)" (*STP2*, 193; *STP*, 196–97; italics added). Because *conduite* brings forth both the act of governing *and* the behavior or comportment of the governed in a mutually influencing relationship, Foucault concludes that "conduite des âmes" is "the least bad" translation for *oikonomia psuchōn*, and that it is only on the basis of this conceptualization that we can analyze how pastoral power "opened up and how [it] was burst open, broke up, and assumed the dimension of governmentality, or how the problem of government, of governmentality, was able to arise on the basis of the pastorate" (*STP2*, 193; *STP*, 197). In other words, in order to account for the transformation of the pastorate—in order to properly account for how one resisted it and, at the same time, brought into existence a new domain of knowledge/power—Foucault draws our attention to the pastorate as a domain not of governmentality but of conduct. By employing the term *conduct* he is drawing attention not merely to the activities of the governors but also of the governed, and to the notion that the space between these two can never be totally collapsed. The practices of governance do not act *directly* on the governed, thus they are never performed perfectly. Rather, since they act upon the *conduct* of the governed, a conduct which is always in part about how the governed *conduct themselves* within such activities, these two sides of the field of power here described are interrelated *but not reducible to each other*.[14] In emphasizing a *relationship* rather than an act, Foucault has opened up a new line of inquiry: how freedom is exercised not only in tactical resistance to governance, but also as an activity on oneself characterized as a *mode* or *manner* of being (*se conduire, se comporter*) that brings into existence a new domain of thought and action. He writes that on the basis of this new analysis, we have something new to study: not merely institutions, nor governing rationalities, nor even revolutionary actions against these first two. Rather, we can also look to the alterations in the *way* or *manner* in which people conducted themselves in relation to the first two. Foucault asks, "Just as there have been forms of resistance to power as the exercise of political sovereignty, and just as there have been other, equally intentional forms of resistance or refusal that were directed at power in the form of economic exploitation, have there not been forms of resistance to power as conducting?" (*STP2*, 195; *STP*, 198). These "revolts of conduct," Foucault states, are of a different type than political or economic revolts of governance since they are not aimed at the overthrow, or reversal of power exercised by a form of sovereignty (*STP2*, 196; *STP*, 198). Rather, they are much more diffuse, subtle, and localized—consisting often in the modification of an activity *within* a given domain of activities and experiences (he provides examples from war, religion, and medicine). Individuals continue to perform the actions assigned to them—the practices of governance in a specific domain of activity. But by changing *their conduct*, the way they relate to themselves within their given roles and duties, these people not only modify the field but, over time, bring into being a new field. Foucault struggles to find an appropriate term for this kind of intentional practice of freedom within a range of prescribed possible activities, referring to "insoumission" (insubordination), "dissidence," and "inconduite" (misconduct) before settling on "contre-conduite," defined as something more than passively not behaving oneself properly, but less than becoming a full adversary to governing power in the hopes of replacing it (*STP*, 205; *STP2*, 201).

This introduction of the concept of "conduct" and its dual senses brings to light a general transition in Foucault's thought in this period.

It is a move away from "governmentality" toward "conduct," from the "war model" to the "game model," from freedom as tactical and reactionary to freedom as relational and creative, from freedom as defined by *what* we do, to freedom defined in relation to *how* we do what we do—a kind of relationship to what one is doing. Of course, the introduction of the term is not a radical break with previous analysis. But this is partially demonstrative of precisely his point. What begins as a small shift in emphasis, in the way Foucault rephrases himself in relation to his own work, slowly transforms into a new question and new research agenda. We might say that by highlighting the term *conduite* Foucault has modified *his* conduct, the results of which cannot be fully seen from the standpoint of this current formulation.[15] Even at this early stage, however, we see Foucault repositioning himself in relation to a new emerging thesis. He begins to reposition his work, opening up the possibility of thinking about power and freedom in terms other than merely moral (i.e., whether a particular act is "good," and thus can be named as an act of freedom, or "bad" and thus reducible to mere power). Instead, we might also think of Foucault's "conduct" in *ontological* terms—as modes of being which are *disclosive* of a domain of objects.[16] In comments offered in 1978, Foucault suggests as much by arguing that, "philosophy might still play a role on the side of counter-power . . . on condition, in short, that it stops posing the question of power in terms of good and evil, but poses it *in terms of existence.*"[17] Here, I believe we can see Foucault reposition himself away from questions of the constituting power of subjects and toward an analysis of the *kinds of relationships* that open space for a working out of alternative possibilities (relationships of power and conduct). He is, I suggest, moving toward an analysis of freedom as characteristic of a certain relationship between entities, not as a property of the subject (a free will), nor as a particular kind of action by the subject (an act of resistance). Put more succinctly, this is the freedom of *situations* not *subjects*: the freedom of "world."

In sum, then, we can observe a slow transition in terminology that tracks a parallel change in the predominant themes and questions for analysis. Foucault begins with a study of (1) the "arts of government" and the related institutions of the modern nation-state. He then isolates and generalizes one feature of these arts: (2) "governmentality" as a form of punitive rationality not reducible to modern state governance proper, but also observable in previous eras, in other domains. Finally, when following this thread of governmentality back to the emergence of pastoral power, Foucault concedes that "governmentality" as a "singular generality" cannot account for the slow modification of relationships of power over time. In order to do this, he introduces the notion of (3) "conduct" in order to highlight the irreducible space between acts of governance and the comportment or self-conduct of the governed. In other words, "conduct" raises the question of the space of freedom in terms of existence.

5.1.c. Experience and Thought

I am fascinated by history and the relationship between
personal experience and those events of which we are a part.
I think that is the nucleus of my theoretical desires.

EW1, 124; DE2, 1347

While Foucault struggled to find an appropriate vocabulary for "conduct," he was returning to and reformulating his use of the terms *experience* and *thought*. These last two terms provide another crucial point of departure for the interrogation of his work in relation to ontology. Foucault returned to the notion of "experience" (after having nearly abandoned it from *L'archéologie du savoir* to *La volonté de savoir*), because taking his object of study as the "historically singular forms of experience" (and not, say, domains of knowledge or practices of governance operating directly on bodies) allowed him to incorporate the element of contingency and freedom as a space of possibilities within such "experiences," thus providing for the ontological *condition* of such knowledge and power practices. Interestingly, this move to "forms of experience" roughly parallels Kant's move to transcendental finitude (as outlined in Chapter One). Just as Kant redefined subjective finitude positively, making it the condition of possibility for knowledge and thus freedom qua autonomy, Foucault makes a similar move away from subjective finitude toward historical contingency in the presencing of the forms of experience defined ontologically.[18] As I will argue later, this opens up space for what Heidegger called "the ontological difference"—the distinction between that which is present within a given clearing (the domains of knowledge and practices of governance in a given era) and "that which presences."[19] Although Foucault did not take up this possibility, it is opened by his use of the term *experience* and is a route of thought worth pursuing in order to better make sense of his later writings on freedom and ethics. To begin this discussion, we might look to the relatively obscure text known as the "unpublished" preface to volume 2 of *Histoire de la sexualité*, perhaps Foucault's most Heideggerian piece.[20]

Foucault states that the object of the work in *Histoire de la sexualité* was to analyze sexuality "as a historically singular form of experience" (*EW1*, 199; *DE2*, 1397). Of course, as he himself anticipates, it is not altogether clear what a "form of experience" refers to, but it does seem to conjure a relation back to his earliest works on madness, unreason, and the like as phenomenological studies of "experience" within historical-cultural milieux. In fact, Foucault himself makes the link explicit. He writes that "to study forms of experience in this way—in their history—is an idea that originated with an earlier project, in which I made use of the methods of existential analysis." However, he concedes this project failed for two reasons. First, "its theoretical weakness in elaborating the notion of experience," and second, "its ambiguous link with a psychiatric practice, which it simultaneously ignored and took for granted" (*EW1*, 200; *DE2*, 1398).[21] The emergence of "experience" as the primary locus of investigation is surprising, then, given that Foucault himself specifically repudiated use of the term.[22] He is confronted by a difficult task in renewing the term. If "experience" failed to serve as a stable locus of investigation before, then how can the task of studying it as a "historical singularity" proceed more successfully? In Foucault's own words, the challenge is to analyze experience without merely resorting to a "general theory of the human being" (the transcendental response), or a "philosophical anthropology and a social history" (the positivist response). The struggle is to think forms of experience without reducing them to either the ahistorical experiences of a transcendental subject or merely the "products" of a deterministic set of historical forces.[23]

Foucault explains that in order to accomplish this task what was required was "to bring to light the domain where the formation, development, and transformation of forms of experience can situate themselves—that is, a history of thought" (*EW1*, 200; *DE2*, 1398). So, we can see in this passage that Foucault has returned to a second major theme which was virtually nonexistent in his "middle" writings (especially so in *Discipline and Punish*). Not only has the concept of "experience" returned as important, but "thought" has also taken up a newly revamped role and these two concepts appear to be internally related. That is to say, part of what defines the specificity of the phrase *historically singular form of experience* for Foucault is that it is inhabited by "thought." Elsewhere, he even goes so far as to claim that "neither those determinations nor those structures can allow for experiences . . . except through thought. There is no experience that is not a way of thinking and cannot be analyzed from the viewpoint of the history of thought; this is what might be called the principle of irreducibility of thought" (*EW1*, 201; *DE2*, 1399). This appears to differentiate "forms of experience" from *épistémès*, for example, which Foucault defined in *The Archaeology of Knowledge* without reference to "thought" as such. There, he defined *épistémès* as

> the total set of relations that unite, at a given period, the discursive practices that give rise to epistemological figures, sciences, and possibly formalized systems; the *way* in which, in each of these discursive formations, the transitions to epistemologization, scientificity, and formalization are situated and operate; the distribution of these thresholds . . . the lateral relations that may exist between epistemological figures or sciences insofar as they belong to neighbouring, but distinct, discursive practices. The episteme is not a form of knowledge (*connaissance*) or type of rationality which . . . manifests the sovereign unity of a subject, a spirit, or a period; it is the totality of relations that can be discovered, for a given period, between the sciences when one analyzes them at the level of discursive regularities. (*AK*, 211; *AS*, 250; italics added)

At least if we take Foucault's statement on *épistémès* in *The Archaeology* to be authoritative, it appears that *épistémès* do not attempt to engage at the level of the "discursive practices" themselves—interpreting, for example, their meaning and use within their respective domains or in relation to their specific epistemological figures. Rather, *épistémè* is a concept introduced to point to a set of relations between *different* discursive practices with the aim of demonstrating a general unity, located not in "the existence of the object . . . nor the constitution of a single horizon of objectivity. . . . It would be the interplay of the rules that make possible the appearance of objects during a given period of time" (*AK*, 36; *AS*, 46). Examining these "rules of formation" allows for a mapping of structural similarities across discursive fields (such as the fields of life, labor, and language presented in *Les mots et les choses*) *without* engaging with the practices which gave rise to the archeological units in each field. By contrast, "historically singular forms of experience" are meant to transpose this question precisely down to the level of the practical activities of subjects within a domain and to inquire into the mutability of such practices insofar as they produce possibilities of self-to-self relations that were previously impossible. By evoking "experience," not from the standpoint of the phenomenology of the individual subject, but rather as a domain of practices that share a broad family resemblance, Foucault has moved away from studying how a body of knowledge came to gain its status as a science both through the vertical relationship between its discursive practices and its epistemological objects, on the one hand, and the horizontal integration of it with other domains of knowledge in a given epoch (archeology as form of historical epistemology), on the other. He moves away from this form of analysis toward the study of disciplinary practices on bodies and the tactical games of reversal and resistance to such governmentality (a genealogy), and finally, to a study of the ways in which subjects relate to themselves as a practice of self-transformation which, in turn, discloses a new domain of objects or entities to which one relates (a historical ontology). This periodization might be further analyzed through the tripartite division of knowledge, punitive rationality and thought.[24]

Beginning with the reflections in the "unpublished" preface to volume 2 of *The History of Sexuality*, we can track three different ways in which Foucault formulates the relationship between "thought" and "experience." The first relationship is the most closely aligned with his early writings on *épistémès* and the human sciences. In this sense, thought refers to the totality of what appears as meaningful knowledge within a field of experience and the operations by which this knowledge gains status as a science. Thought here refers to that which is eligible for claims about truth and falsehood. For the sake of terminological clarity, we might refer to this as a body of "knowledge."

The second use of the word thought actually brings Foucault closer to the hermeneutic tradition. This second sense is evoked when he speaks of thought as something that "inhabits" our activities. He writes,

> "Thought," understood in this way, then, is not to be sought only in theoretical formulations such as those of philosophy or science; it can and must be analyzed in every manner of speaking, doing, or behaving in which the individual appears and acts as knowing subject [sujet de connaissance], as ethical or juridical subject, as subject conscious of himself and others. In this sense, *thought is understood as the very form of action*.... The study of forms of experience can thus proceed from an analysis of "practices"—discursive or not—as long as one qualifies that word to mean the different systems of action *insofar as they are inhabited by thought* as I have characterized it here. (*EW1*, 200–201; *DE2*, 1398–99; italics added)

Elsewhere, in the published preface to volume 2 of *The History of Sexuality*, Foucault puts an even stronger hermeneutic slant on this formulation, defining the task of philosophy as such: "to know to what extent the effort to think one's own history can free thought from what it silently thinks, and so enable it to think differently" (*UP2*, 9; *UP*, 17).[25] Thus, Foucault not only appears to find a form of thought embedded within everyday practices, but also positions "philosophy" as a specific, specialized activity whose aim is to make this implicit thought *explicit*—to turn its silence into voice.[26] Paradoxically, perhaps, the introduction of "what we silently think" as a kind of meaning embedded within our practices returns Foucault to the very thing he criticized in *Les mots et les choses*. Recall that Foucault there associated the modern *cogito*, which he sought to historicize and subject to critique, with the "ceaseless task": to "traverse, duplicate, and reactivate in an explicit form the articulation of thought on everything within it, around it, and beneath it which is not thought, yet which is nevertheless not foreign to thought, in the sense of an irreducible, an insuperable exteriority ... the constantly renewed interrogation as to how thought can reside elsewhere than here, and yet so very close to itself; how it can *be* in the forms of non-thinking" (*OT*, 353; *MC*, 482).[27] This attempt to get "behind" or "beneath" our activities to reveal the hidden "unthought" at work is the task of hermeneutic inquiry. This formulation brings

Foucault, if only momentarily (we shall see below that he almost immediately reverses his position on this question), closer to Heidegger's notion of preontological understanding.[28] Furthermore, Foucault's use of the term *thought* during this period to describe a feature of everyday practices that is not itself reducible to consciously held ideas or concepts, leads him to offer a provisional definition of the "human being" in a manner similar to Heidegger's use of Dasein. Foucault states that his goal is to study "the human being" as that which "problematizes what it is, what it does and the world in which it lives" (*UP2*, 10; *UP*, 18). This echoes, intentionally or not, Heidegger's definition of Dasein as that for whom its existence is an issue as well as the notion that this particular kind of being (i.e., Dasein) is defined by the relationship between its preontological understanding and its self-interpreting activity (not, therefore, by a substance metaphysics which attempts to identify a fixed nature).[29]

Even while briefly reintroducing this hermeneutic use of the term thought, Foucault almost immediately qualifies this and introduces a final third sense of the term. It is this third sense of the word which sees Foucault attempt to cast his analysis in terms of ontology by suggesting there may be a mode of relating to oneself that (to employ Heideggerian terminology) reveals our revealing-in-action. This is the third sense of thought: a movement of the self in relation to itself which simultaneously discloses us as already within and constituted by meaningful relations (of subjects, objects, and practices), *and* as capable of bringing forth new worlds. Foucault writes, "By 'thought,' I mean what establishes, in a variety of possible forms, the play of true and false, and consequently constitutes the human being as a knowing subject [sujet de connaissance]; in other words, it is the basis for accepting or refusing rules, and constitutes human beings as social and juridical subjects; it is what establishes the relation with oneself and with others, and constitutes the human being as ethical subject" (*EW1*, 200–201; *DE2*, 1398). So, in this formulation at least thought appears as what might be called a "constituting event." It is not reducible either to knowledge as a body of systemized possible claims of truth or falsehood, a science, or to a preontological understanding inhabiting all meaningful activity. Rather, Foucault repeatedly states that thought *establishes* and *constitutes*. More specifically, thought is what establishes and constitutes an epistemic field or horizon of intelligibility which, through its determination of what can count as meaningful within the "play of true and false," subsequently constitutes the human being as a subject. So, we might say that thought opens up a domain of knowledge and action which, in turn, sets out the range of possible forms of subjectivity which we inhabit. Thought in this instance is a constituting event.

But how exactly does this thought arrive? What makes it possible? Here is where we see Foucault attempting to navigate between the two problematic poles of: (1) the philosophy of the constituting subject, which seeks the possibility of thought in transcendental consciousness (as with Descartes, Kant, or Husserl); and (2) historical teleology, which seeks the possibility of thought in the unfolding of a rational telos working within our worldly activities themselves, whether we consciously comprehend them or not (as with Hegel or Marx). Certainly, Foucault seems to agree that the disclosure of a domain of knowledge and action occurs according to certain "concrete determinations of social existence" (*EW1*, 201; *DE2*, 1399), such as material or economic structures. However, he also claims that such forces are never entirely determinant because the process of disclosure by which such forces come into play—by which they take their force and structure—is internally related to the process by which thought comes into existence: "neither those determinations nor those structures can allow for experiences . . . except through thought. There is no experience that is not a way of thinking and cannot be analyzed from the viewpoint of the history of thought; this is what might be called the principle of irreducibility of thought" (*EW1*, 201; *DE2*, 1399). When we ask, however, what thought means in this context, we must not understand it as a single form of cognitive reflection disengaged from the embodied practices of the subject, nor a secret "rule," "theory," or "picture" that we are implicitly or unconsciously drawing upon to guide our actions. Rather, *thought* here refers to a supposed movement of the self-in-the-world back upon itself. Since this movement is not universally given, but is rather a relational practice *within* a historically singular form of experience, "thought has a historicity which is proper to it. . . . This is what could be called the principle of singularity of the history of thought: there are events of thought" (*EW1*, 201; *DE2*, 1399). And finally, since the forms of thought in a given period themselves make possible new relations between the self and itself, the historical disclosure of thought contains within it the immanent possibility of its own transformation. This is what Foucault calls the "third principle": "critique—understood as analysis of the historical conditions that bear on the creation of links to truth, to rules, and to the self—does not mark out impassable boundaries or describe closed systems; it brings to light transformable singularities. These transformations could not take place except by means of a working of thought upon itself; that is the principle of the history of thought as critical activity" (*EW1*, 201; *DE2*, 1399; translation modified). In light of this third and final reconstruction of *thought* Foucault reexamines his previous work. Looking back to the studies of madness and psychiatry, he describes his project as being one of outlining "a locus of experience that I tried to describe from the point of view of the history of thought," even while admitting that, "the use that I made of the word 'experience' was very floating" (*EW1*, 202; *DE2*, 1400; translation modified). The new formulation of *experience* is now understood not from the standpoint of the phenomenology of the individual subject: as something that occurs "within" the subject. Rather, it is understood as a historically singular domain of possible thought and action in relationships between subjects and object, subjects and subjects, and subjects and themselves, which contain possibilities for its immanent transformation. On this basis, Foucault seeks to demonstrate how a history of such experiences will be the foundation for the possibility of a history of *being*, since such a domain not only forms an "ensemble of rules, procedures, means to an end" (the ethical-political concern), but also "*determines a domain of objects* about which it is possible to articulate true or false propositions" (*EW3*, 230; *DE2*, 845; italics added). It is only with an eye to historically singular experiences, and their related forms of thought or transformable singularities, that a history of being and truth can proceed. Again evoking very Heideggerian language Foucault writes,

> What I have tried to maintain for many years, is the effort to isolate some of the elements that might be useful for a history of truth. Not a history that would be concerned with what might be true in the fields of learning, but an analysis of the "games of truth," the games

of truth and error through which *being is historically constituted as experience; that is, as something that can and must be thought.* (UP2, 6–7; UP, 13; italics added)

In stating that "Being" is historically constituted as "experience," Foucault has obviously altered his analysis from previous works considerably. This formulation in particular appears to be offering a more generalized account of ontology, even though the level of investigation remains primarily historical or ontic. Foucault begins his work at the level of the specific practices that together, over time, produced stabilized effects that could be analyzed as historical forms of experience. The clearest example of this is that of modern sexuality. However, here we see that there is a general thesis about how this historical work connects to questions of fundamental ontology. For Foucault it seems that a horizon of intelligibility through which Being is made manifest to us is not exclusively (nor even primarily) presented through a set of consciously reflected-upon concepts or principles. "Being" as a horizon of intelligibility is not reducible to a body of knowledge or science to be investigated only through a mapping of structural regularities between discursive fields. Nor, however, can it be reduced to the practices of governance (what is done *to* us by others). Rather, Being is, for Foucault, revealed as experiences, not from the standpoint of the individual phenomenological subject, but as a range or field of possible ways of thinking and acting (i.e., a *world*). Historically singular forms of experience cannot be investigated in the way that other objects might be. They are not "things" we can stand back from, look at, and analyze as they constitute the ontological ground of the forms of subjectivity that we inhabit. Hence, to study the historically singular forms of experience is to write a "historical ontology of oneself."

The question remaining in this, however, is: what makes possible the movement by which a historically singular form of experience comes to be problematized? It is not enough to simply assert that experience is problematized and that this movement of problematization is the work of thought. Rather, we must examine *how* the ontological ground of oneself can be investigated *at all*, how it comes to be *at issue* for the subject in the first place. Only through this can we clarify Foucault's position in relation to freedom.

5.2. FREEDOM IN THREE STAGES: CONTINGENT EVENT, THOUGHT, SPIRITUAL EXERCISE

In this remaining section, I will now briefly analyze three stages in Foucault's final analysis of the question of freedom, drawing upon his later writings. These late writings are so rich and complex a great body of literature on them has already been produced.[30] Hence, my aim here is not to summarize all the lines of inquiry investigated within them. Rather, my aim is to think through these late works in relation to the question of ontology and freedom.

Foucault develops his work in three basic moves. First, he begins with an account of freedom as conditioned on the irreducibility of contingent eventalization, a notion most closely aligned with the "war model" discussed above. Next, seeing limitations in this analysis, Foucault moves to a notion of freedom as grounded in thought-as-problematization. Freedom, in this stage of analysis, consists in grasping conceptually the historical conditions of possibility for a given domain of experience. This is what Foucault calls the principle of the irreducibility of thought. The final stage of Foucault's analysis, however, consists in moving beyond even this toward a study of the *spiritual practices* by which the ethical transformation of the subject takes place. These practices are referred to as "spiritual" precisely because they do not consist in merely affirming the unity or autonomy of the subject as the locus and ground of truth, but rather are taken up as means by which the subject can bring itself into alignment with a domain of experience both projected and actual. I argue, in other words, that these practices are ontologically disclosive.

This reading begins with the watershed piece "The Subject and Power," which sets out the frame of reference for Foucault's last writings. This article is a particularly important piece for the general discussion at hand because it is the first time that Foucault attempts to set out in what way we might speak of "freedom" in relation to the domains of experience and practices of thought discussed elsewhere. Whereas in the *Sécurité, territoire, population* lectures Foucault made room for a new form of resistance, or counterconduct, he did not fully explain how this new conduct was possible or how it altered his previous analysis of power. This is precisely what he attempts in "The Subject and Power."

As part of his "autocritique," Foucault revises and refines his use of the term *power*. Under the model of war, seen most clearly in *Discipline and Punish*, power refers to a vast array of strategic activities of governance, not embedded merely in ideological formations but also in direct manipulation of the physical body. Power seems ubiquitous and unmediated. In "The Subject and Power," however, Foucault narrows his use of the term to only one precise *kind* of relationship within the total possible range of relations between social agents. Specifically, "what defines a relationship of power is that it is a mode of action that does not act directly and immediately on others. Instead, it acts upon their actions: an action upon an action, on possible or actual future or present actions" (*EW3*, 340; *DE2*, 1055). In an interview from the same period, Foucault gives an example to clarify what kind of action and what kind of relationship he is thinking of:

> Power is a set of relations. What does it mean to exercise power? It does not mean picking up this tape recorder and throwing it on the ground. I have the *capacity* to do so—materially, physically, sportively. But I would not be exercising power if I did that. However, if I take this tape recorder and throw it on the ground in order to make you mad, or so that you can't repeat what I've said, or to put pressure on you so that you'll behave in such and such a way, or to intimidate you—*well, what I've done, by shaping your behaviour through certain means, that is power.* . . . I'm not forcing you at all and I'm leaving you completely free—that's when I begin to exercise power. . . . [Power] takes place when there is a relation between two free subjects, and this relation is unbalanced, so that one can act upon the other, and the other is acted upon, or allows himself to be acted upon.[31]

So, we can see that Foucault is not defining power here through the notion of "capacity." My *capacity* to throw a tape recorder, for example, is not power. Rather, power is when I do something such as throw a tape recorder *so as* to influence the behavior of others with whom I am in an already existing relationship. Of course, it is possible to use other human beings as mere objects, to relate to them as Foucault suggests one might relate to the tape recorder in the example above. However, in this case we are not speaking about a relationship of power. Rather, this would be mere domination or violence (*EW3*, 340; *DE2*, 1005). Hence, at minimum, "power" requires recognizing and relating to the other within the relationship as something capable of responding. In a word, it is to relate to something or someone as though it were a "free subject."

This leads us to a second major clarification Foucault makes. He states, "When one defines the exercise of power as a mode of action upon the actions of others, [the 'conduct of conduct'] when one characterizes these actions as the government of men by other men—in the broadest sense of the term—one includes an important element: freedom. Power is exercised only over free subjects, and only insofar as they are *free*" (*EW*3, 341–42; *DE*2, 1056). The important thing to note is that "freedom" here does not denote a property or capacity of the subject. Rather, it is a feature of the *relationship to which one is subject*. Now, one might imagine the following objection to this characterization of freedom by pointing to an inherent difference between, for example, a human being and a tape recorder. In the case of the tape recorder, if I smash it to the floor certainly I am not treating it as something capable of a response to my action. Thus, my action does not attempt to influence the action of a free subject. However, a critic might object, there is *nothing* I can do that would constitute the tape recorder as a free subject. The "freedom" (or nonfreedom) of the tape recorder is not a function of the relations between us, but rather is a property of the object *prior to* the relationship. It is possible to treat a human as either a free subject or merely an object, but it is not possible to treat a tape recorder as a free subject. This demonstrates that "freedom" *does* refer to some inherent capacity of particular kinds of entities, namely those with an autonomous will which is not reducible to the forces to which it is subject. However, it is precisely this notion of freedom as a property of the subject that an ontological form of analysis seeks to displace. We might begin to see this more clearly when we point out that not only are there all kinds of nonhuman entities to which we relate as though they are capable of some kind of original response (constrained as it may be by various factors, such as the case of many nonhuman animals, for instance), but also by the fact that in many cases humans are treated as though incapable of such responses (such as the case of, for instance, a person in a coma). The point is that "freedom" actually names not a specific inherent property or capacity of certain entities, but rather refers to what Foucault calls "a field of possibilities in which several kinds of conduct, several ways of reacting and modes of behaviour are available" (*EW3*, 342; *DE2*, 1056). Furthermore, it is the relationship—the back and forth of actions upon actions—that not only sets out a range of possible future actions, but also, over time, constitutes the *being* of the entity in question. When I attempt to exercise "power" in a relationship with something, rather than merely exercising physical force, I am in part *recognizing* that entity as something capable of a range of possible responses while simultaneously attempting to shape and alter this range. I am recognizing this entity as a subject, but I am also *subjecting it,* in the sense that I am attempting to give the range of possible modes of thinking and acting by which this entity comes to be in the world in a specific form.

While Foucault focuses on human beings and their constitution as "subjects" within specific historical forms of experience (e.g., sexuality), what is truly radical about his suggestion is that many kinds of entities can be related to as subjects in this sense. Foucault chooses to focus on the modes of *subjectification* and leaves undeveloped the relations of *objectification* by which other kinds of entities appear to us as objects, things, or equipment. Heidegger (as we have seen) places emphasis on the latter, and leaves the modes of subjectification relatively undeveloped. However, these two kinds of analyses are complementary and, together, provide a more comprehensive account of historical ontology. Indeed, Foucault states explicitly that his analyses of the modes of subjectification are the complement to Heidegger's analysis of the modes of objectification. He writes: "For Heidegger, it was through an increasing obsession with *techné* as the only way to arrive at an understanding of objects that the West lost touch with Being. Let's turn the question around and ask which techniques and practices form the Western concept of the subject, giving it its characteristic split of truth and error, freedom and constraint."[32] (We will return to this juxtaposition of subjectification/objectification in Chapter Seven, situating it in the context of a longer discussion of critical theory of reification.)

. . .

A third point of analysis is then clearly delineated by Foucault—what we might call the periodization of the techniques of subjectification and the particular forms of resistance they engender. While there are forms of resistance that struggle against violence—say, for instance, slave revolts in which people resist being treated as mere physical objects for labor—there is also a specific kind of resistance to the subjectification discussed above. Foucault states that his aim is to study the emergence and predominance of these kinds of struggles: "struggles against subjection [assujettissement], against forms of subjectivity and submission" (*EW3*, 331; *DE2*, 1046). Furthermore, the need to study this particular kind of struggle is not itself due to the inherently foundational, privileged, or transcendental status of such struggle in relation to other kinds (such as, for example, against religious domination or economic exploitation). Rather, Foucault situates his targeting of this specific kind of resistance within the question first broached by Kant: how can philosophy be something other than a study of universal principles and instead pose the questions, "What's going on just now? What's happening to us? What is this world, this period, this precise moment in which we are living?" (*EW3*, 335; *DE2*, 1050). When Foucault asks himself these questions, his answer is that we (in the modern European tradition) have become "complicated subjects." That is to say, because of the rise of pastoral power, of the government of individualization, of the modern state as both individualizing and totalizing, we recognize ourselves as "subjects"—as entities with a specific set of inherent properties, interiorized but always partially occluded from us, which stand in an internal relationship to the forms of power exercised over us within specific domains of experience (such as sexuality, madness, and reason, etc.). We are *complicated* subjects precisely because these relationships which constrain the range of possible thought and action also presuppose *a range*—and thus, the latent possibility of an original or unique response to our present.

Fourthly, these relationships of power and freedom, of subjection and resistance, themselves "operat[e] *on the field of possibilities* in which the behaviour of active subjects is able to inscribe itself" (*EW3*, 341; *DE2*, 1056; italics added). In other words, it is not a mere matter of *choice* or *will* that determines what can possibly appear as an entity within which such relations of power, subjection, and resistance can take place. Rather—to employ Heideggerian terminology—all "subjects" find themselves always already thrown within a field, or clearing, within which entities appear with which it is possible to have meaningful relations of this kind.[33]

Finally, Foucault famously turned his attention in this final period to one kind of relationship and activity always latent *within* the field of possibilities in a given domain of experience: namely, the relationship of self to self. With the addition of this third axis of analysis (along with the modes of objectification and subjectification, or, alternatively, the techniques of production and signification), Foucault observes that "in all societies there is another type of technique: techniques that permit individuals to effect, by their own means, a certain number of operations on their own bodies, their own souls, their own thoughts, their own conduct, and this in a manner so as to transform themselves, modify themselves, and to attain a certain state of perfection, happiness, purity, supernatural power. Let us call these techniques 'technologies of the self'" (*EW1*, 177; *DE2*, 989–90). The analysis of these new "technologies of the self" are then positioned as not merely parallel or independent from the previous questions of power, domination, and knowledge production, but rather as central to the whole. In the 1981–82 lectures, *L'herméneutique du sujet*, he writes:

> If we take the question of power, of political power, situating it in the more general question of governmentality understood as a strategic field of power relations in the broadest and not merely political sense of the term, if we understand by governmentality a strategic field of power relations in their mobility, transformability, and reversibility, then I do not think that reflection on this notion of governmentality can avoid passing through, theoretically and practically, the element of a subject defined by the relationship of self to self. Although the theory of political power as an institution usually refers to a juridical conception of the subject of right, it seems to me that the analysis of governmentality—that is to say, of power as a set of reversible relationships—must refer to an ethics of the subject defined by a relationship of self to self. Quite simply, this means that in the type of analysis I have been trying to advance for some time you can see that power relations, governmentality, the government of the self and of others, and the relationship of self to self constitute a chain, a thread, and I think it is around these notions that we should be able to connect together the question of politics and the question of ethics. (*Herm.*, 252; *HS*, 242–43)

These five modifications, taken together, might be stated as follows: (1) power is a specific relationship of actions upon actions; (2) it only arises between "free subjects"; (3) a history of these kinds of relationships and the forms of resistance they engender (the resistance to subjectification) can be written; (4) such relations take place within an already existing field of possibilities not reducible to the actions of agents themselves as it is that upon which entities and subjects appear to whom one may related (a clearing); and (5) such relations run *alongside* and interact in complex ways with another kind of relationship—that of self to self, for which a history can be written as well.

We can see above (point 2), that Foucault argues for the necessity of including the concept of freedom within this analysis. What is less clear is how one accounts for this freedom. It may be necessary for the thesis regarding power and the "conduct of conduct"; it may even be necessary for a history of the games of truth and falsehood through which "being is historically constituted as experience." However, to this point, Foucault has merely asserted its *necessity*, we have yet to see on what basis this assertion can be made.

There are, I think, basically three ways in which Foucault attempts to account for "freedom" within the analysis of historical ontology provided in his late works. These three lines of analysis are developed in succession and slowly move us further away from the war model to the game model. The three attempts to account for freedom are what I will call here (1) the principle of contingent eventalization, (2) the principle of the irreducibility of thought, and (3) the ethical-spiritual transformation of the self.

The principle of contingent eventalization refers to the notion that a historically singular form of experience is not characterized by a single telos or *arche* governing it. Rather, it is a contingent set of internally contradictory practices that together, over time, produce a relatively stable set of social relations, institutions of governance, and subjectivities. By stating that the "forms of experience" are internally contradictory, Foucault is attempting to highlight the notion that there is, in fact, no general *épistémè* or bounded gestalt to a particular set of activities that one could ever in a general, holistic manner, get clear of. He is warning against the conflation of relatively stable *effects* of practices and *rules* of use for the domain of experience produced by these effects. "Games" are not hermetically sealed fields of activity, or structuralist totalities. Rather, *game* merely refers here to a general set of activities which are multiple, conflicting and ever changing—what Foucault calls a "regime of practices" (*EW*3, 225; *DE*2, 841). Since a domain of experience is internally contradictory, there is always a latent possibility for what Foucault calls an "event." Events consist in two moments. First, there is a "a rupture [or breach] of [self-]evidence" (*EW*3, 226; *DE*2, 842; translation modified),[34] which makes visible the contingency and singularity of that which was previously taken to be universal and necessary. Second, "eventalization means rediscovering the connections, encounters, supports, blockages, plays of forces, strategies, and so on, that at a given moment establish what subsequently counts as being self-evident, universal, and necessary" (*EW*3, 226–7; *DE*2, 842). It is important to note, however, that this does not yet carry us too far from the model of war, as the "event" is really the product of conflict between competing practices and claims.[35]

The second way in which Foucault seeks to reintroduce "freedom" into his account of the historical ontology of ourselves is through the principle of the irreducibility of thought. The first step in this is a further refining and modification of the concepts of "thought" (following from the equivocal use of the term discussed above) and "problematization." Foucault argues that we can account for the space of freedom within a domain of experience not *only* because such a regime of practices is internally contradictory, but also because *one aspect* of any such regime is defined by practices by which selves relate back upon themselves. In so doing, they are able to slowly modify the conditions under which they find themselves and thus aid in bringing forth a new domain of entities and experiences. As we saw, Foucault begins to analyze this self-reflexivity under the traditional concept of "thought." Thought here appears to reach back to Foucault's early work on historical a priori, since it names the movement by which one *uses* the "event" or "breach of self-evidence" (discussed above) to look out from within a form of experience to inquire into the historical conditions of possibility for such a problematic. This critical movement is what Foucault calls problematization. Foucault specifically links this kind of inquiry to questions of ontology, thereby invoking (while simultaneously modifying) a Heideggerian theme. He explicitly links the study of practices of problematization to the history of truth and to questions of ontology when he writes, for instance, that his work consists in analyzing "not behaviors or ideas, nor societies and their 'ideologies,' but *the problematizations through which being offers itself to be*, necessarily, thought—and the *practices* on the basis of which these problematizations are formed" (*UP*2, 11; *UP*, 19; italics added). The ambiguity with which Foucault employs the term *thought* is further complicated in the interview "Politics, Polemics, and Problematizations." Foucault is worth quoting at length:

> For a long time, I have been trying to see if it would be possible to describe the history of thought as distinct both from the history of ideas (by which I mean the analysis of systems of representation) and from the history of mentalities (by which I mean the analysis of attitudes and types of action [schémas de comportement]). It seemed to me there was one element that was capable of describing the history of thought—this was what one could call the element of problems or, more exactly, problematizations. What distinguishes thought is that it is something quite different from the set of representations that underlies a certain behaviour; it is also something quite different from the domain of attitudes that can determine this behaviour. Thought is not what inhabits a certain conduct and gives it its meaning; rather, it is what allows one to step back from this way of acting or reacting, to present it to oneself as an object of thought and to question it as to its meaning, its conditions, and its goals. Thought is freedom in relation to what one does, the motion by which one detaches oneself from it, establishes it as an object, and reflects on it as a problem.
>
> To say that the study of thought is the analysis of a freedom does not mean one is dealing with a formal system that has reference only to itself. Actually, for a domain of action, a behaviour, to enter the field of thought, it is necessary for a certain number of factors to have made it uncertain, to have made it lose its familiarity, or to have provoked a certain number of difficulties around it. These elements result from social, economic, or political processes. But here their only role is that of instigation. They can exist and perform their action for a very long time, before there is effective problematization

by thought. And when thought intervenes, it doesn't assume a unique form that is the direct result or the necessary expression of these difficulties; it is an original or specific response. . . . *To one set of difficulties, several responses can be made.* And most of the time different responses actually are proposed. *But what must be understood is what makes them simultaneously possible*: it is the point in which their simultaneity is rooted; it is the soil that can nourish them all in their diversity and sometimes in spite of their contradictions. . . . But the work of a history of thought would be to rediscover at the root of these diverse solutions the general form of problematization that has made them possible—even in their opposition; or *what has made possible the transformations of the difficulties and obstacles of a practice into a general problem for which one proposes diverse practical solutions*. It is problematization that responds to these difficulties, but by doing something quite other than expressing them or manifesting them: in connection with them, it develops *the conditions in which possible responses can be given*; it defines the elements that will constitute what the different solutions attempt to respond to. (*EW1*, 117–18; *DE2*, 1416–17; italics added)

This dense passage requires parsing. The first move that Foucault makes here is to restate his opposition to defining thought as something that "inhabits conduct." This would seem to remove him from the Heideggerian notion of thought as "preontological understanding," and thus away from the idea that a history of truth can be written from the perspective of a historical hermeneutics of the underlying cultural understandings of a given era.[36] Instead of defining thought as that which inhabits our activities, Foucault seems to return to a quasi-Kantian account—arguing that "thought" is a "stepping back" from oneself, an objectifying gesture in relation to oneself that permits freedom in relation to oneself. But this is a considerable distance from the formulation that Foucault gave but a few years earlier (especially in the preface to volume 2 of *The History of Sexuality*). "Being" no longer offers itself to be understood through a series of problematizations. Rather, it is "the subject" that thinks, "the subject" that makes a movement of distancing in relation to itself, thus bringing forth the problematization on the basis of which an understanding of being is possible. When Foucault wrote in the preface to volume 2 of *The History of Sexuality* that his genealogy of the subject and truth could only proceed through a study of "the problematizations through which being offers itself as that which can and must be thought" (UP2, 19) it appeared as though he had effected a close rapprochement with Heidegger.[37] We are reminded in particular of Heidegger's famous *es gibt*—the notion that Being "gives itself" to man in the form of gift, which Heidegger specifically employs to undermine the philosophy of the constituting subject. But in the long passage quoted above, this language drops out and Foucault returns to a definition of "thought" and "problematization" as a reflective activity by which *the subject* constitutes itself. Thus, as Béatrice Han-Pile has noted, while Foucault spoke of "historical ontology" in his late works, he almost always speaks of it as the "historical ontology *of ourselves*": that is, "an ontology understood from the perspective of a self-constitution of the subject."[38]

Han-Pile, and others,[39] have argued that because Foucault's notion of historical ontology is ultimately grounded in a reflective activity of the self-constituting subject, it cannot be brought into productive relationship to Heidegger's understanding of ontology. However, I believe this reading misses opportunities to draw out ontological analysis in late Foucault beyond this framework. It is true that Foucault employed a notion of thought and problematization that relied upon such a reflective self-constitution and that he made this movement of thought at least the *condition* of freedom. Still, it is also true that Foucault did not confuse this movement—this motion—with freedom itself. For example, we can note that in the passage quoted above, from "Politics, Polemics and Problematizations," Foucault states that thought "develops *the conditions in which possible responses can be given*" (italics added). The movement of self-objectification *enables* a set range of possible responses to a specific problematic, but it is not these responses themselves. The bringing forth of "diverse practical solutions" made possible by thought is thus analytically distinct from the movement of thought itself. It is to these "diverse practical solutions," not to thought or problematization, that I believe we must look for a grounding of freedom in ontology rather than in the philosophy of the constituting subject. By looking to these practices themselves (not what hidden reflective activity brings them forward *as possible solutions*), and by demonstrating that they both project and support a nonreflective comprehension of self and world, we can develop an analysis that makes "freedom" a feature of the relationship of mutual constitution between subject and world, rather than a feature of the intellectual activity of the constituting subject.[40] It is to the redescription of Foucault's analysis of ethical-spiritual practices as the ground of an ontological analysis of freedom that I now turn.

SIX

THE SUBJECT OF SPIRITUALITY

> It is not so much what you are doing as how you are doing it.
> When we properly understand and live by this principle, while
> difficulties will arise—for they are part of the divine order too—
> inner peace will still be possible.
>
> **Epictetus**

> The transition from *aletheia* to *ethos* (from true discourse to
> what will be the fundamental rule of conduct) begins of course
> with listening.
>
> **Michel Foucault**

IN THIS CHAPTER, by drawing out critical possibilities in Foucault's late work in relation to Heidegger, I articulate the interrelationship between an ontological analysis of selfhood and care and a historical analysis of subjectivity. In the previous chapter, we saw that rather than thinking of freedom as a feature or property of the subject, Foucault's late position was more that it named a particular kind of *situation* or *relationship* to a determinant field or clearing of meaning and action. Freedom is "worldly" in this sense.[1] Yet ambiguities persist. In particular, it is not clear what makes this kind of relationship possible, what brings it into being and sustains it. At first read, Foucault's answer appears to be that it is "thought" which makes free relations possible: to oneself, to others, to the historically singular domains of experience that delimit the horizon of one's intelligible world. The capacity for thought permits the dislodging of the relatively solidified discursive effects that are constitutive of the forms of experience and their related modes of subjectivity. However, stopping there and leaving the analysis at this level leaves one with a position that, while perhaps not antithetical to Heidegger's interrogation of ontology, at least stands in some direct tension to it. For while thought is given different formulations in different parts of Foucault's work (from a science or body of knowledge with discursive structural regularities, to a hermeneutic unthought implicit within all action, to a movement of problematization that seeks the historical a priori), the emphasis remains focused on a relatively individualized and intellectualized concept, a "cognitivist picture" connoting an activity of the mind that has an effect on organizing and ordering experience of the world. This implies, at least, that Foucault bypasses or possibly even rejects Heidegger's critique of cognitivism and the epistemological tradition. And yet Foucault repeatedly stated, particularly in his late works, that Heidegger's work—especially Heidegger's interrogation of the relationship between freedom and truth—was of utmost importance to him.

In this chapter I develop an alternative reading in three basic moves. First, I investigate what I will refer to as the "ontological commitments" of Foucault's analysis of spirituality and care of the self. In the second part of the chapter, I develop a working distinction in Foucault's writings between "selves" and "subjects," which is then used to demonstrate linkages to Heidegger's own account of selfhood and the critique of transcendental subjectivity. Part three attempts to draw out the implications of these developments, particularly with regard to a historical analysis of subjectivity in the West. Since both Heidegger and Foucault are committed to an understanding of selfhood and freedom as ontologically grounded in relations of care, a historical form of analysis that can account for the concealing of this ground is called for. Foucault's history of subjectivity, with particular reference to Descartes and Kant, is read alongside Heidegger in light of this challenge.

6.1. SPIRITUALITY AND CARE

In this section I will attempt to draw out some of Foucault's ontological commitments as evidenced by his late work (beginning with the 1981–82 lectures, *L'herméneutique du sujet*, to the end of his life in 1984) and connect these to the earlier discussion of Heidegger on selfhood and freedom. The aim here is threefold: (1) to reconstruct a general ontological analysis of selfhood in late Foucault; (2) to use this analysis to resolve Foucault's equivocation regarding the status of "thought" as demonstrated in the previous chapter; and (3) to demonstrate the constructive relationship Foucault's analysis of care of the self can have with Heidegger's ontology of care. Central to my argument is that Foucault makes certain ontological commitments which he himself did not render fully explicit. I will summarize these here, proceed to elaborate upon each, and then situate them in relation to the previous discussion of Heidegger. These commitments include the following:

1. "Selfhood" is not understandable through reference to either a substance metaphysics or a determinant set of formal properties that stand in a transcendental relation to the field of action by the self. The self does not stand in a transcendent relation to the field of action (as a "subject," over against objects and other subjects), but rather gains its very being through the practical activities in which it is always already engaged, within an already existing world of entities which it does not itself constitute.

2. Modification of modes of practical involvement is, therefore, also *self*-modification.

3. *One* of these activities of (self)modification is the work of thought (outlined in the previous chapter).

4. The work of thought presupposes the existence of pre-reflective practices by which the world and the self (which become the object of problematization for thought) gain their existence in the first instance.

5. These prereflective practices within a world are situated in an already existing context of meaning, referred to previously in Heidegger as a "clearing." Such a clearing, furthermore, references not merely the existence of entities but also the ethical relatedness between things which one does not assign through choice, but rather amid which one finds oneself. These relations of meaningful connectedness are what Heidegger called "Care" [*Sorge*].

6. The practice of freedom, therefore, is defined not by a disengagement or detachment of the self from its worldly activities (since such activities are the ontological ground of selfhood), but rather is a particular *mode* of engagement that discloses the latent possibilities for change and (self)transformation from within our basic practices themselves. It is by engaging in its worldly activities in a

considered, intentional and careful manner that the self may disclose new possibilities and bring itself within the domain of these new possibilities, thus effecting a transformation of itself. Foucault refers to this mode of engagement as a "spiritual" one, and the collection of such considered practices as the care of the self.

6.1.a. Spirituality

In order to further explicate and defend the above claims, we might take as our point of departure Foucault's distinction between philosophy and spirituality, introduced in the 1981–82 lectures *L'herméneutique du sujet*. Philosophy, in Foucault's precise sense of the term here, refers to "the form of thought that asks, not of course what is true and what is false, but what determines that there is and can be truth and falsehood and whether or not we can separate the true and the false. We will call 'philosophy' the form of thought that asks what it is that enables the subject to have access to the truth and which attempts to determine the conditions and limits of the subject's access to the truth" (*Herm.*, 15; HS, 16). We might highlight for our purposes here Foucault's reference to philosophy as a "form of thought" that takes as its central preoccupation the separation of truth from falsehood and an investigation of the conditions under which either arise (the possibility of verification).

While recognizing that philosophy has been a central part of the Western cultural tradition since at least Socrates,[2] and even acknowledging the centrality and importance of the injunction *gnōthi seauton* (know thyself), Foucault nevertheless insists on the greater importance of spirituality, at least to Classical Greek, Hellenistic, Roman, and early Christian cultures. Each of these periods, in their own ways, of course had practices, doctrines, and schools of philosophy. However, according to Foucault, during these periods the philosophic injunction to know thyself always appeared *within* the more general framework of the *epimeleia heautou* (care of oneself). Philosophy was a specific way of life and domain of practices, perhaps even an exceptional one. However it was taken up as merely "*one* of the forms, *one* of the consequences, as a sort of concrete, precise, and particular application of the general rule: you must attend to yourself, you must not forget yourself, you must take care of yourself" (*Herm.*, 5; HS, 6). These practices of care of the self understood the relationship between the "subject" and "truth" through a predominantly "spiritual" framework. Foucault defines the term spiritual as follows:

> I think we could call "spirituality" the search, practice, and experience through which the subject carries out the necessary transformations on himself in order to have access to the truth. We will call "spirituality" then the set of these researches, practices, and experiences, which may be purifications, ascetic exercises, renunciations, conversions of looking, modifications of existence, etc., which are, not for knowledge but for the subject, for the subject's very being, the price to be paid for access to the truth. (*Herm.*, 15; *HS*, 16–17)

He goes on to list three main characteristics of spirituality in this sense:

> [1] Spirituality postulates that the truth is never given to the subject by right. . . . [2] It postulates that for the subject to have right of access to the truth he must be changed, transformed, shifted, and become, to some extent and up to a certain point, other than himself. . . . [3] Finally, spirituality postulates that once access to the truth has really been opened up, it produces effects that are, of course, the consequence of the spiritual approach taken in order to achieve this, but which at the same time are something quite different and much more: effects which I will call "rebound" [de retour], effects of the truth on the subject. (*Herm.*, 15–16; *HS*, 17)

Spiritual practices are an answer to the practical questions: What must be done to myself such that I may become the kind of subject capable of apprehending the truth? What modifications must be made to my being? How must I transform myself? Philosophic activities (dialogue, contemplation, etc.) aim not so much at this preparatory work of self-transformation as an interrogation of what is or isn't actually true. They are not, therefore, in competition or opposition to spiritual practices as Foucault defines them, but rather refer to one domain of activities or way of living that one could engage in secondarily to engaging in the spiritual.

The classic example of a spiritual practice in this sense (an example to which Foucault repeatedly refers) is meditation. We might imagine a spiritual agent engaged in meditative practices whose aim, for instance, is to center the self, to make one more calm, balanced, aware of the present moment, and the like. An interlocutor might approach this person and ask: "Why do you meditate? Is it true that meditation has this effect on the person? Is the meditative life truly the best way of life?" These kinds of questions are, of course, classic philosophic questions. They can be important, interesting, even unavoidable. However, such questions (at least from the standpoint of this "spiritual practitioner") stand in a secondary and derivative relationship to actual meditation. Because the meditative practices are meant to affect my very *being* (make me a more calm, balanced, present-aware person), their effects are present even in the answering of the question (i.e., I respond in calm, balanced, and present-aware *manner*). In other words, the search for knowledge about the self and the world can be undertaken in various ways, and spiritual activities upon ourselves in the midst of these explorations make such diverse ways of being possible.[3]

One of the implications of bringing to light the centrality of these spiritual practices for Foucault is that it helps reorient and resituate the previous discussion on "thought." Relatively few commentators have adequately tied these two strands of Foucault's thought together. Readers (often following from Foucault's own equivocations) have frequently insisted that his analysis of freedom depends most centrally on the model of critique as the apprehension of the historical a priori: that there is a mode of thought that consists in the reaching out from within a singular form of experience to grasp the historical conditions of possibility of this as a problematic. They further argue that it is only through a history of such movements, a history of such problematization, that the history of being can be constituted.[4] Contrary to this reading, however, I suggest that insofar as this analysis remains focused on the reflective relationship of the self-constituting subject, it has not properly understood the ontological ground of such thought. To do this would require an analysis of freedom as a feature of the *ēthos*, or mutually constituting relationship between subjects and objects disclosed through those *basic practices* that comprise prevailing modes of practical involvement in the world which, in turn, make possible the self-reflective movement named by Foucault as thought. We would need to transpose the question from the level of philosophy, thought, and the *questioning of being* to the level of spirituality and *transformation of being*. Placing attention on this second level of analysis requires looking to Foucault's analysis of spirituality, not philosophy, since it is focused, not on the interrogation of truth (what is or is not true, in this case vis-à-vis the historical a priori), but rather on the *transformation of the very being of the subject of knowledge* (what must be done to the self in order for it to enter into the games of truth at the present).

When we take as our point of departure the *spiritual* activities by which selves are constituted as subjects capable of apprehending truth we can see more clearly that, for Foucault as for Heidegger, the ontological ground of selfhood and freedom is the basic practices that continually disclose a self and its world within its already existing ethical relations. There are two large sets of implications that flow from these ontological commitments. The first is a stance on what counts as *ethics*. We saw above that Foucault defined as spiritual practices those activities done on the self such as to transform the very being of the self, making it capable of apprehending a truth. It remains to be highlighted, however, that these transformative practices are themselves already *ethical* practices. Put succinctly, ethics refers to the intentional, self-directed exercise of spiritual practices. Ethics names the working out of the possibilities already latent within our activities (our walking, our eating, our sexual practices, etc.) in an intentional, conscious manner. Hence Foucault's claim that while "freedom is the ontological condition of ethics," ethics is the "considered form" or the "conscious practice of freedom" (*EW1*, 284).[5]

This helps us develop Foucault away from the tradition of autonomy and toward ontology since, contrary to this formulation, the "working out" of alternative possibilities in spiritual activities does not consist in a stepping back, a gesture of detachment or disengagement of the subject from its worldly relations. Such a thesis would presume a "remainder" of the subject not itself embedded within already existing relationships and activities.[6] The subject in this detached, cognitivist model is adequately prepared for the apprehension of truth, its proper self interests and thus free will, because it relies upon a feature of itself (the will, the categories of intuition, etc.) which are *universal* and *unchanging*. However, if one takes the above position vis-à-vis the ontology of selfhood, then a philosophy of ethics oriented around autonomy in this sense is untenable. Instead, an ethics that derives from the ontology of care must take as its point of departure a particularized mode of engagement or relationship in and to the activities of disclosure that constitute the self. When these activities take on an intentional or attentive quality, then they can be understood to be *ethical* practices. This is why for Foucault (as for Heidegger) freedom consists not in the autonomy of the subject vis-à-vis its worldly activities, but rather an engagement in those activities. This is, however, a particular *kind* of engagement. It is an engagement that is care-full. This is why, for instance, Foucault argues in the third volume of *The History of Sexuality* that the particular practices of cultivation of the self (manifest in, say, practices of sexual austerity) were "dominated by the principle that says one must 'take care of oneself'" (CS, 43; SS, 61). This "taking-care," however, was not understood along a corrective or curative model, but as an attentive or ever-present cautiousness in whatever one is doing. The *souci de soi* consists in *"an intensification of the relation* to oneself by which one constituted oneself as the subject of one's acts" (CS, 41; SS, 57–58). It is an engagement that is attentive to the *ethopoetic* nature of our activities, attentive to the fact that activities are themselves already imbued with meaning and that they are creative: disclosing the world in which we are always already thrown. The field or range of possibilities latent within any given set of practices is itself the ontological clearing which grounds the possibility of freedom. When this freedom (latent possibilities in a field of worldly practices) is engaged in an attentive, care-full manner, the self discloses itself as that which may bring forth a world that is simultaneously projected and actual, utopian and present.

If we think not of "free subjects" and rather in terms of "free relations," embodied by a mode of comportment with specific practices of cultivation, then we are offered quite a different picture from that of the model of autonomy which has come to prevail in so much of practical philosophy since Kant. Many commentators have specifically associated Foucault with this Kantian tradition, and there is considerable evidence in Foucault for such a reading.[7] However, I do not think that this is the only possible reading. Particularly when read in relation to Heidegger, another Foucault emerges, one whose work leads away from precisely this preoccupation with self-governance by the will. For if the "will" is the center of the practices of care of the self, this implies that there is a strong ontological distinction between the true, interior self and the merely phenomenal self. It also implies a strong ontological distinction between the self and the world of relations. We cultivate our "will" (true, inner self) such that we can look at our external determinations (passions, appetites, social relations, etc.) and properly determine which are "our *own* projects" and which are not "our own."

The radical thing about Heidegger and Foucault is that they show us how the strong distinction between "my own" projects and those merely given to me by social contexts is untenable. This is because, for both of them, such projects are not reducible to the discrete, "choice-acts" of agents *on* a field of possibilities. Such a view would miss how the force and meaning of an act gains its standing because it appears within a preexisting context, clearing, or field. If this is the case, they argue, then freedom is not the absence of constraint on the choice options of subjects, because the *meaningfulness* of action requires limitation, restraint, and resistance. As previous chapters have attempted to show, action takes place within this space opened up between possibility and constraint. This space Heidegger referred to as *Spielraum*; this action Foucault named as *conduite*. This situated freedom, then, does not hinge on me being ontologically distinct from my social world (self-sufficient), nor does it rely on me focusing on and cultivating one feature of myself as the transcendent condition for agency within such relations (the will). Rather, freedom consists in an "ethical attitude"—what Heidegger would call a *mode* of being and what Foucault would call the *conduct* of our conduct—toward the field of practical involvement. This mode, they further suggest, reveals (a) my-self as the locus of a series of basic practices, and (b) the possibilities latent within them for thinking and acting otherwise. This "ethical attitude" or mode of comportment is one of the senses in which we might say that we can "take care" within our relations.

6.1.b. Care

As a further point of creative engagement between Heidegger and Foucault, we might look to their respective uses of the term *care*. Disambiguation of the term care might be a helpful way of illuminating the distinction to be made between the approach taken by Heidegger and Foucault and that taken by theorists of autonomy and free-will.

Care in this context tends to denote (at least) three different things. First, care may refer to a special, willful relationship with an ethical component. This is the sense of the term I evoke when I say that I need to "take care" of a child. Certain of Foucault's feminist critics have, for instance, accused him of not paying enough attention to how much our subjectivity is formed by these kinds of relationships.[8] Others have taken Heidegger to task for similar reasons.[9] These critics may or may not be right in their claims that Heidegger and Foucault lack an account of this kind of "willful caring for others." As a generalized critique of Heidegger's concept of *Sorge* or Foucault on *souci*, however, these criticisms seem misplaced. This particular kind of relationship is surely not what either thinker is trying to get at through their use of the term. This kind of relationship is not *Sorge*, nor is it *souci*, in the specific uses of those words within the works discussed here. Rather, it is closer to what Heidegger called *Fürsorge* (often translated as "solicitude").[10]

Second, on the other end of the spectrum from the first sense of the term, we have the meaning evoked by Heidegger's use of *Sorge*. When Heidegger uses the term care he means, at least in the first instance, something like "ontological involvement." This just means that we are always already involved in a world that *matters* to us, in relation to other entities that are *meaningful* to us.[11] In fact, to go one step further, we can say that "the subject" *is* these care-full or meaningful relations. In the sense of this "being in concern-full relations," we cannot *not* care. In fact, we *are* care (as in, we are our concern-full relations). This is why, in the first instance, *Sorge* is ontological and "pre-ethical."

Finally, somewhere between these two positions is Foucault's *souci*. We can get at this third sense of the term, an admittedly creative use of Foucault's *souci de soi*, when we ask how we might realize *Sorge* (above). The polysemic term *realize* is perhaps helpful in the context of this discussion because it captures nicely two sides to *souci de soi* that Foucault purposefully wants to merge. To "realize" something can mean both "to become aware of" it and "to make it real." I think that the *souci de soi* may be read as attempts to realize *Sorge*. That is, when we become aware of the fact that "we" (subjects) *are* only insofar as we are embodied in concern-full relations with other entities and other selves, then we "make manifest" this concern-full relation. When I say that we "become aware," I don't mean that we "think" this in the traditional philosophical sense, grasp its essence conceptually in our minds. Rather, I mean that we attempt to weave these truths (*logoi*) into our mode of comportment, our very being (*bios*), such that it is made manifest. In this way, the "ethics of the care of the self" can be thought of as introducing the kind of superordinate criteria of relating to oneself we first encountered with Heidegger. It rests upon a distinction not between existentially involved agents always already engaged in concern-full relations with others versus detached, disembedded selves. Rather, it is a distinction between modes of relating to this condition of existential engagement. In the latter case, although we may fall away from a particular, heightened awareness of our basic condition of involvement, this in no way means we fall away from involvement itself. By the same token, to trouble over, become concerned with, or "care for" ourselves in and through our basic condition of involvement is precisely to *realize* ourselves in a new way. Of course, to "realize" oneself in this way is paradoxical. It amounts to saying that one must exert great effort to realize what one already is. Hence the centrality to both Heidegger and Foucault of the famous aphorism, inherited from the Greeks but prominent too in Nietzsche: "You must become what you are."[12] They "realize" *Sorge* in the two senses that they (a) make us understand, ground our knowledge of, care-full relations, and (b) they *just are* those relations, thus they make *Sorge* manifest. The division between "the world" (i.e., concern-full relations) and the self falls apart at this point. Hence, for Heidegger, care [*Sorge*] in the ontological, worldly sense, and care-of-the-self are two sides to the same coin. In fact, he specifically states that "the expression 'care for oneself' [Selbstsorge] . . . would be a tautology" (*BTa* §41, 237; *SZ* §41, 193).

6.2. OF SELVES AND SUBJECTS

At the beginning of this chapter I suggested that Foucault's distinction between philosophic and spiritual activities in *L'herméneutique du sujet* advanced two new lines of inquiry. The first was theoretical: an investigation of the general ontology of selfhood in relation to thought and care. I have attempted to read Foucault's invocation of the language of care in a way that draws out the potential parallels to Heidegger.

There is, however, another line of inquiry: the historical. To get at this analysis, we might begin by asking how it is that this understanding of care and selfhood (with its related distinction between spiritual and philosophic practices) came to be concealed. If relations of care are primary to activities of thought, then how and when was this relationship concealed? To answer such a question requires a historical form of critical analysis.

This historical analysis takes as its point of departure a distinction between the terms *subject* and *self*. The potential for reading Foucault's *souci de soi* in terms of historical ontology has been covered over and misread partially because of his own slippage in the use of *sujet* and *soi* when speaking of care. Yet there is an important distinction at work here. The shift from late medieval to early modern conceptions of selfhood marks a movement away from "selves" as inseparable from their existence within a space of ethical concerns—a moral order—toward "subjects," whose primary orientation revolves around the inward search for indubitable premises that can then serve as the basis for the reconstruction of the activity of knowing itself.[13] The term *subject* thus evokes the Cartesian and Kantian traditions. It typically denotes an entity, distinct from mere "objects," capable of reflection upon the world and itself. The capacity for reflective reason is the defining feature of this subject and the ground of the possibility of knowledge about the world beyond it. Commentators on Foucault have, paradoxically, condemned him for *both* attacking and unproblematically employing the "subject." To take but one example, Linda Alcoff has written that,

> It is not simply the transcendental notion of subjectivity that Foucault is opposing, that is, a subject that is transhistorical and universal, but the notion of a subject as a being with a kind of primordial interiority that is autonomous or spontaneous in some ontological sense. This is why Foucault says that historicizing the subject is insufficient and that we must dispense with the constituent subject altogether. . . . What his analysis undermines is the conceptualization of the very internal life of consciousness that has been taken, within the Cartesian tradition, to be the ultimate authority, a level of reality about which we can have more direct knowledge than any other and that generates a knowledge least open to interpretation and illusion.[14]

Alcoff speaks to the fact that Foucault's work represents a fundamental challenge, not only to the Cartesian notion of subjectivity as the ground of knowledge, but also the very notion of interiority so central to the hermeneutic tradition and what Foucault calls "pastoral power" (and, we might add, the humanist notion of "mankind").[15] And Foucault himself makes this critique explicit. He states in no uncertain terms:

> One has to dispense with the constituent subject, to get rid of the subject itself, that's to say, to arrive at an analysis which can account for the constitution of the subject within a historical framework. And this is what I would call genealogy, that is, a form of history that can account for the constitution of knowledges, discourses, domains of objects, and so on, without having to make reference to a subject which is either transcendental in relation to the field of events or runs in its empty sameness throughout the course of history. (EW3, 118)

But, we might note, Foucault's critique here is more nuanced than it is normally taken to be. Foucault specifically targets the notion of the *constituent* subject. He critiques "subjectivity" per se only if "subjectivity" is taken to refer to an entity that stands in a position *transcendental* to a field of events, in its historical invariability. Amy Allen, for one, has—I think persuasively—pointed out that "Foucault's aim is not to get rid of the concept of subjectivity altogether; instead, he sets aside any conception of the subject *as constituent* in order that he might better understand how the subject *is constituted* in a particular way in this particular cultural and historical milieu."[16] While this may be true for the vast majority of Foucault's writings, in particular the archeological and genealogical studies, in his later writings Foucault does seem to persist in speaking of the ways in which subjects *constitute themselves*. This has led to the persistent critique that the question of constituent agency has haunted his analysis of freedom, for if it is not "the subject" who acts and affects the course of history, then *who* or *what* is doing this acting?

In the 1984 interview where Foucault declared Heidegger "the essential philosopher" for him, he was asked to clarify this question of the subject. Since Foucault had specifically stated that he was interested in the ways in which subjects constitute themselves, and that this work of self-constitution proceeded through "thought," it appeared to many as though a quasi-transcendental notion of consciousness had been reintroduced. The interviewer put this directly to Foucault, asking if he understood the subject to be "the condition of possibility of an experience." Foucault responded in an (uncharacteristically) unequivocal manner:

> Absolutely not. The experience is the rationalization of a process, itself provisional, which results in a subject, or rather in subjects. I would call subjectivization the process through which results the constitution of a subject, or more exactly, of *a subjectivity which is obviously only one of the given possibilities of organizing a consciousness of self*. (FL, 472; DE2, 1525; italics added)

Note that Foucault specifically draws attention to the fact that the particular mode of subjectivity derived from a host of practices of governance, languages of interpretation, and activities of self-constitution is only *one* mode among many. There is, in other words, a range of possible forms of subjectivity that correspond to any particular historical form of experience. Thus, for Foucault, while there may be "subjects" in relation to forms of experience (and forms of thought specific to these), there is nothing we could call "the subject" as a singular, transcendental condition for experience (nor an invariable mode of thought as the condition for this subject). Subjects still act, still have agency in Foucault's account, but they do so not by drawing upon a universal "core" (a will, ego, or *cogito* in its historical invariability). Rather, subjects exercise agency by drawing upon the resources disclosed *to* them through the basic practices that constitute the world of practical involvement. Forms of subjectivity are the outgrowth of the more basic modes of practical involvement in which one finds oneself, but they are not *determined* in some unmediated, direct way by these modes of engagement since, as I argued previously, a clearing or field of possible meaning and action presupposes a certain "play space" within which agency is actualized. It is better then to speak of "modes of becoming subject" (or subjectification) than of "the subject" in its being: a shift from a question of *what* to *how*. The sharp distinction between *constituting* and *constituted* subject breaks down at this point, but it does so through recourse to the notion that the constitution of subjects brings with it capacities and possibilities of agency.[17]

Further clarity on this question may be achieved by making a more careful distinction between self and subject than Foucault sometimes offered. This also will help to illuminate connections to Heidegger's own critique of the philosophy of the constituting subject. This distinction is already there in Foucault's own work, but it is not always carefully delineated and consistently employed. Furthermore, the inattentiveness to this distinction on the part of commentators has led to some missed opportunities for bringing out the richness of Foucault's work.[18] We might parse out this distinction in three moves. First, let us reserve the term *subject* for a special and specific kind of entity with a determinate and invariable set of properties, the most important of which is a certain capacity for reflection on itself (self-consciousness). It is clear that Foucault wants to critique the idea of the subject in this sense, primarily by demonstrating that the supposedly determinant and invariable set of properties that define the subject (including self-reflective consciousness) are, in fact, historically variable and *constituted* by practices on and by the self. In other words, it is the ethical activities of (self)transformation—the *spiritual activities* on the self—that make a particular kind of subject possible, in a specific place, at a specific time. Thus, while there is no singular subject with a fixed ahistorical set of properties, there are various *subjectivities*—ways of life in which selves take certain properties to be invariant, determinant, and necessarily central to their identity. These selves draw upon resources from within the background field of practices with an unquestioning reliance. Insofar as we require such a background field, these properties *are* determinant in this sense: they define the horizon of the possible. As Foucault states, "There are two meanings of the word 'subject': subject to someone else by control and dependence, and tied to his own identity by a conscience or self-knowledge. Both meanings suggest a form of power that subjugates and makes subject to" (*EW3*, 331; *DE2*, 1046). We might say, to use slightly different vocabulary, that one is embedded within a certain form of subjectivity, not because it is imposed externally, but precisely because it is taken up by the subject herself as the limit of meaningful possibilities.[19] One example of this from Foucault is his analysis of the formation of "sexual subjectivities" in the West whereby "sex-desire" was taken up as a central, necessary, and defining feature of identity and agency. The "hermeneutics of the subject" refers to the various sciences to emerge that attempt to locate the most important or determining properties of subjectivity such that we may correspond our actions properly to who we "really" are.[20] So, to restate, while Foucault rejects the notion that there is a "subject" with a fixed set of invariable properties, he does not reject the notion of historical forms of subjectivity, understandable not by reference to internal properties but rather through the various practices of subjectification which bring a solid form of subjectivity into being. In fact, the study of these modes of subjectification comprises the heart of Foucault's work.[21]

The second move in the differentiation between subjects and selves is to ask a historical question: has it always been the case, in all places, in all times, that people thought of themselves as having a set of determinant inner properties to which they must correspond? Foucault's answer to this is clearly no. For Foucault, the point of studying Classical Greek, Hellenic, Roman, and early Christian practices of the self is clearly not to bring them back.[22] Rather, it is to throw into relief the specificity of the modern, Western notion of subjectivity and its relationship to both truth and agency or freedom. The notion that humans were a special kind of entity whose determining property was an ahistorical form of reflective reasoning that provided the sufficient and necessary condition of possibility for knowledge of the world and, through this, free agency, is something that Foucault locates historically at the birth of the modern era. As we have already seen, according to Foucault, prior to the emergence of "the subject" (even in its various modern forms: sexual, delinquent, etc.), premodern European civilizations understood the ground of truth and freedom not to be grounded first and foremost in the injunction *know thyself*. Rather, before *know thyself* became the precondition for knowledge and free, ethical action, *care for thyself* was paramount. In the model of care of the self, one does not seek to determine the determinant properties of the subject. Instead, one seeks to bring oneself under a domain of already existing ethical relationships and, in so doing, to *become* a true, proper, free or ethical self. The self here *is* only insofar as it corresponds to these already existing ethical relations. Thus, when Foucault speaks of *care* of the *self*, this is not to be understood as a minding of the subject, defined by its essential properties. Rather it is to be understood as an attentiveness to the immanence of the self in relation to its worldly activities: "the self with which one has the relationship is *nothing other than the relationship itself*. . . . It is in short the immanence, or better, the *ontological adequacy* of the self to the relationship" (*Herm.*, 533; *HS*, 514; italics added).[23]

By suggesting above that this differentiation of self from subject in Foucault revealed certain "ontological commitments," a possible line of constructive dialogue is opened up in relation to Heidegger. Specifically, we can see that the notion of the self in Foucault functions somewhat like a historicized version of Heidegger's Dasein. Heidegger's tools and methods are certainly different, but the target is the same: to displace the modern, Western notion of the subject as a substance with a set of determinant formal properties. In its place, they suggest, we might think of ourselves as ontologically grounded in basic practices and relations of care. In *Being and Time* Heidegger thought he could demonstrate the fallacy of subject-centered epistemology through recourse to transcendental hermeneutic phenomenology. By examining our everyday activities, the normal way in which we move through the world, Heidegger thought it possible to demonstrate the fact that we are not first and foremost detached "minds" encountering a world. Rather, we are more basically (his term is "primordially") simply *in a world* of practical involvement—acting, coping seamlessly. Models that attempt to reconstruct the conditions of knowledge from the standpoint of a detached subject will inevitably miss the mark therefore. For Heidegger, before we are subjects, before we are being-conscient, we are more simply (and, paradoxically, more fundamentally) being-there [*Da-sein*].[24] (In the final, concluding chapter, we shall explore this critique of "cognitivist subjectivity" in relation to social theories of reification.)

Heidegger began developing this thesis in his earliest works,[25] refined it considerably in *Being and Time*,[26] and maintained it even after "the turn."[27] What changed was less the thesis than his methods of analysis. Heidegger came to see that, ironically, his use of transcendental hermeneutic phenomenology to demonstrate the priority of fundamental ontology to epistemology actually reinscribed some of the very problems he was attempting to break free of. Specifically, he lacked an account of *how* the subject came to be paramount (an analysis of the processes of subjectification in the West) and how, on his own account, a critique of the subject required a complementary mode of historical analysis.[28] In this sense, by pursuing the thread of his own work,

Heidegger came to modify his own position in a manner analogous to the slow transformation we observed in Foucault's writings in the previous chapter. Along a parallel track, Foucault too attempts to displace the philosophy of the constituting subject through recourse to the historical a priori and the notion of thought-as-problematization. Like Heidegger, however, this ironically committed him to a position that reinforced certain features of this very problematic. A more complete analysis would proceed at the level of the ontological involvement of Dasein, not the self-constitution of the subject through "thought." Ontological involvement is what makes this "thought" possible, and Foucault's analysis of the activities of care appears to be his attempt at just such a study.

When we read Foucault alongside Heidegger with an eye to revealing similarities in what I have been calling their ontological commitments, I think we can state the following: Both thinkers argue that our primary experience of the world and of ourselves is not mediated by consciousness but is, instead, derived from a practical relationship within an already existing world. Basic technological-practical activities prefigure conceptualization and thematization. This foundation leads in two directions with respect to the question of freedom. On the one hand, it leads to an analysis of our relations *within* the clearing. When we investigate this, we see that both Heidegger and Foucault see a particular clearing or field of practical involvement, not as a determinant ruled-based set of patterns, but as a sphere of *possibilities*, given as it is to a "play space" within which agency is realized. Freedom in this sense is a space of possibilities within which we act. On the other hand, it also leads to an analysis of our relations *to* the clearing. On this level, we are asking a question of how might we relate *to* the modes of practical involvement in which we find ourselves, *how* we take up our possibilities. Freedom in this sense is a "right relation" to the world, one which discloses those possibilities referred to in the first part.

On first read, these might appear to be two discrete categories or ways of thinking about freedom. However, as I have attempted to unfold through the preceding discussion, they are in fact mutually interrelated. Heidegger attempted to show the interrelationship of these two senses in his late work when he spoke of freedom as a relationship *to* the clearing that preserved the freedom *of* the clearing. For instance, in

"Building, Dwelling, Thinking," he writes, "The word for peace, *Friede*, means the free, das *Frye*; and *fry* means preserved from harm and danger, preserved *from* something, safeguarded. To free actually means to spare. . . . To dwell, to be set at peace, means to remain at peace within the free, the preserve, the free sphere that safeguards each thing in its essence" (*BW*, 351; *GA*, 7: 150–51). As Julian Young notes in his careful parsing of this passage, Heidegger (probably quite intentionally) slides between two different valences of the relationship between dwelling and caring.[29] At first it appears as though dwelling denotes being taken care of, safeguarded against, or protected. Later in the same passage, however, dwelling is said to indicate a *caring-for*. In other words, the one who dwells is both the *object* and the *subject* of caring.

What this suggests is that our *mode* of being (peaceful, careful, etc.) is related to our *possibilities* of being (the range or "free sphere" of thought and action): action is indebted to the "home" built for it. In my reading, this relates directly to Foucault's use of the term *conduite*. The previous analysis of this term discussed how it emerged from within a host of other considerations with regard to the "arts of government" and "governmentality" (Chapter Five). Read now in light of Heidegger's reflections, however, we can see the true philosophical originality and import of Foucault's terms. *Conduct* understood as a noun, refers us to the first sense of freedom mentioned above—as the range of possibilities disclosed to us from *within* a clearing or field. It is *what* we can do. However, our "conduct" understood as a verb, refers us to the second sense of freedom above—the *relationship* to our field of practical involvement. It is *how* we do what we do. Thus, with Foucault's suggestion that a history of the "conduct of conduct" can be written—a study of the modes by which selves comport themselves within their basic practices disclosed by a field of practical involvement—he is offering us the clearest articulation to date of how a *historical ontology of freedom* might proceed.

6.3. THE HISTORY OF SUBJECTIVITY

If it is the case, however, that the ontological thesis regarding selfhood and practical involvement is convincing, then this thesis rebounds upon itself, seeking an analysis of its own (historical) conditions of possibility.

In other words, the articulations of spirituality, care, and selfhood given above demand on their own terms to be taken up as *practical interventions* in a world with its own determined conditions, limitations, and possibilities. In reading both Heidegger and Foucault under the sign of "historical ontology," I have been arguing that their approaches consistently attempt to reveal the interrelatedness of (1) claims to knowledge about the world; (2) the disclosure of a domain of entities about which it is possible to make such claims; and (3) an ethical positioning of the subject of knowledge in relation to the world thus interpreted. Together, these three features comprise a "clearing" or "field" of practical involvement—what is sometimes called a "practical system."[30] In arguing that a "fundamental" ontology—which proceeds to sketch out the general form of this analysis—unfolds on its own terms into a "historical" ontology, I have suggested that there is a continuity (though not a total commensurability) leading from Heidegger to Foucault and that the historical ontology of freedom must proceed not from the reconstruction of the universal conditions of knowledge required for the rational determination of action, but rather through an analysis of the specific configurations of knowledge, techniques of objectification and subjectification, and ethical practices of self-transformation given over through a practical field of possibilities. Finally, I have argued, this requires relating to other philosophical projects, not merely as a collection of arguments about the world, but as a set of practical relations *within* the world and *to* oneself. This history remains, however, forever incomplete. This is partially due to the fact that the scope of the study would be nearly infinitely wide but also, and more importantly, because the redescription and rearticulation of the past tradition out of which this historical ontology derives is itself an *ongoing* practical task. Yet even if the task is never complete, we are nevertheless driven back to the outset of this discussion.[31] I will, therefore, attempt to demonstrate how the analysis of freedom in relation to historical ontology requires a subsequent repositioning in relation to its own past, its own alternatives.

From this new vantage point, the emergent preoccupation with attunement and ethopoetic transformation of the self in Heidegger and Foucault is not merely an *alternative* account of freedom, running alongside that of autonomy and the philosophy of the transcendental subject. Rather, the historical ontology of attunement and spiritual transformation stands in an internal relationship to the tradition of autonomy and transcendental subjectivity in the West. It does so in two senses. First, historical ontology can offer an alternative reading of the history of autonomy and transcendental subjectivity, one that sees this tradition as also always engaged in spiritual transformation of selves (into subjects) and things (into objects), but as *one that attempts to conceal this very transformation*. From this standpoint, the history of subjectivity in the West is that of a spiritual tradition which conceals its own activities of ethical (self)transformation. Through this lens, we might read not only Heidegger's account of the rise of modern *technē* as an ethopoetic revealing that conceals itself, but also Foucault's account of disciplinary society as a complementary form of analysis focused on the modes of subjectification (rather than Heidegger's emphasis on modes of objectification). (In the next chapter, I shall suggest that this formulation has resonances too with social theories of reification that view this phenomenon as a form of "forgetting.") Second, historical ontology is internally related to the model of the autonomous, transcendental subject because it understands this not merely to be an alternative theoretical "model," but precisely as *the world* out of which historical ontology emerges. In this sense, the practice of articulating historical ontology and spiritual transformation is not merely attempting to *describe* the world alternatively; it is itself an attempt at a *spiritual transformation* from within the prevailing mode. This is why Heidegger and Foucault both situate their own accounts of freedom within the general rubric established by Descartes and Kant. To merely assert one could "leap over" the epistemological model, to simply "do otherwise" without first preparing the ground, would be to return to an understanding of the subject as "detachable" from its worldly conditions.[32] As a way of organizing this resituated relationship to the history of subjectivity in the West, we will look exclusively at the similarities between Heidegger and Foucault with respect to their analyses of Descartes and Kant.

. . .

Reading Foucault and Heidegger's historical ontology through this lens of spiritual transformation reveals new insights and new potential for alternative interpretations. In this section, I will examine Foucault's "double reading" of Descartes and Kant with an eye to elucidating parallels to Heidegger's history of Being in the West. The aim here is to demonstrate how Foucault's history of subjectivity might complement and complete Heidegger's own attempts to situate historically his ontological analysis. In this I am returning to a theme first presented in Chapter Three. There I suggested, following on work by Béatrice Han-Pile, that a quasi-Heideggerian form of historical analysis might be possible if it were to posit that there are some modifications "at the ontic level that are so considerable that they act on the very ontological structure of our existence and modify it."[33] These modifications would not be modifications on the level of consciousness, but would rather unfold on the level of practical involvement. Hence the corresponding form of historical analysis would proceed through an analysis of the *basic practices* that make up the prevailing modes of revealing in a given epoch. I will read Foucault's treatment of Descartes and Kant, not as traditional interpretations of their "philosophy," but rather as interpretations of their "spirituality." By this I mean that Foucault takes up these two important figures in the Western tradition as exemplars in transformations of the practical relationship to the self. In so doing, he gives a concrete demonstration of the forms of making—the practical knowledges, or *technē*—through which modern "man" comes to know itself through a fashioning of itself. This complements Heidegger's analysis of the history of Being in the West as unfolding through *technē*, not only by providing more concrete historical specification of these transformations, but also by providing a new axis of analysis: that of the relationship of self to self.[34]

6.3.a. "Le moment cartésian"

A key transition in the history of subjectivity in the West according to Foucault is what he calls "le moment cartésian." The general shift in subjectivity that Descartes exemplifies revolves around a new relationship between the "subject" and "truth" such that truth is, at least in principle, accessible without modification or effect on the subject itself. Truth becomes something knowable to any subject, regardless of the transformation of the subject itself through practices. Foucault calls the point at which this transformed relationship became possible the "le moment cartésian," not to single out Descartes as a singular, historical event to which all such analytics of truth and pastoral power can be traced, but rather as an exemplary instance of a general transformation in European thought and cultural practices. Specifically, the Cartesian moment is the moment which

> placed self-evidence [l'évidence] at the origin, the point of departure of the philosophical approach—self-evidence as it appears, that is to say as it is given, as it is actually given to consciousness without any possible doubt. . . . What's more, by putting the self-evidence of the subject's own existence at the very source of access to being, this knowledge of oneself (no longer in the form of the test of self-evidence, but in the form of the impossibility of doubting my existence as subject) made the "know yourself" into a fundamental means of access to truth. (*Herm.*, 14; *HS*, 16)

This reading of Descartes actually began years earlier for Foucault, developed in his 1972 exchange with Derrida over the interpretation offered in *Histoire de la folie*. In his response to Derrida, "Mon corps, ce papier, ce feu," Foucault suggested that Descartes needed to be subjected to a "double reading." On the one hand, we might read a text such as *The Meditations* as an example of Cartesian reasoning. From this standpoint, we investigate the text as an instance of the Cartesian *cogito* at work: as a subject who, through the power of his own reasoning alone, grasps truth through a careful application of the methods of knowing. Beginning from first premises—"clear and distinct ideas"— the author of *The Meditations* merely follows proper logic to a set of conclusions via proper syllogisms. In Foucault's parlance, this is a modern "philosophical" reading of *The Meditations*.

There is, however, another reading. The "double reading" of *The Meditations* also consists in investigating them as a *practice of self-constitution*, or a spiritual exercise. This second reading "refers less to the signifying organization of the text than to the series of events (acts, effects, qualifications) which the discursive practice of meditation carries with it: *it is a question of the modifications of the subject by the very exercise of discourse* (*EW*2, 405; *DE*1, 1125; italics added). Recalling the original sense and spirit of the term *meditations*, Foucault reminds Derrida that "a 'meditation' produces, as so many discursive events, new utterances that carry with them a series of modifications of the enunciating subject. . . . In meditation, the subject is ceaselessly altered by his own movement. . . . In short, meditation implies a mobile subject modified through the effect of the discursive events that take place" (*EW2*, 405–6; *DE1*, 1125). So, rather than focus exclusively on what Descartes said, on the status of the text and its argument as a truth claim, Foucault also inquires into *how* this person and this text *gain status* as sufficient grounds for possible truth. In other words, he is interested in what needs to be done, performed on the self, such that it can be taken seriously as a self-contained sufficient entity capable of apprehending truth through the exercise of its own faculties, independent of external aid or modification. This process of becoming a "subject" of knowledge and truth, requires first, Foucault argues, a set of spiritual exercises or "meditations."

The final step in Foucault's reading is to ask what is required of the *reader* at the level of spiritual transformation such that the text and this subject (Descartes) can appear as self-contained possible grounds of truth. Hence, he suggests, we can read *The Meditations*, not only as a logical system or argument to follow, but also as "a set of modifications forming an *exercise*, which each reader must effect, by which each reader must be affected, if he in turn wants to be the subject enunciating this truth on his own behalf" (*EW2*, 406; *DE1*, 1126). Hence, Foucault's reply to Derrida is about much more than just how to read Descartes. It is also in part about how "we readers" constitute ourselves in different ways through the particular kinds of interpretations we offer. Derrida, Foucault charges, not only fails to read Descartes in relation to those spiritual practices which were the precondition for the supposed access to truth offered in *The Meditations*, but also that in so doing, Derrida is actively constituting himself as a "subject" capable of accessing truth without prior or ongoing spiritual transformation. Hence, from Foucault's standpoint, in this sense at least, Derrida is quite Cartesian.[35] This analysis of Descartes as a transformative figure, but one whose very form of self-transformation is a concealing one, remained largely consistent throughout his late writings.[36]

6.3.b. Kant, Humanism and Teleological Anthropology

Although Descartes clearly looms large for both Heidegger and Foucault with respect to questions of truth, epistemology, and subjectivity, with respect to the question of freedom and its relation to ethics, Kant remains the primary point of reference. In Chapter One, I sketched out how the Kantian understanding of freedom might be taken up as an alternative theoretical model or discourse to that of situated freedom. Now, however, it is incumbent upon us to reread Kant under the rubric of historical ontology itself. That is to say, to take up the Kantian philosophy of freedom not merely as a theory but as a practical relationship to the world. Just as Foucault subjected Descartes to a "double reading," so too he suggests we may take up Kant in two registers.

On the one hand, Kant formalizes the critical philosophy of the enlightenment—the attempt to define the transcendental a priori conditions of possible experience and, through them, subject (moral) action to rational determination. In this way, he stands as the single most important contributor to thinking about freedom in terms of a philosophy of transcendental subjectivity. It was this more standard reading of Kant that was offered in Chapter One. However, another reading is also possible, one which is hopefully more accessible to us having run through Heidegger and Foucault. On this second reading, Kant is also understood as the initiator of a certain "ontology of actuality," defined less by a formal transcendental argument and more by a certain ethical attitude or relationship to oneself enabled by a specific spiritual exercise or *askēsis*.[37]

In this "second reading" what makes Kant so significant to the historical ontology of freedom is not so much his insights into epistemology—his attempts to secure the truth of the power of reason through a demonstration of its limits.[38] Rather, what is revealed through a second-order reading of Kant is that the truth of this relationship (between freedom and obligation) is revealed only through a more basic *ethical* or *spiritual transformation* of the subject of knowledge. The task of Kantian practical philosophy, viewed from this vantage, is not merely to describe and defend this transformation, but rather to aid in its realization.

As we have seen, according to Foucault (and, we might add, Heidegger) the Cartesian moment represents the emergence of a certain practical relationship to the world characteristic of the modern West that takes as its point of departure the notion that the self-certainty of the subject (i.e., of self-consciousness as such) is the foundation of all knowledge. Within this model, the acquisition of knowledge is not linked to a specific ethical mode of being in the world, an ethos. Under Foucault's reading, however, Kant reintroduces this ethical dimension to knowledge acquisition. Kant is therefore working *within* the Cartesian subject-centered philosophical tradition, but he also works *against* it in important ways. In a 1983 interview, Foucault stated:

> After Descartes, we have a subject of knowledge which poses for Kant the problem of knowing the relationship between the subject of ethics and that of knowledge. There was much debate in the Enlightenment as to whether these two subjects were completely different or not. Kant's solution was to find a universal subject that, to the extent it was universal, could be the subject of knowledge, but which demanded, nonetheless, an ethical attitude—precisely the relationship to the self which Kant proposes in *The Critique of Practical Reason*. (*EW1*, 279)

To this, interviewers Hubert Dreyfus and Paul Rabinow asked, "You mean that once Descartes cut scientific rationality loose from ethics, Kant reintroduced ethics as an applied form of procedural rationality?" Foucault responded,

> Right. Kant says, "I must recognize myself as universal subject, that is, I must constitute myself in each of my actions as a universal subject by conforming to universal rules." The old questions were reinterpreted: How can I constitute myself as a subject of ethics? Recognize myself as such? Are ascetic exercises needed? Or simply this Kantian relationship to the universal which makes me ethical by conforming to practical reason? Thus Kant introduces one more way in our tradition whereby the self is not merely given but is constituted in relation to itself as subject. (*EW1*, 279)

So, what specifically is this "ethical attitude" and this "action of self-constitution" that Kant offers? To answer this, we must look to Foucault's most famous statement on the topic: "What Is Enlightenment?"

According to Foucault, one of the most important things Kant did was provoke a new kind of questioning about the present. While acknowledging that "it was certainly not the first time that philosophic thought had sought to reflect on its own present" (*EW1*, 304; *DE2*, 1382), Foucault nevertheless suggests that Kant's reflections on the Enlightenment are unique insofar as they define the *Aufklärung* as an *Ausgang*, an exit. Unlike other reflections on modernity that Kant offers, in which the present is defined in relation to "questions of origin or defines the internal teleology of a historical process" (*EW1*, 305; *DE2*, 1385) (the mode of teleological freedom outlined at the beginning of this work), here Foucault claims that Kant grasps his present *without* assigning it a predefined role "on the basis of a totality or of a future achievement" (*EW1*, 305; *DE2*, 1385). So if the *Aufklärung* can be defined as an exit and an event in the present, but without making this event part of a large historical anthropology, what kind of "exit" is it? In a word, it is an exit from "immaturity" (personal and collective). The exit from immaturity involves, for Kant, the realization that submission to the proper use of reason is different from mere obedience to authority. What is at stake for Kant is the transformation from naïve to mature moral consciousness. Submission to reason involves, for the mature subject, the realization of its objective interests. It cannot, therefore, be seen as an obstacle to the true freedom of the subject.

Of course, Foucault does not praise this specific aspect of Kantian practical philosophy. Indeed, he finds much that is problematic here, for two main reasons. First, as numerous other commentators have noted, Kant's ethic is bound up with the emergence of the juridical subject and the model of law-governance that Foucault seeks to problematize and denaturalize. In his demonstration of the continuing import of the juridical form of subjectivity to neo-Kantian practical philosophy, James Tully usefully outlines the main contours of this model:

> The juridical subject is the individual or collective subject of rights and duties. Juridical subjects coordinate their moral and political action by means of laws or norms. The laws are legitimate or just in so far as they are universal and based on the agreement or consent of those who subject themselves to them. The juridical practical systems are the legal and political institutions of European societies in which power is exercised through the law in a primarily prohibitive manner by and over agents who are constituted as law-governed bearers of rights and duties. Juridical forms of knowledge are law-centred theoretical, jurisprudential and legislative codes and their traditions of interpretation, modes of application, systems of punishment and theories of revolution against unjust constitutions.[39]

Thus, in his construal of freedom as self-governance as the basis for proper moral action, Kant sets up an antinomy between autonomous and heteronomous legislation that undergirds much of the juridical form of subjectivity. Since Kant defines maturity in terms of a relationship of governance, whereby one can only be said to be acting morally if one is acting according to a law given to oneself, he drives the movement toward a form of subjectivity in which discrete individuals interact with each other through self-authorized contract and consent. The threat to one's own autonomy comes, therefore, from a recognition of the deep (we might say, ontological) interdependence of subjects and their surrounding context of meaningful thought and action. The notion that free agency is actualized through the mobilization of resources disclosed to the subject, but not of their own choosing or legislation, is antithetical to such a model. The juridical model of subjectivity reinforces a long-standing contest against obstacles to "pure" self-determination, including nonrational features of the self such as the passions and the body.[40] As Andrew Cutrofello argues,

> Kant subscribes to the juridical model of power, and he fashions critique on a juridical model so that it might serve as an instrument for resisting domination. Hence, the political stakes of critique consist primarily in a battle of laws. At the same time, Kant recognizes the emergence of disciplinary power, which, however, he continues to construe on a juridical model. As the key to critical philosophy's struggle with disciplinary power, Kant invokes a new form of discipline. Thus the juridical battle between power (heteronomy) and critique (autonomy) becomes a struggle between two sorts of discipline—a discipline of domination (heteronomy) versus a discipline of resistance (autonomy).[41]

The aspect of this model that Foucault takes issue with is not, of course, a relationship of discipline over oneself per se. As many of his later writings attest, he is deeply interested in the various ways in which subjects come to work on themselves through practices of self-discipline. Foucault's central argument, as James Tully puts it, is that the juridical model, "by focusing our attention on the problem of the mode of subjection and the elaboration of a universal code, causes us, as both theorists and participants in juridical games, to overlook processes of subjectivisation in politics and, in an analogous fashion, practices of ethical self-formation in morality, precisely what a 'critical' philosophy should concentrate on."[42] In this manner, Kant's challenge—that we discipline ourselves in order to produce subjects who experience their freedom in terms of universal laws of reason—represents both an *extension* and a *concealing of* the thesis regarding spirituality and care. It is an extension of it insofar as Kant advocates an ethical transformation of the subject as the precondition for the apprehension of knowledge about the world. It is, however, also a concealing of this very move through a positing of the necessary and universal structure of this relationship—one found, not created, through the relationship to the self itself. Hence, Foucault writes,

> It seems to me that this is very clear in Descartes, with, if you like, the supplementary twist in Kant, which consists in saying that what we cannot know is precisely the structure itself of the knowing subject, which means that we cannot know the subject. Consequently, the idea of a certain spiritual transformation of the subject, which finally gives him access to something to which precisely he does not have access at the moment, is chimerical and paradoxical. So the liquidation of what could be called the conditions of spirituality for access to the truth is produced with Descartes and Kant; Kant and Descartes seem to me to be the two major moments. (*Herm.*, 190; *HS*, 183)

Thus, for Kant a certain form of governance—of the self over itself—takes its place as the necessary and universal condition for ethics. This particular relationship then serves to anchor the second major aspect of the Kantian model to which Foucault objects:[43] the notion of a developmental anthropology whereby Kant attempts to reconcile the empirical and transcendental (or anthropological and critical) sides of his project through recourse to the notion of a purposiveness in nature that guides rationalization in human history. As Foucault writes: "Through these different practices—psychological, medical, penitential, educational—a certain idea or model of humanity was developed, and now this idea of man has become normative, self-evident and is supposed to be universal. Humanism may not be universal but may be quite relative to a certain situation. . . . What I am afraid of about humanism is that it presents a certain form of our ethics as a universal model for any kind of freedom" (*TS*, 15).

Yet, despite all this, there is something Foucault clearly finds interesting and important in Kant's reflections on the *Aufklärung*. This is not the Kant involved in the critical project of delimiting the necessary bounds of reason as such. Nor is it the Kant who proposes a disciplinary model of the juridical subject, wedded to a teleological anthropology leading through the stages of history from savagery to civilization. Instead, the Kant that Foucault is most impressed and interested in is the one who suggests that an *ethical attitude* of attentiveness to the present moment is the precondition for access to truth and, in so doing, reintroduces a dimension of spirituality to critical philosophy. This is the limited sense in which we can see that Foucault's work is still "Kantian." As Ian Hacking writes,

> Among the radical novelties of Kant was the notion that we *construct our ethical position*. Kant said we do this by recourse to reason, but the innovation is not reason but construction. Kant taught that the only way the moral law can be moral as [sic] if we make it. Foucault's historicism combined with that notion of constructing morality leads one away from the letter and the law of Kant, but curiously preserves Kant's spirit. Kant founded his metaphysics of ethics on the idea of freedom. That was another innovation.[44]

When we look to his reading of "What Is Enlightenment?" we can see that there are two main aspects to this innovation that Foucault finds promising. First, although Kant's work does get taken up in the direction of the disciplinary model of the juridical subject under the rubric of universal reason, Kant himself acknowledges that the apprehension of this reason requires a prior ethical transformation of the subject of knowledge. As such, Kant reintroduces the spiritual dimension that Foucault seeks to trace through the Western history of subjectivity.[45] Foucault writes that "from Kant on, I believe that there again, one will see that *the structures of spirituality have not disappeared*, neither from philosophical reflection nor perhaps from knowledge" (*Herm.*, 28; *HS*, 29). We might see an example of this if we look closely at Kant's own words. According to Kant, the Enlightenment "is man's emergence from his self-incurred immaturity. Immaturity is the inability to use one's own understanding without the guidance of another. This immaturity is self-incurred if its cause is *not lack of understanding*, but lack of *resolution and courage* to use it without the guidance of another."[46] Immaturity is not a state of cognitive deficiency—a lack of understanding or knowledge. Rather it is a different practical relationship to oneself, the state in which *one does not fashion oneself* as a subject of universal reason. In other words, an ethical relationship to oneself is the precondition of the development of understanding, thus reintroducing the question of the relationship between the epistemological subject and the ethical subject, which Descartes had foreclosed.

The second important feature that Foucault extracts from this text requires a certain historicizing of Kant. Foucault does not think that we can constitute ourselves as moral agents through recourse to an ahistorical property of the subject—the will, universal reason, or the like. Rather, we constitute ourselves as moral agents by drawing upon resources disclosed *to* us in the particular historical and cultural location of the present. This requires, therefore, a particular attentiveness to *what is possible in the present*. This attentive questioning of our actual condition is therefore the precondition for an ethical self-fashioning. This is the second major innovation that Foucault draws from Kant. When Kant attempts to respond to the present moment as he understands it, Foucault notes that the very preoccupation with the present is *itself an ethics*. Kant reveals in his writings here a deep concern for *what is actually happening*. This is, for Foucault, itself an important and unique feature of the modern critical ethos.

Thus, what Foucault finds most important about the Enlightenment is this attitude, this "mode of relating to contemporary reality" (*EW1*, 309; *DE2*, 1387). Contrary to those who interpret Foucault as merely advocating a willful destruction, or overcoming of all tradition, he specifically and cautiously refers to this ethos as one in which "the high value of the present is indissociable from a desperate eagerness to imagine it, to imagine it otherwise than it is, and to transform it *not by destroying it but by grasping it in what it is* . . . [through] an exercise in which extreme attention to what is real is confronted with the practices of a liberty that *simultaneously respects this reality and violates it*" (*EW1*, 311; *DE2*, 1389; italics added). What I have suggested throughout this chapter is that one meaningful vocabulary for such a relationship to the present is that of care. As outlined above, this is not a "taking care" in the sense of a healing relationship—returning us back to some originary state of pure, healthy, unalienated being. Rather, it is a relationship of care in the sense of an attentiveness to what *actually is* and through this, to the latent possibilities for transformation from within. It is, in this sense, a relationship of care that is a practice of freedom.

Foucault clearly sees in Kant, just as in Descartes, potential for precisely this kind of opening up to new possibilities. In order to achieve this, he reads the two thinkers against themselves, demonstrating how they foreclose certain possibilities and, often despite themselves, open up new ones. A guiding thread to this narrative has been Foucault's analysis of how Descartes and Kant *constitute themselves* through their respective projects and so contribute to the ongoing history of spiritual transformation in the West. We draw resources from this past precisely in order to challenge it, demonstrating its strength in certain respects through a simultaneous revealing of its limitations. Of course, this involves taking up the question of limits differently from the critical tradition as Kant construed it. Certainly, Kantian philosophy is a reflection on limits, on finitude. However, for Kant this limit is taken up through the experience of the necessary and the obligatory. For Foucault, however, the reflection on limits is experienced not only in submission to necessity, but rather, more fundamentally in transgressive possibilities engendered by the experience—in brief, through the projection of possibilities beyond the limit. Hence the relationship Foucault attentively attempts to draw between truth and freedom.

> But if the Kantian question was that of knowing [savoir] what limits knowledge [connaissance] must renounce exceeding, it seems to me that the critical question today must be turned back into a positive one: In what is given to us as universal, necessary, obligatory, what place is occupied by whatever is singular, contingent, and the product of arbitrary constraints? The point, in brief, is to transform the critique conducted in the form of necessary limitation into a practical critique that takes the form of a possible transgression. (*EW1*, 315; *DE2*, 1393; translation modified)

In short then, we might say, along with Amy Allen, that what Foucault calls for is "a critique of critique, which means not only a criticism of

Kant's project for the way in which it closes off the opening in thought that it had created but also a critique *in the Kantian sense of the term*—that is, an interrogation of the limits and conditions of possibility of that which Kant himself took as his own starting point, namely the transcendental subject itself."[47]

By focusing on Descartes and Kant as central figures in the transformation of Western philosophy, Foucault brings his analysis into closer conversation with Heidegger's history of Being in the West. He does so, furthermore, by focusing on the ways in which Descartes and Kant not only helped to bring forth a new relationship between truth and subjectivity in the West—one that took "the subject" as a self-contained, complete entity requiring no modification in order to access the truth of the world—but also, perhaps paradoxically, concealed the spiritual exercises required to bring this new relationship into being. For Foucault, Descartes inaugurates a new form of subjectivity in the West, but does so precisely by concealing the spiritual transformation required to inaugurate such a "subject." When Foucault claims that, with Descartes, "evidence is substituted for ascesis" (*EW1*, 279), he is (intentionally or not) echoing a major theme in Heidegger. Heidegger and Foucault both effectively argue that the emergence of Cartesian epistemology and Kantian practical philosophy must not be critiqued merely as "philosophic mistakes." Rather, they represent a *world of practical involvement* with mutually implicating practices of subjectification and objectification. Furthermore, what is particularly problematic about this mode of revealing is not that it is "wrong" or does not correspond to reality. Rather, the issue at stake is that this is a mode of revealing that conceals its own conditions of appearance, thus prevailing over other possibilities and concealing the latent possibilities of transformation from within. Foucault has two major fears about the transformations exemplified by Descartes and Kant—both of which are very much in line with Heidegger's own analysis of certain pathologies in the modern, Western relationship to Being. First, though very subtly, Foucault suggests that the "Cartesian moment" permits a new form of instrumental relationship to the "objects" of the world. Just as Heidegger claims that truth in the post-Cartesian era gets reduced to objectification and repetition, Foucault also argues that "the Cartesian type of knowledge cannot be defined as access to the truth, but is knowledge [connaissance] of a domain of objects. So, if you like, the notion of knowledge of the object is substituted for the notion of access to the truth" (*Herm.*, 191; *HS*, 184). Elsewhere, again echoing a Heideggerian theme, Foucault comments that the changes that Descartes inaugurated "make possible the institutionalization of modern science" (*EW1*, 279). Unfortunately, although Foucault does express some reservations about the prevalence of this mode of objectification, he does not elect to take the question up in any substantial way.

More significant, however, is Foucault's second worry: that the Kantian legacy has been taken up in a one-sided or uneven manner. He suggests that post-Kantian practical philosophy betrays an almost singular preoccupation with the critical project of circumscribing the limits of knowledge and the correlated relationship of self-governance as the precondition for freedom at the expense of an "ontology of actuality" grounded in an ethical attitude of attentiveness and care. The domain of knowledge and action brought into being by the Cartesian and Kantian moments is, for Heidegger and Foucault, uniquely problematic because it purports to delimit the entire horizon of the intelligible (truth *as such*), and is thus dangerously totalizing. For Foucault, this means that the relationship to truth, while not *actually* disconnected to the ethical and spiritual transformations of the self, is presented as such:

> The relationship to the self no longer needs to be ascetic to get into relation to the truth. It suffices that the relationship to the self reveals to me the obvious truth of what I see for me to apprehend the truth definitively. Thus, I can be immoral and know the truth. I believe this is an idea that, more or less explicitly, was rejected by all previous culture. Before Descartes, one could not be impure, immoral, and know the truth. With Descartes, direct evidence is enough. After Descartes, we have a nonascetic subject of knowledge. This change makes possible the institutionalization of modern science. (*EW1*, 279)

The analysis of a Cartesian and Kantian form of subjectivity that conceals the conditions of its own appearance, transforms our very relationship to truth, and is enabling of a totalizing form of (Western) science, is all very much in line with Heidegger's own critique. The passage above stands in a complementary and constructive relationship to Heidegger's own characterization of Descartes, in whose work "man's claim to a ground of truth [is] found and secured by man himself.... To be free now means that, in place of the certitude of salvation, which was the standard for all truth, man posits the kind of certitude by virtue of which and in which he becomes certain of himself as the being that thus founds itself on itself" (N4, 97; GA, 6.2: 125–26). This permits humanity to enter into a new era in which freedom is no longer understood as a correct *relation* to the world, but rather asserts the "new freedom of self-assured self-legislation" (N4, 100; GA, 6.2: 129).

For Heidegger, this is represented in the emergence of our understanding of reality as a "world-picture." The ontology of the world-picture that has come to prevail over the Western world is, furthermore, the outgrowth of a more basic technological involvement, a set of activities that both transform "things" into "objects" and, in so doing, also serve to constitute "Dasein" (our located, particularized being-in-involvement within a world) as a "subject" (the locus of a set of determinant properties). We might say, to transpose Foucault's language into Heidegger—that this technological involvement is a *spiritual* one, insofar as it reconstitutes the very being of the subject of knowledge such that a new relationship to truth is made possible. Cartesian and Kantian *philosophy* merely represents the philosophical expression of a mode of being or relationship in the world, one in which reality is an object represented to the knowing subject.

This stance toward the world has a twofold set of consequences. Philosophically, it produces a host of problems beyond which we struggle to see. The attempt to found knowledge upon this model of representation leads, ironically, to the very anxiety over relativism and subjectivism that this model was meant to lay to rest. This relates back to the problems of (self)concealment (discussed in Chapter Three) which Heidegger seeks to dissolve rather than solve by way of reminding us of the ontological preconditions for such problems.[48] Unfortunately, when it comes to the most general level of analysis—the emergence of "the subject" as the organizing point for questions of truth and freedom in Western thought—Heidegger provides little detail with regard to its historical emergence and effect (an area in which Foucault is more helpful). Nevertheless, it is clear that Heidegger identifies a similar problematic here. Since from within the Cartesian-Kantian world-picture, only that which can be represented to the cognizing subject as indubitable counts as being, ethical relationships to the world are reducible to questions of epistemology. If epistemological questions cannot be definitively settled in the face of radical skepticism, then radical nihilism threatens not only knowledge claims but also our ethical relationship to the world itself (i.e., the world loses meaning and ethical import).

Practically, Heidegger and Foucault both suggest that the Cartesian-Kantian model leads to a relentless totalization of one (technological) mode of social, spatial and temporal ordering. If reality can be reduced to a world-picture, then it can be objectified. World-pictures can then be compared and contrasted in terms of their adequacy. This leads, for Heidegger, to the demand that *only* the most adequate picture as an absolute set of criteria be employed to filter and order our relationship to the world. He writes,

> The interweaving of these two processes—that the world becomes picture and man the subject—which is decisive for the essence of modernity illuminates the founding process of modern history, a process that, at first sight seems almost nonsensical. The process, namely, whereby the more completely and comprehensively the world, as conquered, stands at man's disposal, and the more objectively the object appears, all the more subjectively (i.e., peremptorily) does the *subjectum* rise up, and all the more inexorably, too, do observations and teachings about the world transform themselves into a doctrine of man, into an anthropology. (*OBT*, 70; *GA*, 5: 93)

Hence Heidegger's claim that the mode of revealing that is modern technology—the mode of revealing intertwined with the age of the world-picture—demands a challenging-forth, an ordering of things and selves which must be exclusive and total. The tragic irony of this is that this mode of revealing further masks itself qua mode of revealing, thus covering over Dasein's special relationship to its world. Instead of taking up this mode of revealing as a working out of possibilities latent within the world—as a creative, care-taking activity—the modern technological subject purports merely to be responding to the objective reality of the world as such. Thus, even while most actively marshaling reality, the modern subject denies this as an active engagement. Hence Heidegger's claim that the truly insidious thing about modern technology is not *what* it does to the world (though he clearly thinks this is disastrous as well), but rather that the *way* in which it does this serves to cover over the very horizon of historically transmitted practices that make such a mode of being possible. Modern technology conceals itself by concealing the background practices that are its historical condition of possibility. He states, "The essential unfolding of technology threatens revealing, threatens it with the possibility that all revealing will be consumed in ordering and that everything will present itself only in the unconcealment of standing-reserve" (*BW*, 339; *GA*, 7: 34). In a similar manner, Foucault's concern with the rise of "disciplinary society" is not that it engages in this or that activity which one could consider bad—though, again, there may *also* be concern on this level. Rather, Foucault's concern is that the particular way in which the human sciences' purported capacity to define and describe the truth about the subject masks the background micropractices that made such a "subject" possible in the first place. Thus, the human sciences conceal their historic relationship to institutions of power that are not merely *reflective* of modes of subjectivity, but also *productive*—what Foucault called the "political technology of the body." For Foucault, just as for Heidegger, the ultimate expression of this ordering/concealing is the constitution of "Man" as the locus of teleological humanism and the philosophy of the constituting subject.

SEVEN

OBJECTIFICATION, REIFICATION, SUBJECTIFICATION
HISTORICAL ONTOLOGY AND SOCIAL CRITICISM

THE PRIMARY AIM OF THE CURRENT STUDY has been to provide a philosophical explication of historicity and situated freedom in Heidegger and Foucault, emphasizing points of connection and convergence between these two thinkers despite their differently positioned intellectual projects. In this final, concluding chapter, we turn more directly to applications for social and political theory. While the matter has already been raised in several other sections of the book, this final chapter seeks to recapitulate the preceding discussion by foregrounding more explicitly the following question: Of what utility is a general, ontological conception of situated freedom with regard to the tasks of social criticism? What work can a historical ontology of ourselves do in the service of such critique and, perhaps just as importantly, what work can it *not* perform?

In order to address these questions, I propose returning to the set of concerns raised in the concluding section of Chapter Three. There, via Herbert Marcuse's early critical appropriation of Heidegger, we considered some of the possible modes by which insights from ontological and historical-materialist analyses could be integrated and synthesized. That chapter concluded by noting that the particular project undertaken by Marcuse had largely ended in failure. The chasm between Heidegger and Marx proved too wide. The Marxist desire for a radical act that could foreclose exploitation universally—wedded to a Hegelian conception of the Absolute—conflicted too fundamentally with Heidegger's insistence upon finitude, contingency, and historicity without teleological resolution. Thus, resoluteness, which Marcuse had rendered as "radical action," could be operationalized as a concept in the service of sociohistorical change only in a limited sense, that is, only in relation to a specific oppositional context, with the constrictors of its particular factically given time and place. Marcuse's attempt to translate Marxist notions of historically necessary action into Heideggerian terms ran up against the proviso that struggles against pathologically distorting forms of praxis (e.g., alienation, reification, etc.) could only be local: the movement of history is an open-ended process of radical transcendence, recovery, and return that cannot, even in principle be definitively and finally overcome. This would not mean that certain forms of revolutionary overturning of are not called for—even necessary, in the specific sense with which Marcuse employed the term—but it does demote them from any pretensions to a definitive realization of nonalienated being.

In the intervening chapters (Chapters Four, Five, and Six), we then turned to Foucault as a possible alternative means of concretizing the Heideggerian insights into historicity and ontological freedom, pursuing the intuition that bridging these two thinkers would be an easier task than the Marx-Heidegger synthesis sought by Marcuse and others. Through his critical histories of spiritual practices, I argue, Foucault ultimately both completes and transgresses the original impulse found within Heidegger's work pertaining to the relation of historicity and freedom. For in the final analysis, Foucault does not attempt to provide a general, definitive "theory" of freedom, finitude, and historicity. He does not attempt to provide us with the final vocabulary through which such questions must necessarily be articulated. Not only does such a final vocabulary not exist, codification of this sort would *foreclose*, rather than instigate, the ever-present need for self-problematization since it would falsely present itself as located above and beyond the field of contestation itself, rather than in situ. For Foucault, there can be no definitive vocabulary, even for situated freedom, since it is embodied in relational ethical practices of self-transformation, not in the language we employ to designate them. Instead, Foucault provides us with a complex set of exemplary practices in which agents were able to problematize their own relationship to their particular context of thought and action.

This is a more proper example of the kind of *authentic historicizing* we initially encountered in Chapter Three, since its purpose is not to provide examples for imitating, but exemplars for following. We have moved then from the assumption that a general theory of freedom is necessary toward a historical, perspectival survey of the actual practices by which humans call into question the field of meaning into which they are thrown. The connection drawn between the attentive, ethical conduct of oneself as the (historical) condition of possibility for the transformation of our experience of the world is the justification I take for redescribing the general analysis here as a "historical ontology of freedom." I would argue that this form of analysis is, ironically, a more authentic capturing of the original spirit of Heidegger's insights into historicity and freedom than Heidegger's own epochal *Destruktion* of Western metaphysics.[1]

At the same time, it is important to recognize a certain nagging concern with regard to this form of critical-historical work, a concern that likely persists despite the reconstructive recasting of Heidegger and Foucault in the previous chapters. The concern is that a historical, perspectival survey of the various modes of "care of the self," even when situated in relation to an ontology of care, fails to provide us with the kinds of tools we require for the robust forms of social criticism we desire in the present. It provides a general survey, but no "theory," examples but no definitive, final criteria for classification and replication. There is no blueprint to follow. This general objection can be further disarticulated in its positive or negative forms. In its positive iteration, the concern is often advanced that this form of historical ontology fails to provide positive content for the explication of normatively preferred social order. There is no definitive content posited here. Put negatively, the portrait of situated freedom and historical ontology may be thought not even to equip us with the means to *invalidate* any particular field of activity or thought. It rules nothing out. The latter is a less demanding standard than the former, but at the heart of both is a similar concern: all particular social and political forms may be considered equally representative of an ontology of finitude and, as a result, we are left with no reasons for preferring one iteration over another.

This concluding chapter resists this interpretation. In this chapter, we will therefore return to the general question of relating ontology and social criticism, resituated now in light of our explication of Foucault's historical ontology. For the purposes of this chapter, I shall return to the question of social transformation we opened up in Chapter Three. The focus here is on how contemporary critical theories of reification are recast in light of our traversing Heidegger and Foucault. This recasting is employed as a means of throwing into stark relief what utility one can (and cannot) extract from ontological analyses (fundamental or historical) for the purposes of social criticism. Central to my claim is that while the picture of situated freedom and historical ontology provided cannot provide the kind of programmatic, positive morality desired by some, it does not follow from this that it is useless as a tool of social criticism. It does, however, force us to adjust our picture of critique.

7.1. CRITICAL THEORIES OF REIFICATION

As a means of entering into these questions, let us return to a theme introduced in Chapter Three: the relationship between ontology and critical theories of reification. By *critical theory of reification*, I am referring to those analyses concerned with critiquing modes of social organization and/or socially mediated praxis in which human relationships are thought to have taken on the character of thing- or object-like relations in some relevant sense. Various attempts have been made to provide such an analysis, most especially from those working in the tradition of western Marxism, particularly because thinkers in this tradition have been convinced that under capitalism, social life is pathologically experienced as instrumentalized or object-like. In Chapter Three, we examined Marcuse's particular attempt to recast this in Heideggerian terms; in his words, the "taking-on-oneself of the law of the thing rather than letting one's own Dasein happen."[2] Variations of this concern can also be found in a host of other thinkers from across the twentieth century, many of whom have already been mentioned in passing here, including Georg Lukács, Jean-Paul Sartre, Lucien Goldman, and, as I will discuss further in a moment, Axel Honneth.

For each of these thinkers, a critical theory of reification is importantly a *social* theory. None wish to restrict themselves to a picture of reification as either mere "category error" or as the function of "moral failure." By category error, I mean instances of literal misclassification as a result of the failure to recognize something that does not properly exhibit the characteristics of an object for something that does (in whatever relevant sense). This is not the sense in which we will use *reification* here, excluding therefore cases of literal misclassification in which an X is taken for a Y. Additionally, reification is not used in a moralistic sense, that is, to signify a morally problematic action on the part of one individual against another. It is of course possible to employ a species of this language to reference precisely this sort of morally problematic behavior. It can, for instance, be found in feminist analysis that highlights the sexual objectification of women in terms not wholly dissimilar from those employed by reification theorists.[3] More generally, this moralistic idiom of "objectification" is evident in a tradition of thinking generally derived from or heavily indebted to Kant, in which thinkers raise objections to treating humans instrumentally, rather than as autonomous agents in their own right.[4] Although it might be possible to speak of some species of objectification in terms of category errors or morally abusive action, this is not, however, what the reification theorists we are concerned with here are trying to get at. Instead, the thinkers mentioned above are unified in their use of the term as a means of characterizing a *form of life*, that is, in reference to much broader phenomenon integrated across an entire set of social relations, not reducible to a cognitive error, nor to the direct, intentional activity of any one particular agent taken in isolation.

Although we have first raised the question of reification here in the context of Marcuse's early writings on the possibility of a "phenomenology of historical materialism," the ur-text for this discussion is more properly Georg Lukács's "Reification and the Consciousness of the Proletariat," the 1923 essay that forms the heart of the book *History and Class Consciousness*.[5] Apart from being credited with rehabilitating the Marxist tradition by situating its philosophical foundation in the Hegelian language of dialectics (as opposed to the comparatively crude "scientific" positivism and economic reductionism that prevailed in, for instance, certain variants of Soviet social science of the period), Lukács is also recognized for having found in Marx's theory of commodity fetishism the seeds of a general social theory of reification.

Marx, of course, had previously used the term *verdinglichkeit* to refer to the kind of relationship observable in certain spheres of capitalist social relations.[6] Perhaps most famously, in the analysis of the commodity form from the opening sections of *Capital*, Marx employs the term to characterize a dual-sided phenomenon. The first sense, clearest in the notion of commodity fetishism, references the process by which productive social relations come to be congealed in objects, which then seems to have independent, "free-standing" worth and value. In a famous passage from this section of *Capital*, Marx invites us to examine the "residue of the products of labour," saying:

> There is nothing left of them in each case but the same phantom-like objectivity; there are merely congealed quantities of homogeneous human labour, i.e. of human labour-power expended without regard to the form of its expenditure. All these things now tell us is that human labour-power has been expended to produce them, human labour is accumulated in them. As crystals of this social substance, which is common to them all, they are values—commodity values [Warenwerte].[7]

Elsewhere, he adds,

> The mysterious character of the commodity-form consists therefore simply in the fact that the commodity reflects the social characteristics of men's own labour as objective characteristics of the products themselves, as the socio-natural properties of these things. Hence it also reflects the social relation of the producers to the sum total of labour as a social relation between objects, a relation which exists apart from and outside the producers. . . . As against this, the commodity-form, and the value-relation of the products of labour within which it appears, have absolutely no connection with the physical nature of the commodity and the material [dinglich] relations arising out of this. It is nothing but the definite social relations between men themselves which assumes here, for them, the fantastic form of a relation between things. (*Capital*, 164–65)

Since these commodities seem to have a "life of their own," inasmuch as they relate to one another in a manner that appears independent of human intervention and/or decision (e.g., we do not simply "decide" the value relation between commodities; value is supposedly reflected by an objective price set by the market), these things come to take on the character of quasi-spiritual entities for us—removed and floating above and around us. As Marx puts it, "I call this the fetishism which attaches itself to the products of labour as soon as they are produced as commodities, and is therefore inseparable from the production of commodities" (*Capital*, 165). As this passage attests, the fetishistic attachment to commodities as objects which appear to have value in and of themselves, divorced from the social relations that have produced them and which continue to circulate them, is inherent to what it means for something to be a commodity under capitalism; it is not something "added on" afterward on an ad hoc basis. It is in reference to this "congealed" or hypostasized commodity value that we may initially speak of reification.

But insofar as thinking about *verdinglichkeit* through the lens of commodity fetishism encourages us to think about the objectified relationship between myself and this object (which is in reality not static, but the expression of a dynamic relationship of production), it is only a vehicle for getting at the deeper problem. The real reason why commodities take on this character under conditions of capital has nothing to do with my subjective relationship to the object itself. Rather, it has to do with the separation and isolation of workers from each other under conditions of a social division of labor. As Marx puts it, "Objects of utility become commodities only because they are the products of the labour of private individuals who work independently of each other" (*Capital*, 165). Insofar as the phenomenon of commodity fetishism on the one level (my relationship to an object of purchase) points us toward a deeper analysis of objectification on another level (the relationship between laborers), it paradoxically conceals and reveals the truth of the situation. In other words, while on the one hand commodity fetishism is "false" (because it falsely represents the value of something in it), on the other hand it is "true" in the sense that it is a proper expression of the transformation of labor itself into a chain of equivalence, that is, the leveling of the qualitative distinctions between different laboring activities and their ultimate fungibility under capitalism. All differences of labor are leveled as they come to be ultimately expressed in units of empty time (i.e., in hourly wages). A commodity is, after all, an abstract unit of exchange between isolated individuals, divorced from their actual relationship to production—not because of a moral failure on the part of an isolated individual, but because under the complex, diffused, and dispersed conditions of production in capital, it is impossible for this *not* to be the case.

Georg Lukács picked up and expanded upon this insight from Marx. For Lukács, the discussion of commodity fetishism in *Capital*, volume 1, "contains within itself the whole of historical materialism and the whole self-knowledge of the proletariat seen as the knowledge of capitalist society." (Lukács, 170). So Lukács's innovation was in taking Marx's work on commodity relations and expanding it into a general theory of reification, one that not only transverses all sectors of society (political, cultural, economic), but also operates on two registers. Lukács calls these two registers the "objective" and "subjective" levels. The *objective* level refers to the impersonal forces that appear to hold sway over our society without coming effectively under the control of any particular human agent. The classic example of this is our everyday experience of "market forces," which appear to us as autonomous and independent of direct human conscious planning or control. On the *subjective* level, Lukács argues that although such semi-autonomous forces appear to us as "objective" external laws of a world we cannot control, they are, in effect, routed through us. Anticipating Foucault, Lukács suggests that the set of social relations comprised by capitalism are attended by a set of relationships of the self to itself, that is, the manner in which we conform ourselves and adapt ourselves to the impersonal forces of the market in order to best avail ourselves of whatever advantages they might bring. They therefore form an ensemble of habits and practices that together comprise a "subjectivity," including a stance or relation to oneself. In this case, "a man's [sic] activity becomes estranged from himself, it turns into a commodity which, subject to the non-human objectivity of the natural laws of society, must go its own way independently of man just like any consumer article" (Lukács, 87).

Part of the explanation behind the popularity and impact of Lukács's work is precisely his decision to elevate reification from a localized phenomenon to a general social form. Subsequent thinkers in the Western Marxist tradition have found this useful because, for Lukács, reification does not signify a mistaken act (in isolation) but a mistaken form of life, wherein "mistaken" refers not to the idea that it has violated a set of moral principles that we hold, but rather that it does not conform to certain ontological facts. Under capitalism, we increasingly view and experience our own society not as the product of our own creative construction, but rather as constituted by a set of impersonal, autonomous laws (i.e., the laws of the market) to which we must conform. This mode of seeing and experiencing the world as constituted by external, objective, impersonal, and autonomous forces is what Lukács calls "the reification of consciousness," and it is his central proposition that this has come to constitute our "second nature" (Lukács, 86). Importantly, however, for Lukács the world isn't *actually* an external, impersonal set of forces over against all human subjectivity, but is instead the product of our productive, creative powers. Our "second nature" of interpreting the world *as though* it were this autonomous sphere is false then in the sense that it doesn't conform to reality.

However, Lukács's thesis has also always been controversial since it appears to be quite totalizing. Lukács is clear that he sees reification as permeating our entire society—penetrating even into family life and the sphere of religion, for instance. He argues: "The qualitative difference between the commodity as one form among many regulating the metabolism of human society and the commodity as the universal structuring principle has effects over and above the fact that the commodity relation as an isolated phenomenon exerts a negative influence at best on the structure and organization of society" (Lukács, 85). In positing the commodity as a "universal structuring principle" of capitalist society, Lukács is thus not only suggesting that reification effects a kind of de-differentiation of social spheres, leveling all domains of the social by permeating each. He also commits himself to an account of the conditions under which such a critical analysis is *itself* possible, since one of the domains to be subjected here will be the theoretical analysis of society itself. One of the radical implications of Lukács's generalization of Marx's basic thesis therefore is that reification also permeates philosophy and critical theory. This amounts to an even stronger claim than the "de-differentiation of spheres" or "generalization" thesis, for Lukács concludes that the distorted form of praxis that mediates social relationships between agents is also mirrored in, and reinforced by, a false picture of human subjectivity and agency contained within prevailing philosophical idioms and modes of critical reflection. And so he contends that modern critical philosophy itself "springs from the reified structure of consciousness" (Lukács, 110–11). More specifically, Lukács is concerned that a philosophical tradition we have inherited persists in conceiving of the human as first and foremost a detached, isolated, atomistic agent who apprehends the world through an act of "cognitive grasping." Lukács calls this the "contemplative stance," and for him it is not coincidental that this philosophical model of the self seems to echo the kind of atomistic, competitive, utility-maximizing agents that capitalist economics represents us as, and indeed compels us to become. The "unified economic structure" of capitalism permits a "unified structure of consciousness that embrace[s] the whole society . . . [to be] brought into being." What is this "unified consciousness"? It is the stance of the "passive observer of society", who "lapses into a contemplative attitude *vis-à-vis* the workings of his own objectified and reified faculties" (Lukács, 100). Thus, this contemplative attitude or stance does not merely mistakenly frame us through a "cognitivist" model of subjectivity. It is not a category error of the sort mentioned in the opening passages here. Rather, it is *symptomatic* of a form of life that exhibits a distorted form of praxis. Hence, there is a mutually reinforcing logic between (1) a model of subjectivity as first and foremost cognitivist; (2) an epistemological model (originally derived from the natural sciences) in which we are thought to gain most certain understanding of the world when we "stand back" from it, objectify it as precisely the set of impersonal laws and forces that (not coincidentally) reflect the picture of a detached individual in a market society; and (3) the practical experience of those market forces which increasingly reorganize our social praxis itself. As Lukács puts the point, under such conditions, "all human relations (viewed as the objects of social activity) assume increasingly the objective forms of the abstract elements of the conceptual systems of natural science and of the abstract substrata of the laws of nature. And also, the subject of this 'action' likewise assumes increasingly the attitude of the pure observer of these—artificially abstract—processes, the attitude of the experimenter" (Lukács, 131). Elsewhere, he calls out the "dogmatic assumption," that would posit this "rational and formalistic mode of cognition [as] the only possible way of apprehending reality" (Lukács, 121).

In so framing his analysis, Lukács actually synthesizes at least two different ways of thinking about reification: one that operates as social criticism (of capitalist society), the other which operates as a critique of traditional epistemology. However, this is also where certain problems arise in his formulation. For "reification" refers here to two slightly different phenomena. On what I will call a *vertical axis*, reification reflects a false philosophical anthropology, namely, a false understanding of what humans essentially and basically are. Namely, we are *not* isolated, atomistic agents who apprehend the world in cognitive detachment, but rather are engaged and existentially involved agents who encounter the world first and foremost through our practical activities. So reification is a false picture of ourselves, where "false" is something like "does not correspond to social ontology as it *really* is." On the other hand, *reification* is also employed here as a term of reference for a phenomenon on a *horizontal axis*, that is, a relation *between social agents*. On this horizontal axis, the term names a pathological form of social organization that is historically contingent, namely, capitalism. Capitalism falsely isolates social agents and instrumentalizes the relations between them. On this level, however, capitalism is thought to be pathologically reified in a slightly different way than on the vertical axis, since it is precisely the problem that under capitalism our lives *have actually* taken on this reified character.

To get clearer of the slippage, we might consider what it means for something to be "nonreified" in these examples. In the first (vertical) axis, nonreified means engaged, involved praxis, which we have said *always already* exists. But on the second (horizontal) axis, nonreified means noncapitalist in some society that is *yet to come*. The point of criticizing a cognitivist epistemological model of human subjectivity and action is to assert that noncognitivist, practical coping activities are always already more basic to human modes of Being-in-the-world than this particular theoretical model admits. By contrast, the point of criticizing a capitalist mode of social organization is to bring about its overturning, to realize a nonreified form of life in some as yet actualized form. Dispelling reification of the first sort will involve realizing what has always been there (but for its concealing in some way). Dispelling reification in the second sense will entail radically transforming our world so as to bring about that which is not yet the case.

7.2. HONNETH AND HEIDEGGER

In his most recent attempt to reactualize the language of reification, German philosopher and social theorist Axel Honneth has attempted to revive reification theory and, in so doing, to navigate through these challenges. In this project, he has directly enlisted Heidegger as another importance resource.[8] This isn't entirely unexpected or novel for, as we have already noted, Heidegger does advance concern for a pathology that takes the form of something like the "reification of consciousness" in a manner not entirely dissimilar to that seen in Lukács, at least with respect to what Lukács called the "contemplative stance."

There are two explicit references to the "reification of consciousness" in *Being and Time*, and, apart from Marcuse's early work, there have been other attempts to build off of these enigmatic comments toward a critique of capital. Interestingly, the two references bookend *Being and Time* as a whole, appearing in the introduction and then on the very last page. I quote them in their entirety:

> One of our first tasks will be to prove that if we posit an "I" or subject as that which is proximally given, we shall completely miss the phenomenal content [Bestand] of Dasein. *Ontologically*, every idea of a "subject"—unless refined by a previous ontological determination of its basic character—still posits the *subjectum* along with it, no matter how vigorous one's ontical protestations against the "soul substance" or the "reification of consciousness." The Thinghood itself which such reification implies must have its ontological origin demonstrated if we are to be in a position to ask what we are to understand *positively* when we think of the unreified *Being* of the subject, the soul, the consciousness, the spirit, the person. (BTa §10, 72; SZ §10, 46)

> The distinction between the Being of existing Dasein and the Being of entities, such as Reality, which do not have the character of Dasein, may appear very illuminating; but it is still only the *point of departure* for the ontological problematic; it is nothing with which philosophy may tranquilize itself. It has long been known that ancient ontology works with "Thing-concepts" and that there is a danger of "reifying consciousness." But what does this "reifying" signify? Where does it arise? What does Being get "conceived" "proximally" in terms of the present-at-hand *and not* in terms of the ready-to-hand, which indeed lies *closer* to us? Why does this reifying always keep coming back to exercise its dominion? What *positive* structure does the Being of "consciousness" have, if reification remains inappropriate to it?

> Is the "distinction" between "consciousness" and "Thing" sufficient for tackling the ontological problem in a primordial manner? Do the answers to these questions lie along our way? And can we even *seek* the answer as long as the *question* of the meaning of Being remains unformulated and unclarified? (BTa §83, 487; SZ §83, 437)

Much has been made of these passages, most famously by Lucien Goldman, who suggested that they not only provide material for the construction of a bridge between Heidegger and Lukács, but also, perhaps more adventurously, that a hidden conversation was already taking place between the two thinkers.[9] Venturing onto this terrain is not required here, though perhaps provisionally we can acknowledge that Heidegger may provide resources for a critique of reification whether or not he intended to do so.

A project that would draw upon Heidegger for the purposes of a critique of reification could gain inspiration from the fact that Heidegger offers independent reasons for framing Dasein as fundamentally non-Thinglike. Specifically, Heidegger is very critical of an inherited tradition of thinking that posits a model of human subjectivity and agency in which we are thought to encounter reality, first and foremost, in the stance of observation, or cognitive detachment. As Honneth observes, contrary to such a "contemplative stance," viewed through the lens of *Being and Time*, "the subject no longer neutrally encounters a reality that remains to be understood, but is existentially interested in a reality that is always already disclosed as having qualitative significance."[10] As we have already seen, Heidegger calls the organizational structure of this invested, engaged relationship with the world Care. Heidegger has some more specific appeal here for someone such as Honneth because *Being and Time* does not restrict the problem of reification on the vertical axis to a deviation located exclusively in capitalism, but instead sees the tendency to occlude the basic structure of Care as symptomatic of a more general tendency, that is, a learned habit of framing the world cognitively by means of the subject-object opposition. This makes more explicit than Lukács the idea that, although reifying pictures of human subjectivity and agency are problematic, they are more like forms of false self-interpretation, but ones that nevertheless leave the basic structure of Care intact. For Heidegger, an objectifying picture of human relatedness to the world cannot actually eliminate Care, since we have just asserted that Care is primordial in the sense of always already structuring Being-in-the-world. As such, we are left with the realization that reification has not eliminated the other, nonreified form of praxis but has merely concealed it from our awareness. This is why Heidegger must introduce a set of superordinate distinctions between modes of *relating to* the more basic structure of Care, rather than a primary distinction between Care and non-Care. Hence, too, Heidegger's preference for the language of a "forgetfulness" of Being, since this implies that basic relations of Being-in-the-world have not been obliterated, but merely occluded from conscious view.[11]

Thus, while a plausible Heideggerian approach to the question might agree that such a distorting phenomenon as the "reification of consciousness" exists in our contemporary situation, such a position would nevertheless disagree with Lukács on the ultimate scope, source, and solution to this problem. Lukács sees the "reification of consciousness" as the byproduct of a distorted form of praxis, produced by the historical and sociological context of modern capitalism, and thus in need of a practical, dialectical overturning by another, revolutionary, noncapitalist praxis projected into the future as a possibility yet to be realized. By contrast, Heidegger would see the "reification of consciousness" as the byproduct of a forgetting of our more basic Being-in-the-world, a forgetting made manifest in an epistemological model that stands in need of an ontological critique, one which can more modestly "remind" us of what is already latent within our worldly activities by demonstrating to us the more basic or primordial nature of the structure of Care.

It is perhaps for this reason that Heidegger has found an unexpected ally in Axel Honneth. In recent publications, Honneth not only reintroduces Heidegger to a discussion of reification, he suggests that this is necessary in order to overcome some of the limitations in Lukács's approach.[12] Specifically, Honneth argues that Lukács's work suffers from an unacknowledged split between two different pictures of nonreified praxis. On the one hand, Honneth reads Lukács as positing a picture of nonreified, "true" human praxis as consisting in those instances "where an object can be thought of as the product of a subject, and where mind and world therefore ultimately coincide with one another" (Honneth, 27). Echoing a common criticism of Lukács, Honneth thus reads the

Hungarian Marxist's work as an odd materialist reworking of Fichte, whereby ideal (nonreified) praxis embodies a relationship of total identity between self and world, in this case because the externalization of the self through laboring activity is undisturbed by any distortions.

Rejecting such an Idealist picture, Honneth offers a second, alternative reading of Lukács on nonreified praxis. In this "unofficial" version, Lukács "doesn't contrast reifying praxis with a collective subject's production of an object, but with another, intersubjective attitude on the part of the subject" (Honneth, 27). In this case, then, undistorted praxis is not found in a relationship of identity between self and world, but in a relationship of mutual recognition between self and other in which the dialectic of identity/difference is normatively transformed (rather than transcended altogether) through a form of praxis in which "humans take up an empathetic and engaged relationship towards themselves and their surroundings" (Honneth, 27). These two nonreified pictures conform then to what I have termed the verticle and horizonal axes of the problem.

The gains to be had from drawing upon Heidegger are not reducible to the general overlap between *Being and Time* and *History and Class Consciousness* when it comes to the idea of an epistemic stance of detachment as embodying a mode of reification (a position that would be shared by many other thinkers when stated as this high level of generality).[13] More specifically, Honneth finds in *Being and Time* a more complete and immediate account of a nonreified relation (i.e., Care) since, for Heidegger—unlike for Lukács—this is not projected into some future yet to come and thus necessarily unspecified. Honneth objects to the totalizing tendencies in Lukács's account mentioned above, whereby capitalism is thought to eliminate *any* possibility of engaged, true praxis. Since Lukács (supposedly) views capitalism as destructive of any such true relations, he "*cannot* conceive of his project as unveiling an already present possibility of human existence, but instead as sketching a future possibility" (Honneth, 31). As a result, Lukács appears rather oddly to enter into the critique of capitalism backward: he offers an account of *distorted* praxis first, while delaying any account of its undistorted form to a future date. For Honneth, however, this is insufficient, both logically and practically. Logically, the very identification of distorted praxis seems to presuppose the conceptual grasping of its genuine or undistorted form. Moreover, from a practical standpoint, it is difficult to see from whence we are to derive resources for the overturning of capitalism's distortions if they have been entirely eliminated here and now. Lukács's answer was, of course, to suggest that the contradictions of capitalism would produce the conditions of its own overcoming in the form of a unified, self-conscious, collective proletariat subject. Lukács found some light in his otherwise very dark portrait of capitalism only by asserting that the basic contradictions of capitalism—specifically the "rigid opposition of subject and object" (Lukács, 351)—would produce a form of consciousness capable of grasping itself as both subject and object (i.e., the proletariat). Hence, for Lukács, the complete penetration of the commodity form into all dimensions of society is presented as producing paradoxical results. On the one hand, "it [becomes] increasingly difficult and rare to find anyone penetrating the veil of reification," yet, on the other, the "commodity can only be understood in its undistorted essence when it becomes the universal category of society as a whole" (Lukács, 86). This is a familiar refrain in Marxist thought: the purity and depth of the alienation processes of modern capitalism actually permit, paradoxically, for new possibilities of overcoming them, a set of circumstances not possible in earlier, less strict forms. In light of the past ninety years of debate and practical struggle to bring about such a unified, collective subject, however, this response seems inadequate for us today. No such unified subject of history has emerged. In fact, Lukács himself came to see this framing as inadequate, subjecting his earlier work to a form of autocritique.[14]

Thus, Honneth turns to Heidegger's conception of Care as a superior rendering of genuine praxis for precisely the reason that Care is meant to signify an already existing reality. The critique of reification does not take the form of a projection into the future, but rather appears now as a reminder of what is always already the case. As a result, "we are left with the realization that reification has not eliminated the other, non-reified form of praxis but has merely concealed it from our awareness" (Honneth, 31). In this Heideggerian rendering, then, reification does not refer to a distortion in our more basic Being-in-the-world, but rather to a second-order "false interpretive habit," or mode of self-understanding and self-appropriation with regard to our basic praxis that remains intact nevertheless. As Honneth puts it: "The habit, which has become second nature, of conceiving one's relationship to oneself and to one's surroundings as an activity of neutral cognition of objective circumstances, bestows over time a reified form on human activity, without ever being able to eradicate the original 'caring' character of this activity completely" (Honneth, 33).

The costs of translating reification into this Heideggerian register are substantial, however. Namely, we run back into the problem identified previously in Chapter Three. As we move toward a general, ontological theory of Being-in-the-world, the project begins to lose utility as a tool of social criticism. After all, since no particular society can be thought of as any more or less a manifestation of Care, we would have to say that capitalism is just as much a manifestation of an engaged, existentially invested mode of Being-in-the-world than any other postcapitalist society to come. The realization of Care could not be thought of as uniquely manifest in any particular sociocultural world, and thus cannot have the narrow, normatively favored connotation that Honneth imports into it. Put another way, whatever term we wish to use for a nonreified form of life (whether we wish to employ the term Care for this or not), it cannot denote both (1) a primordial, genuine mode of human praxis in the sense of engaged practical involvement in the world over against the distorted picture of detached, observational status; and (2) a specific, normatively preferred social relationship. In the first sense of the term it is genuine in the sense of always already the case. In the second sense, it is genuine in the sense of normatively preferred among a range of possible alternatives as yet to come.

Axel Honneth's formulation of the matter brings this problem into sharp relief. For Honneth does not merely refashion Heidegger's ontological conception of Care as a means of critiquing and intervening in a narrow rendering of reification along the vertical axis mentioned above. Rather, he also finds in Care a model for normatively favored relations of reciprocity on the horizontal axis, that is, between social agents. Even more ambitiously, for Honneth, "realizing Care" translates into a specific programmatic moral regime. To accomplish this, Honneth rather quickly analogizes from Heideggerian Care to the Hegelian model of Recognition, arguing that both are properly thought of as affirming the notion of practical involvement in general (as opposed to a cognitivist model) as well as affirming a specific, normatively privileged kind of practical involvement (over against normatively deficient forms). Hence, Care is equated to Recognition, and then both to an "intersubjective stance" that embodies "an element of affective disposition, even of positive predisposition" toward others (Honneth, 35). From a general ontology of praxis, or deep involvement in practical activities over against a cognitivist picture of agency, we are meant to arrive deductively at a robust, programmatic morality that, in effect, appears as a Kantian kingdom of ends, albeit cloaked in a mixture of Heideggerian and Hegelian language.

Deducing a positive morality from a general ontology is, however, a dubious prospect. For, as we have already intimated here, adopting Heidegger's thesis on Care (understood as the structure of Being-in-the-world, however translated into the language of existential involvement, practical coping, etc.) does not commit one to any particular positive moral or political stance. Honneth glosses over this problem by conflating Care and Recognition, but the central tension remains, a verdict confirmed by many of Honneth's immediate interlocutors for this work, such as Judith Butler, Jonathan Lear, and Raymond Geuss.[15] The point here is that "affirming Care" means only affirming the general fact of existential involvement in a world, while remaining agnostic with regard to the particular ethical-political valence of this involvement. For this reason, Care does not equal Recognition, since the latter is meant to provide additional positive content. In fact several commentators have drawn fairly dire conclusions for the very idea of relating ontological and sociopolitical matters per se, not restricting themselves to the particular formulation given by Honneth recently. The farthest-reaching conclusion to be drawn from this attempt to reformulate reification in a Heideggerian idiom is that fundamental ontology can have precisely *no* connection to practical philosophy, however creatively reformulated. Raymond Geuss arrives at this conclusion in his critical review of Honneth's work. He writes:

> From the fact that care for the world is prior to cognition, it does not follow that I must have a basically affectionate, optimistic, or fostering attitude toward anything in the world in particular. To love, to hate, or to be indifferent, detached, neutral, and so on are all ways of being "care-fully" engaged. To repeat, the priority of care, con-

cern, and so on has, precisely because it is quasi-transcendental, no
... effect on how we ought to act concretely toward individuals,
groups, or nature. ... If care (or recognition) is a precondition of
everything and anything, including hatred or indifference, it cannot
be the basis of an ethics or social criticism. Sartre spent his whole life
trying to prove Heidegger wrong about this, and failed.[16]

Any attempt to derive practical, sociopolitical utility from the general Heideggerian critique of the epistemological-cognitivist model will have to contend with this objection, and part of the rationale behind our traversing this long thread from Lukács to Honneth consists in putting the challenge as starkly as possible. This is, as we have seen, a persistent issue plaguing the existential- or phenomenological-Marxist tradition extending from Marcuse in the 1920s and 1930s to Sartre in the 1960s and 1970s. However, while it is important to identify and take stock of such challenges, it is likewise important to avoid overinflating them. While the specific project undertaken by Honneth may appear unconvincing, it does not flow from the acknowledgement of its particular limitations that we must necessarily concede the futility of the general endeavor itself (*pace* Geuss).[17] Instead, we may build constructively from this long conversation that emerged over the course of twentieth-century Critical Theory as a means of resituating the previous discussion, demonstrating an alternative possible route.

Throughout this work, I have pursued the intuition that Foucault's historical ontology might prove a more useful resource for unpacking the concrete implications of Heidegger's broad ontological thesis. In light of the above attempts to translate Heidegger's ontology into sociopolitical terms of critique through the language of reification, let me now turn to showing how a reconstructed Foucauldian perspective may serve us better.

7.3. Reification and *Assujettissement*

It is perhaps counterintuitive to suggest Foucault as a resource for rethinking matters of reification, even in light of our creative reappropriation of his thought undertaken in previous chapters. Foucault does not frequently employ the language of objectification in general, even less so the more specific "reification." Instead, he appears intentionally to opt for the inverse language, producing a theory of *subjectification*, or *assujettissement*. Moreover, Foucault appears repeatedly to commend a practice of freedom and "care of the self" that entails an intentional *self-objectification*. Does he not invite us to imagine ourselves as objects of aesthetic self-fashioning, analogizing between the human self and paintings, even lamps and houses?[18]

Given the considerable explication of Foucault's work in the previous chapters (especially Chapter Six), it is hopefully clear that any initial objectification / subjectification opposition will reveal itself as superficial. For, as we have seen, in his later works on the "ethics of the care of the self as a practice of freedom" and on the "aesthetics of existence," Foucault attends precisely to the ossifying tendencies of a certain conception of subjectivity in the West—what he retrospectively terms the "objectivizing of the subject" [*l'objectivation du sujet*]—in a manner not entirely dissimilar to Heidegger's critique of the cognitivist picture (*EW*3, 326; *DE*2, 1042). What these two thinkers share, not only with each other, but also with a host of other thinkers across the twentieth century, is a critical interrogation of the question of "the subject" as defined by a set of transhistorical properties. In this way, they continually attend to how it is that "the subject" cannot be analyzed with tools developed and derived from the study of objects, as for instance on the model of the natural sciences. The subject is not merely another type of object. Heidegger's way of reminding us of this fact is to avoid discussing "the subject" at all, opting instead to speak of Dasein, a mode of Being-in-the-world that does not have "properties" (analogous to objects), but rather "existentials." For his part, Foucault likewise declines to investigate "the subject" as such, and instead undertakes an analysis of the particular, historically mediated practices of *subjectification* that constitute us as subjects in different ways over time. The movement from a static, transcendental-deductive methodology to a dynamic, situated existentialist one in regards to the study of subjectivity is a major paradigm shift in twentieth-century thought that cannot be easily rescinded.

Despite their general suspicion of hypostasized images of the subject, however, and their shared critique of a cognitivist picture of selfhood that does precisely this, both thinkers refuse to treat this picture of subjectivity as merely a moral failure or an epistemic error. Rather, they "provincialize" the transcendental subject as one possible practical relationship to the self, but one with a particular history in the West such that it remains occluded to itself. In Chapter Six, I unpacked the particulars of this story insofar as Heidegger and Foucault converge in terms of their respective readings of the contribution of major figures such as Descartes and Kant to this historical inheritance. Now we might recast this slightly. A cognitivist approach comprises a false picture of subjectivity, true, but this is not merely a false "theory." Rather, it is also a distorted practical attitude to oneself, a mode or manner in which we come to relate to ourselves as "objectlike" in some relevant way. This distorted picture of subjectivity is more like a false interpretive habit, one that nevertheless cannot obliterate the more basic dynamic relations or sense in which selfhood is embedded, relational, and practically-holistically disclosed in action. While subjectivity can never be a fixed, static term of reference, it is possible to adopt a learned habit of self-relating that restricts us to some manner or another of acting *as though* this were the case. In this situation, we are not freeing ourselves from a distorted essence (since there is no essential subject in *this* sense), but rather from a habitualized mode of thinking and acting that falsely presents itself as though it were essential. We are self-limiting then through a hypostasized (or reified) mode of self-relation that is contingent and singular, rather than universal and necessary. It is in light of this interpretation that we can perhaps make better sense of what Foucault meant when he interpreted his role as consisting in showing "people that they are much freer than they feel."[19] This is to say, the particular kind of critical project to emerge here is one that seeks to *remind* us of our rootedness in a set of complex practices which are always more contingent, contestable, and mutable than they may first appear.

Seen from this vantage point, we can affirm the general Heideggerian point with regard to Care, and the always already existentially involved, practically coping self of Dasein, while *also* discovering Foucauldian resources for sociopolitical critique. This requires, however, another move, namely that we shift our understanding of social criticism. Following Geuss's reply to Honneth above, it is true that a positive, programmatic morals cannot be deductively arrived at from a general ontology. From the idea of the self as embedded, relational, and existentially involved, we cannot arrive deductively at a moral code that provides a final, definitive, ideal realization or codification of this basic social ontology. However, we need not conclude that the elaboration of a concept of reification in the ontological sense can have *no* utility for social criticism, only that social criticism need not take the form of a positive programmatic vision.

Foucault provides a key intervention here because he (1) also accepts the "anticognitivist" picture shared by many of the thinkers above; (2) employs this "anticognitivism" as a tool of negative social critique; without (3) turning this into a project of positive philosophical-anthropology, that is, by trying to deduce from the general claim about ontological involvement a positive programmatic morality. He does so by way of (4) shifting from providing a general "theory" of freedom toward a survey of exemplary modes of enacting freedom in particular locales. This permits us to bring to light some of the sociopolitical implications of historical ontology without overreaching toward a full-blown, programmatic moral philosophy of the sort that Honneth wishes to deduce from ontology.

This is, of course, a narrower and more modest imagining of the critical intellectual than the one we find in many other thinkers, for it cannot, even in principle, provide a definitive answer to the question of "freedom" taken in the general. Whereas Hegel, Schopenhauer, and Nietzsche sought an overcoming of the gap between objective knowledge and a finite subject in a final, absolute moment—either the achievement of Absolute Spirit, the total renunciation of the self, or the assertion of the *Übermensch*—Foucault sees the self as engaged in perpetual self-transformation. An appropriately reconstructed historical ontology of freedom does not aim, then, at a final vocabulary or theory that would reveal a state of being that was fully self-transparent and absent of conflicting interpretation. Rather, it aims to study the various relations between the "modes of subjectification" and "modes of objectification" that make up the present field of possibilities in which one is situated. We take up previous models, languages, and philosophical projects, not merely as a set of principles or concepts about which one can either be "for" or "against." Rather, we will attempt to see these alternative traditions—in this case, the philosophy of the constituting subject and of teleological anthropology following from Descartes and Kant—as both an *ethical poiesis* (a work performed on oneself) and as a *technē* (a practical activity of relating to the world with a corresponding rationality). Seen from this vantage point, then, these alternatives are not merely negative foils we might attempt to discredit and discard. Rather, they are the practical world in which we find ourselves, or what Foucault would call the "form of problematization," out of which our own spiritual practices of resistance and transformation emerge. We thus appropriate from them even as we critique and transgress them. An understanding of freedom as a particular relationship to our practical world of involvement, and the spiritual practices of self-transformation that help attune us to the possibilities of the present field, allows us to see that freedom is not something that will ever be "achieved" in some final, absolute moment. Rather, because it is linked to the very problematization it diagnoses and resists, it is a relationship that cannot be exhaustively determined.

Effecting this shift in perspective means that the ongoing project of writing a "historical ontology of ourselves" is no panacea for all of the possible experiences of constraint and domination, even those we might more narrowly group under the heading of objectification or reification. But it is not meant to be. Instead, it is intended to be leveled at one *particular* range of modes of self-objectification in the modern West, those closely associated with the false interpretive habit of viewing subjectivity through the ossifying lens of object types and classifications, especially cognitivist ones. Whereas Heidegger tended to view this self-objectification as a general tendency in the Western philosophical tradition, Foucault connected it up more directly to specific, concrete cases in which human modes of subjectification congealed into rigid typological classifications—the mad, the delinquent, the abnormal, the sexual deviant.[20] The critique of such classificatory schemes can be thought of as existing in a kind of "family resemblance" with the various critical theories of reification adopted throughout the twentieth century, since it aims at freeing us from the picture of subjectivity as reducible to "object types" and the restrictive effects of this ossification. As David Owen reminds us, such classificatory systems do permit of a certain type of individualization, but only in the sense of viewing a specific individual as a unique *example* of a general typology (for instance, being the only case of a subspecies of delinquent).[21] What such schemes do *not* leave room for is an *expressivist* self, one whose identity and subjectivity is uniquely formed in and through action with others in particular, concrete situations (rather than being presocial, or formed in advance of the activity of self-articulation).[22] Bringing to the fore a critical, historical ontology aimed at highlighting the practices of freedom immanent within modes of subjectification may help us mediate between the two axes described above (vertical and horizontal), because one species of the horizontal pathologies is recast as practices which embody the denial of selfhood as practical, relational expression in and through action and, hence, represent human subjectivity as thinglike in the relevant sense. In this case, social criticism aims less at legislating what we ought to become and more at reminding us what we already are, reminding us of our already existing relations of indebtedness/transgression, or our situated, worldly freedom.

REFERENCE MATTER

NOTES

CHAPTER ONE: OVERVIEW OF THE PROBLEMATIC

The epigraph to this chapter is drawn from G. W. F. Hegel, *The Philosophy of Mind*, trans. William Wallace (Oxford: Oxford University Press, 1971), section I, subsection C, §482, 239.

1. Peter Sloterdijk, *The Critique of Cynical Reason* (Minneapolis: University of Minnesota Press, 1987 [1983]), xxvi–xxvii.

2. Karl Marx and Friedrich Engels, "Manifesto of the Communist Party," in *The Marx-Engels Reader*, 2nd ed., ed. Robert C. Tucker (New York: Norton, 1978), 491.

3. John McCumber refers to this movement as the increased tendency "to construe freedom in terms of situations, not of subjects." *Philosophy and Freedom* (Bloomington: Indiana University Press, 2000), 3.

4. An alternative theory of intersubjectivity that draws more from Hegel and hermeneutic philosophy is Charles Taylor's "recognition thesis" in which freedom is not a function of transcendental will but rather is discursively created and maintained through dialogical relations of mutual respect and reciprocity.

5. For a critique of Habermas along these lines, see Nikolas Kompridis, *Critique and Disclosure: Critical Theory Between Past and Future* (Cambridge, Mass.: MIT Press, 2006).

6. Jürgen Habermas, "Work and Weltanschauung: The Heidegger Controversy from a German Perspective," in *The New Conservatism: Cultural Criticism and the Historians' Debate*, ed. and trans. Shierry Weber Nicholsen (Cambridge, Mass.: MIT Press, 1989), 142–43.

7. Exceptions to this generalization include work by William Connolly, Fred Dallmayr, Günter Figal, Michael Haar, Nikolas Kompridis, Jean-Luc Nancy,

and Leslie Paul Thiele. See Connolly, *Identity/Difference* (Minneapolis: University of Minnesota Press, 1991), esp. chap. 1; Dallmayr, "Ontology of Freedom: Heidegger and Political Philosophy," *Political Theory* 12.2 (May 1984): 204–34; Figal, "An Essay on Freedom: Ontological Considerations from a Practical Point of View," in *For a Philosophy of Freedom and Strife* (Albany: State University of New York Press, 1998), 13–28; Haar, "The Question of Human Freedom in the Later Heidegger," *Southern Journal of Philosophy* 28, supplement (1990): 1–16; Kompridis, *Critique and Disclosure*, esp. part 2; Nancy, *L'expérience de la liberté* (Paris: Galilée, 1988); and Thiele, *Timely Meditations: Martin Heidegger and Postmodern Politics* (Princeton, N.J.: Princeton University Press, 1995).

8. Johanna Oksala, *Foucault, Politics, and Violence* (Evanston, Ill.: Northwestern University Press, 2012), 19.

9. Charles Taylor, *Hegel and Modern Society* (Cambridge: Cambridge University Press, 1979), 154–66.

10. Ibid., 160.

11. Béatrice Han, "Foucault and Heidegger on Kant and Finitude," in *Foucault and Heidegger: Critical Encounters*, ed. Alan Milchman and Alan Rosenberg (Minneapolis: University of Minnesota Press, 2003), 128–29.

12. Ibid., 128.

13. Discussed in more detail below under the heading of "teleological freedom."

14. For a defense and elaboration of Habermas's work in this regard, see David S. Owen, *Between Reason and History: Habermas and the Idea of Progress* (Albany: State University of New York Press, 2002).

15. Immanuel Kant, *Critique of Judgment*, trans. Werner S. Pluhar (Indianapolis: Hackett, 1987).

16. Ibid., §64, 298.

17. Immanuel Kant, "Idea for a Universal History with a Cosmopolitan Purpose," in *Political Writings*, trans. H. B. Nisbet (Cambridge: Cambridge University Press, 1991), 42.

18. I take this reference to Sisyphean deeds from Yirmiahu Yovel, *Kant and the Philosophy of History* (Princeton, N.J.: Princeton University Press, 1980), 101–2.

19. See Kant, *Critique of Judgment*, "Comment" to §86 for the articulation of moral authorship.

20. Ibid., §87, 340.

21. Jürgen Habermas, *The Theory of Communicative Action*, 2 vols. (Boston: Beacon, 1984 [1981]).

22. In this way, at least, the Heideggerian and Foucauldian formulation of freedom through care-full engagement actually resonates more with certain premodern formulations of freedom in terms of *right relation*, than the near exclusive emphasis on self-dependence in post-Kantian practical philosophy. In this way, a dialogue is set up with, for instance, Aristotle. Freedom understood as a right relation with the world, either in terms of harmony, equilibrium, or

nonextremism, can only be understood in relative terms (that is, in relation to the particular factical conditions of the present) and cannot be merely grasped conceptually, but must become a part of oneself—a *hexis*—through the actual engagement with activities in this particular manner.

23. Thomas Dumm, *Michel Foucault and the Politics of Freedom* (Lanham, Md.: Rowman and Littlefield, 2002), 19. Dumm is speaking specifically of Foucault here, but part of my argument is that something similar can apply to Heidegger. Note Dumm's use of Heideggerian language and that Dumm is quoting from a George Kateb article not about Foucault, but rather Nietzsche and Heidegger. See George Katab, "Thinking and Human Extinction (II): Nietzsche and Heidegger," in *The Inner Ocean: Individualism and Democratic Culture* (Ithaca, N.Y.: Cornell University Press, 1992), 127–51.

24. Oksala, *Foucault, Politics, and Violence*, 5.

25. I say simultaneously because the relationship is sustained only in and through the practices. This folds into the general theme of a free relationship only being immanent within practices of freedom.

26. Recent work by philosopher Nikolas Kompridis has been highly suggestive in this manner as well. Kompridis's *Critique and Disclosure* offers a detailed critique of the rather narrow manner in which Habermas construed the supposed unity of reason and in so doing left the philosophical tradition of Critical Theory impoverished (in Kompridis's analysis). As should become clear by the end of this piece, I have found much of Kompridis's account compelling. However, it is a relatively small aside that proved highly evocative for my own work. In the context of a discussion of the Frankfurt school's reluctance to genuinely engage Heidegger's work in a serious way, Kompridis laments that, "the early Marcuse's genuine interest in the possibilities of combining ontological and materialist forms of critical analysis has been left to languish as a historical footnote, even though its considerable potential has barely been developed either by Heideggerians or Habermasians" (33). And, in a footnote to this passage, he adds: "Michel Foucault's critical histories are probably the most successful attempt to bring about such a combination of approaches, but it is probably not quite what Marcuse had in mind" (287 n. 51).

27. Marcuse, "Heidegger's Politics: An Interview," in *Heideggerian Marxism*, ed. Richard Wolin and John Abromeith (Lincoln: University of Nebraska Press, 2005), 165–66. This interview with Fredrick Olafson first appeared in *Graduate Faculty Philosophy Journal* 6.1 (1977): 28–40.

28. Marcuse, "Heidegger's Politics," 168.

29. Ibid., 169.

30. Ibid., 175.

31. See the essays contained in Alan Milchman and Alan Rosenberg, eds., *Foucault and Heidegger: Critical Encounters* (Minneapolis: University of Minnesota Press, 2003). Additional works of this sort include: Hinrich Fink-Eitel, "Zwischen Nietzsche und Heidegger: Michel Foucaults 'Sexualität und Wahr-

heit' im Spiegel neuerer Sekundärliteratur," *Philosophisches Jahrbuch* 97.2 (1990): 367–90; Rainer Forst, "Endlichkeit, Freiheit, Indiviualität: Die Sorge um das Selbst bei Heidegger und Foucault," *Ethos der Moderne: Foucaults Kritik der Aufklärung*, ed. Eva Erdmann, Rainer Forst, Axel Honneth (Frankfurt am Main: Campus Verlag, 1990); Neil Levy, "The Prehistory of Archaeology: Heidegger and the Early Foucault," *Journal of the British Society for Phenomenology* 27.2 (May 1996): 157–71; William McNeil, "Care for the Self: Originary Ethics in Heidegger and Foucault," *Philosophy Today*, 42.1 (1998): 53–64; Allan Megill, *Prophets of Extremity: Nietzsche, Heidegger, Foucault, Derrida* (Berkeley: University of California Press, 1985); Jana Sawicki, "Heidegger and Foucault: Escaping Technological Nihilism," *Philosophy and Social Criticism* 13.2 (1987): 155–73; Michael Schwartz, "Critical Reproblematization: Foucault and the Task of Modern Philosophy," *Radical Philosophy*, no. 91 (September–October 1998): 19–31; William V. Spanos, *Heidegger and Criticism: Retrieving the Cultural Politics of Destruction* (Minneapolis: University of Minnesota Press, 1993), esp. chap. 5; Rudi Visker, "From Foucault to Heidegger: A One-Way Ticket?" *Research in Phenomenology* 21 (1991): 116–40; Krzysztof Ziarek, "Powers That Be: Art and Technology in Heidegger and Foucault," *Research in Phenomenology* 28 (1998): 162–94. For a unique and personalized account, one which insists upon a fundamental incommensurability between Heidegger and Foucault, see Paul Veyne, *Foucault: Sa pensée, sa personne* (Paris: Albin Michel, 2008), chap. 6.

32. This is outlined in considerably more detail in Chapter Four.

33. For a biographical account of Heidegger's influence on Foucault via the former's debate with Sartre, see James Miller, *The Passion of Michel Foucault* (New York: Simon and Schuster, 1993), 46–51.

34. *Michel Foucault: Remarks on Marx, Conversations with Duccio Trombadori*, trans. R. James Goldstein and James Cascaito (New York: Semiotext(e), 1991), 72.

35. "Philosophy and the Death of God," *RC*, 85–86. Originally published as "Qu'est-ce'un philosophe?" in *Connaissance des hommes*, no. 22 (Autumn 1966): 9. Reprinted in *DE1*, 552–53.

36. Michel Foucault, "Subjectivity and Truth," in *The Politics of Truth*, ed. Sylvère Lotringer (New York: Semiotext(e), 1997), 178–79.

37. "C'est plutôt . . . du côté de Heidegger et à partir de Heidegger que j'ai essayé de réfléchir à tout ça" (*Herm.*, 189).

38. Dreyfus and Rabinow, *Michel Foucault: Beyond Structuralism and Hermeneutics*, 2nd ed. (Chicago: University of Chicago Press, 1983).

39. Michel Foucault, "Truth, Power, Self," in *Technologies of the Self: A Seminar with Michel Foucault*, ed. Luther Martin, Huck Gutman, and Patrick Hutton (Amherst: University of Massachusetts Press, 1988), 12 ff.

40. "When I was a student in the 1950s, I read Husserl, Sartre, Merleau-Ponty. When you feel an overwhelming influence, you try to open a window. Paradoxically enough, Heidegger is not very difficult for a Frenchman to understand. When every word is an enigma, you are in a not-too-bad position to understand

Heidegger. *Being and Time* is difficult, but the more recent works are clearer. Nietzsche was a revelation to me. I felt that there was someone quite different from what I had been taught. I read him with a great passion and broke with my life, left my job in the asylum, left France: I had the feeling I had been trapped. Through Nietzsche, I had become a stranger to all that." Ibid., 9–15, 12–13.

41. Klossowski, *Nietzsche et le cercle vicieux* (Paris: Mercure de France, 1969).

42. Evidence that Foucault was already very familiar and influenced by Klossowski can be found in his 1964 essay "The Prose of Actaeon," *EW2*, 123–35. Foucault once described *Nietzsche et le cercle vicieux*, in a letter to Klossowski, as "the greatest book of philosophy I have read in addition to Nietzsche himself." Quoted in translator's preface to Pierre Klossowski, *Nietzsche and the Vicious Circle*, trans. Daniel Smith (Chicago: University of Chicago Press, 1998).

43. Tom Rockmore, *Heidegger and French Philosophy: Humanism, Antihumanism, and Being* (London: Routledge, 1995), 130.

44. Michel Foucault, *Lectures on "The Will to Know" and "Oedipal Knowledge,"* trans. Graham Burchell (New York: Palgrave Macmillan, 2013); *Leçons sur "La volonté de savoir" et "Le savoir d'Oedipe"* (Paris: Seuil, 2011). For the interpretation in relation to Heidegger, see the editor's footnotes and essay by Daniel Defert, "Course Context," 262–86.

45. Louis Althusser, *The Future Lasts Forever*, trans. Richard Veasey (New York: New Press, 1992), 176; *L'avenir dure longtemps* (Stock/IMEC, 1992), 168.

46. This reading of influence is supported by Hans Sluga, "Foucault's Encounter with Heidegger and Nietzsche," in *The Cambridge Companion to Foucault*, 2nd ed., ed. Gary Gutting (Cambridge: Cambridge University Press, 2003), 210–39; and Samuel Ijsseling, "Foucault with Heidegger," *Man and World* 19 (1986): 413–24. It appears to contradict, for instance, Paul Rabinow's claim that "Foucault's encounter with Heidegger was in the existential Dasein stage." Paul Rabinow, "Modern and Counter-Modern: Ethos and Epoch in Heidegger and Foucault," in *The Cambridge Companion to Foucault*, ed. Gutting, 197–214.

CHAPTER TWO: POTENTIALITY AND AUTHENTICITY

1. Charles Taylor, "Engaged Agency and Background in Heidegger," in *The Cambridge Companion to Heidegger*, ed. Charles Guigon (Cambridge: Cambridge University Press, 2006), 202.

2. Although not discussed in this section, it is perhaps important to note that as seemingly obvious as this claim is (i.e., that one is always already in a world), Heidegger is actually making a rather bold statement contrary to the Cartesian and Kantian tradition of thought. First, if Being-in-the-world is a priori and grounds knowledge, then ontology is prior to epistemology. Second, the entire problem of a subject-object distinction is dissolved, as such a subject must already be in a world that it is engaged in for it to even encounter an object as a problem for knowledge. More will be said about this in latter sections of the book relating Heidegger and Foucault to Kant.

3. Note that, in later works, Heidegger diversifies this rather simplistic (though nevertheless helpful) dualism of modes of relating to other beings. In the lectures between 1935 and 1936, for example, Heidegger expands the basic distinction between "thing" and "equipment" to include also "art" and "work."

4. *Befindlichkeit* is difficult to translate from German to English, as both major translations of *Sein und Zeit* attest. First, *Befindlichkeit* has an obvious, common usage in everyday German, as in the question: *Wie befinden Sie sich?* or "How are you? How are you doing?" This means that what could literally be rendered as "How do you find yourself?" is often just translated as "How are you?" the key here being that the verb *Sich Befinden* is made synonymous with *Sein* when translated, which, in this context, is clearly problematic. If one were to translate *Sich Befinden* into French, one would at least have recourse to *Se trouver*.

Second, there are few words in English that can convey a general state of being without importing a psychological or cognitive emphasis. The Macquarrie and Robinson translation (*BTa*) renders *Befindlichkeit* as "State-of-Mind." This is, to my thinking, a good example of importing a cognitive emphasis which Heidegger clearly does intend. By "cognitive emphasis," I mean that *Befindlichkeit* clearly does not refer to a purely mental state. Joan Stambaugh (*BTb*) translates *Befindlichkeit* as "Attunement." Although this is certainly an adequate translation of the term, it runs up against the difficulty of being differentiated from uses of *Gestimmtsein*, which is "Having a Mood" or, sometimes translated also as "to be attuned."

We can see this problem arise in translating, for example, the following passage: "Die Gestimmtheit der Befindlichkeit konstituiert existenzial die Weltoffenheit des Daseins" (*SZ* §29, 137). The Macquarrie and Robinson translation is: "Dasein's openness to the world is constituted existentially by the attunement of a state-of-mind" (*BTa* §29, 176), while Stambaugh translates: "The moodedness of attunement constitutes existentially the openness to world of Da-sein" (*BTb* §29, 129). The word *attunement* has been reversed between the two translations. In Macquarrie and Robinson, it is used for *Gestimmtheit*, while for Stambaugh it is used for *Befindlichkeit*, which necessitates a new (and awkward) term, *moodedness*, for *Gestimmtheit*.

It seems to me that the most literal rendering of *Befindlichkeit* would be "the state or condition one finds oneself in." Although this is clearly long and awkward in English, it is important in the context of the specific discussion above to carefully distinguish between a state-of-mind, a mood, and a more general, *precognitive* condition in which one finds oneself (which includes not only mental states, psychological conditions, but also the world, its equipment, things and other human beings).

The importance of this is clear when we take, for example, another important section: "Seiendes vom Charakter des Daseins ist sein Da in der Weise, daß es sich, ob ausdrücklich oder nicht, in seiner Geworfenheit befindet. In der Befindlichkeit ist das Dasein immer schon vor es selbst gebracht, es hat sich immer schon gefunden, *nicht* als *wahrnehmendes* Sich-vorfinden, sondern als gestimmtes Sichbefinden" (*SZ* §29, 135; italics added). My translation: "An entity of the character of Dasein is its 'there' in such a way that, whether explicitly or not, it finds itself [sich befindet] in its thrownness. In this condition of being found [Befindlichkeit] Dasein is always brought before itself, and has always already found itself, *not* through a coming before itself in *perception*, but rather as a finding itself [sich befinden] as being in a mood [gestimmtes]."

5. "Aus *der her Angehendes begegnen kann*" (*SZ* §29, 137–38; italics in original).

6. "Das Gestimmtsein dezieht sich nicht zunächst auf Seelisches, ist selbst kein Zustand drinnen, der dann auf rätselhafte Weise hinausgelangt und auf die Dinge und Personen abfärbt" (*SZ* §29, 137). Translation: "Having a mood is not related to the psychical in the first instance, and is not itself an inner condition which then reaches forth in an enigmatical way and puts its mark on Things and persons" (*BTa* §29, 176).

7. See note 4.

8. Michael Gelven, *A Commentary on Heidegger's "Being and Time,"* rev. ed. (DeKalb: Northern Illinois University Press, 1989), 86–87.

9. "Sie wirft nicht gleichsam über das nackte Vorhandene eine 'Bedeutung' und beklebt es nicht mit einem Wert, sondern mit dem innerweltlichen Begegnenden als solchem hat es je schon eine im Weltverstehen ershlossene Bewandtnis, die durch die Auslegung herausgelegt wird" (*SZ* §32, 150).

10. Thus, one target for Heidegger is (from his perspective) the neo-Kantian rationalist fallacy of attributing meaning to propositions—understanding meaning as something "added on" to understanding when interpretation is explicitly theorized.

11. My translation. See *BTa* §31, 184–85, and *BTb* §31, 136, for comparison.

12. Stambaugh, for instance, glosses over the term completely in her translation of the passage quoted above from §31, rendering "Der Entwurf is die existenziale Seinsverfassung des Spielraums des faktischen Seinkönnens," as: "Project is the existential constitution of being in the realm of factical potentiality for being" (*BTb* §31, 136).

13. Hubert Dreyfus, *Being-in-the-World: A Commentary on Heidegger's "Being and Time," Division I* (Cambridge, Mass.: MIT Press, 1991), 189.

14. Ibid., 190–91.

15. Here, Heidegger is arguing that the recognition that death cannot be by-passed, both in the sense of an event that cannot be avoided but also as something which cannot be surpassed in importance to determining meaning for living possibilities. Stambaugh's decision to translate *unüberholbar* as "not-to-be-by-passed" rather than "not to be outstripped" perhaps better preserves these two senses of the term insofar as Heidegger is using it to characterize death existentially.

16. This seeing oneself as "objectlike" we will return to in the last chapter through a discussion of reification.

17. "Ein Mensch ist in einem Zimmer *gefangen,* wenn die Tür unversperrt ist, sie nach innen öffnet; er aber nicht auf die Idee kommt zu *ziehen,* statt gegen sie zu drücken." Ludwig Wittgenstein, *Culture and Value,* trans. Peter Winch (Chicago: University of Chicago Press, 1980), 42; my translation, italics in original.

18. The Stambaugh translation has rendered *sich zueigen ist* as "belongs to itself" (*BTb* §9, 40).

19. On the connection between authentic, *autos,* and "done by one's own," see Michael Inwood, *A Heidegger Dictionary* (Oxford: Blackwell, 1999), 23.

20. Whether such acknowledgment can be translated directly into *any* sort of politics, we return to consider in Chapters Three and Seven.

CHAPTER THREE: THE FIELD OF FREEDOM

The epigraph to this chapter is drawn from *The Phenomenology of Perception* (New York: Routledge, 1945), 510.

1. "Vom Wesen des Grundes" was written in 1928, published in *Festschrift für Edmund Husserl zum 70. Geburtstag* (Halle, 1929), and again in *GA,* vol. 9. Historical information on this and other lectures and courses is from Alfred Denker, *Historical Dictionary of Heidegger's Philosophy* (Landam, Md.: Scarecrow, 2000), unless otherwise noted.

2. "Vom Wesen der menchlichen Freiheit: Einleitung in die Philosophie" was offered as a course in 1930 and published in *GA,* vol. 31.

3. "Vom Wesen der Wahrheit" was probably Heidegger's most important piece from the publication of *Being and Time* to the end of World War II; it was certainly the piece that occupied most of his time. It was originally offered as a lecture at Marburg in 1926, then again in Karlsruhe 1930. This version was published in *Nachlese zu Heidegger,* ed. Guido Schneeberger (Bern: Suhr, 1962). A revised version of the essay was delivered in Bremen 1930 and Freiburg 1930, published in *GA,* vol. 9. A course by the same title was offered in 1931–32, given as a lecture in Dresden in 1932 and published in *GA,* vol. 34. Another revised version of the topic was offered as a course in 1933–34, published in *GA,* vols. 36–37, and published by Heidegger in 1943 (Frankfurt am Main).

4. "Schelling: Vom Wesen der menschlichen Freiheit" was offered as a course in 1936 and was published twice: once in Tübingen (1971) and then in *GA,* vol. 42.

5. "Logik" was presented during summer semester of 1928 and is published in *GA,* vol. 26.

6. "To be sure, philosophizing—and it especially—must always proceed through a rigorous conceptual knowledge and must remain in the medium of that knowledge, but this knowledge is grasped in its genuine content only when in such knowledge the whole of existence is seized by the root after which philosophy searches—in and by *freedom*" (*MFL,* 18).

7. For one of the few secondary commentators to read *Being and Time*

through the question of freedom, see Béatrice Han-Pile, "Freedom and the 'Choice to Choose Oneself' in *Being and Time*," in *The Cambridge Companion to Being and Time*, ed. Mark Wrathall (Cambridge: Cambridge University Press, 2013), 291–319.

8. Fred Dallmayr, "Ontology of Freedom: Heidegger and Political Philosophy," *Political Theory* 12.2 (May 1984): 204–34; 208.

9. Ibid.

10. Jürgen Habermas, *Philosophisch-politische Profile* (Frankfurt am Main: Suhrhamp, 1971), 81–82. Elsewhere Habermas condemns *Being and Time* for promoting "the decisionism of empty resoluteness," in *The Philosophical Discourse of Modernity* (Cambridge, Mass.: MIT Press, 1987), 141.

11. Cited and discussed further in Dallmayr, "Ontology of Freedom," 208.

12. Johanna Oksala, *Foucault, Politics, and Violence* (Evanston, Ill.: Northwestern University Press, 2012), 5.

13. Detailed in Chapter Two.

14. This phrase is taken from Günter Figal, "An Essay on Freedom: Ontological Considerations from a Practical Point of View," in *For a Philosophy of Freedom and Strife*, trans. Wayne Kline (Albany: State University of New York Press, 1998), 16.

15. Stephen Mulhall, *Heidegger and "Being and Time"* (London: Routledge, 1996), 96.

16. Charles Taylor puts this point as follows: "We can't turn the background against which we think into an object for us. The task of reason has to be conceived quite differently: as that of articulating the background, 'disclosing' what it involves. This may open the way to detaching ourselves from or altering part of what has constituted it—may, indeed, make such alteration irresistible; but only through our unquestioning reliance on the rest." In "Overcoming Epistemology," *Philosophical Arguments* (Cambridge, Mass.: Harvard University Press, 1995), 12.

17. See, for instance, Charles Taylor's use of Heidegger in "Overcoming Epistemology," "Lichtung or Lebensform: Parallels Between Heidegger and Wittgenstein," "To Follow a Rule," in *Philosophical Arguments*.

18. Note here that "scientific knowledge" is a translation of *wissenshaftliche Erkenntnis* and should be taken in the broadest sense of both terms *scientific* and *knowledge*. That is to say, Heidegger is not talking about "science" in the narrow sense as it is used in modern English (i.e., natural and mathematical sciences, as opposed to the humanities), but in the sense of general reflexive thematized knowledge.

19. In the William McNeil translation of "On the Essence of Ground" found in *Pathmarks* (Cambridge: Cambridge University Press, 1998), the terms are translated as such: *abstecken* = "marks out"; *verfestigen* = "anchors"; and *umgrenzen* = "governs." I don't see the need for these less literal translations.

20. Although "binding" and "obligation" are good translations for these

terms, in this context we might also point to the notions of "connection" and "commitment." This might convey better the sense that, in setting out a range or field of possibility, the "worlding" of the "world" is not a system of governance in the sense of a dictate from someone (or something) to Dasein. Rather, in rendering the world intelligible to Dasein, this process also lays out a series of connections between things, as well as a general commitment which disposes Dasein to comport itself more in some ways than others. Thus, the process "guides" and "shapes" Dasein's thinking and acting without in anyway "obliging," or "forcing."

21. The link between projection's function in marking out a "determinate field" [*bestimmtes Feld*] and the general condition of facticity as an existential of Dasein can be seen by pointing to Heidegger's earlier characterization of Dasein's as defined by its "determinate being" [*Seinsbestimmtheit*] in the section on facticity in *Being and Time* (BT §12).

22. On this theme, see Han-Pile, "Freedom and the 'Choice to Choose Oneself' in *Being and Time*."

23. Maurice Merleau-Ponty, *The Phenomenology of Perception* (New York: Routledge, 1945), 509; italics added.

24. In his critique of Isaiah Berlin's concept of negative liberty, Charles Taylor drew similar conclusions. He wrote, "[The] recourse to signification takes us beyond a Hobbesian scheme. Freedom is no longer just the absence of external obstacle *tout court*, but the absence of external obstacle to *significant* action, to what is important to man. . . . Thus the application even of our negative notion of freedom *requires a background condition of what is significant*, according to which some restrictions are seen to be without relevance for freedom altogether, and others are judged as being of greater and lesser importance." In "What's Wrong with Negative Liberty?" in *Philosophical Papers*, vol. 2, *Philosophy and the Human Sciences* (Cambridge: Cambridge University Press, 1985), 211–29; 218–19 (italics added). Of course, Taylor was himself also strongly influenced by Heidegger. I have written on this topic in "The World of Negative Liberty: Reading Berlin Though Weak Ontology," in *Isaiah Berlin and the Politics of Freedom*, ed. Bruce Baum and Robert Nichols (New York: Routledge, 2012), 216–30.

25. Richard Rorty, "Heidegger, Contingency, and Pragmatism," in *Philosophical Papers*, vol. 2, *Essays on Heidegger and Others: Philosophical Papers* (Cambridge: Cambridge University Press, 1991), 27–49 at 43.

26. William Connolly, *Identity/Difference* (Minneapolis: University of Minnesota Press, 1991), 32–33.

27. Figal, "Essay on Freedom," 18.

28. In this sense at least, the "forms of life" or "worlds" serve the same function as the transcendental subject in Kant. Just as the transcendental subject ordered and formed both the intuitions of things in space and time and inner intuitions of the empirical self for Kant, so too does understanding form the world, within which we find things, others, and ourselves for Heidegger.

29. Rorty helpfully phrases it thusly: "But *what* is forgotten when we forget the 'openness of beings'? Heidegger's familiar and unhelpful answer is 'Being.' A slightly more complex and helpful answer is: that it was Dasein using language which let beings be in the first place." Rorty, "Heidegger, Contingency, and Pragmatism," 45. The fact that it was "Dasein using language which let beings be in the first place" relates back to my response to the first imagined objection to potentiality as a feature of ontological freedom, which, I argued, relied implicitly upon a distinction between the thing-in-itself and the thing-under-description.

30. The language of "absolutization" may be misleading in naming the phenomenon at issue here because it risks presenting the problem of metaphysics as something that humans *do* or *don't do*, rather than a condition, situation or relationship to the world in which we find ourselves.

31. Julian Young, *Heidegger's Later Philosophy* (Cambridge: Cambridge University Press, 2002), 28–29.

32. Leslie Paul Thiele, *Timely Meditations: Martin Heidegger and Postmodern Politics* (Princeton, N.J.: Princeton University Press, 1995), 71.

33. The problem with the language of "values," Heidegger states, is that it is both "subjectivist" and, paradoxically, objectifying of nonhuman reality: "By the assessment of something as a value what is valued is admitted only as an object for human estimation" (*P*, 265; *GA*, 9: 349).

34. To this end, Heidegger concludes the *Letter* by saying, "It is time to break the habit of overestimating philosophy and of thereby asking too much of it. What is needed in the present world crisis is less philosophy, but more attentiveness in thinking; less literature, but more cultivation of the letter" (*P*, 276; *GA*, 9: 364). In the conclusion to this chapter and then again in Chapter Seven, we relate this concern with a Marxist critique of "reification" as a similarly dual-sided phenomenon.

35. A theme which will reappear in many later thinker's work, Foucault included.

36. "The human being is not the lord of being. The human being is the shepherd of being" (*P*, 260; *GA*, 9: 342).

37. Béatrice Han, "Foucault and Heidegger on Kant and Finitude," in *Foucault and Heidegger: Critical Encounters*, ed. Alan Milchman and Alan Rosenberg (Minneapolis: University of Minnesota Press, 2003), 151.

38. Despite anticipating this objection, Heidegger's rather quick gloss over the matter of natality has not shielded him from criticism of this sort. A well-known example of this criticism comes from Paul Ricoeur, who enlists Arendt: "The silence of *Being and Time* regarding the phenomenon of birth . . . is surprising. . . . I wish to mention the theme of 'natality' which, according to Arendt in *The Human Condition*, underlies the categories of the *vita activa*: labor, work, action. Should not this jubilation be opposed to what does indeed seem to be an obsession of metaphysics with the problem of death . . . does not the anguished

obsession with death amount to closing off the reserve of openness characterizing the potentiality of being? Must one not then explore the resources of the experience of the potentiality of being?" Ricoeur, *Memory, History, Forgetting* (Chicago: University of Chicago Press, 2006), 357. While Ricoeur is correct of course that *The Human Condition* shifts focus away from the Heideggerian emphasis on being-toward-death toward natality, it is also necessary to attend to Arendt's revised conception itself. Natality does not function as one end of a temporally stretched structure of being-in-the-world (at the other end of which stands death), but rather functions as a kind of radical inaugural event and thus break from linear, mechanistic temporal succession. Arendt is not talking about the kind of "Being-toward-the-beginning" mentioned by Heidegger in §72 of *Being and Time*. As she puts it,

> With word and deed we insert ourselves into the human world, and this insertion is like a second birth, in which we confirm and take upon ourselves the naked fact of our original physical appearance.... Its impulse springs from the beginning which came into the world when we were born and to which we respond by beginning something new on our own initiative. To act, in its most general sense, means to take an initiative, to begin ... to set something in motion.... Because they are *initium,* newcomers and beginners by virtue of birth, men take initiative, are prompted into action." (Hannah Arendt, *The Human Condition*, 2nd ed. [Chicago: University of Chicago Press, 1998], 177)

In this way, and despite important differences in their approaches, far from being a total break with Heidegger, Arendt's novel thematization of natality links up surprisingly well with Marcuse's creative rendering of Resoluteness in terms of radical action (discussed at length below).

39. Here I have chosen not to follow Macquarrie and Robinson's preference for translating *Geschichtlichkeit* as "historicality," simply because I find the term too cumbersome. However, some confusion may arise here, for two reasons. First, the meaning Heidegger attributes to *Geschichtlichkeit* changes somewhat from his early to later writings. In *Being and Time*, for instance, *Geschichtlichkeit* refers to the condition of "being historical." It gets at what it means for something to be a "historical" object, for instance. However, in later works, as Heidegger comes to recognize that our fundamental experience and understanding of reality itself changes over time, he comes to use to the term to refer to this more radical position on an authentic historizing of ontology or the question of being itself. In short, *Geschichtlichkeit* moves from referring to the "being of history" to the "history of being" [*Seinsgeschichte*]. A second set of confusions arise because other, post-Heideggerian philosophers, as well as English-language translators, have used the terms *historicality* and *historicity* to refer to both understandings of *Geschichtlichkeit*, making it difficult to track in which sense the term is employed. (For an example, see the note below on Marcuse's *Hegels Ontologie und die Theorie der Geschichtlichkeit*, n. 44.) For my purposes, I have used *historicity* to refer to *Geschichtlichkeit* in *Sein und Zeit*, and *authentic historicizing*

to refer to the grasping and disclosing of the "history of being." For a helpful commentary on these issues, see Iain Thomson, "Heidegger and National Socialism," in *A Companion to Heidegger*, ed. Hubert Dreyfus and Mark Wrathall (London: Blackwell, 2005), 32–48, at 45 n. 8.

40. Discussed in SZ §76–77. For a close study of the major debates around "historicity" leading up to and informing *Being and Time*, see Jeffrey Barash, *Martin Heidegger and the Problem of Historical Meaning* (New York: Fordham University Press, 2003).

41. *Of Time and Being*, trans. Joan Stambaugh (New York: Harper and Row, 1972), 24; *Zur Sache des Denkens* (GA, vol. 14), 25.

42. See Chapter One.

43. These essays have been translated and collected (along with a few more recently writings and interviews) by Richard Wolin and John Abromeith, eds., in *Heideggerian Marxism* (Lincoln: University of Nebraska Press, 2005). Hereafter cited in text as "Marcuse, [page no.]."

44. First published as *Hegels Ontologie und die Grundlegung einer Theorie der Geschichtlichkeit* (1932), and again later under the slightly amended title *Hegels Ontologie und die Theorie der Geschichtlichkeit* (Frankfurt am Main: Vittorio Klostermann, 1968); translated into English by Seyla Benhabib as *Hegel's Ontology and the Theory of Historicity* (Cambridge, Mass.: MIT Press, 1987). Note that although the title is translated here using the term *historicity* and not *historicality*, it is referencing the same notion of *Geschichtlichkeit* discussed in Division II of *Being and Time*. See the discussion in note 40.

45. For a general study of the relationship between Heidegger and Marcuse, see Andrew Feenberg, *Heidegger and Marcuse: The Catastrophe and Redemption of History* (New York: Routledge, 2005); Alfred Schmidt, "Existential Ontology and Historical Materialism in the Work of Herbert Marcuse," in *Marcuse: Critical Theory and the Promise of Utopia*, ed. Robert Pippin, Andrew Feenberg, and Charles P. Webel (South Hadley, Mass.: Bergin and Garvey, 1988), 47–67; and John Abromeit, "Herbert Marcuse's Critical Encounter with Martin Heidegger: 1927–1933," in *Herbert Marcuse: A Critical Reader*, ed. John Abromeit and William Mark Cobb (New York: Routledge, 2004), 131–51.

46. "All genuine knowledge is, in the most profound sense, 'practical' knowledge, in that it brings a human Dasein 'into the truth'" (Marcuse, 9).

47. In this regard, Marcuse approvingly enlists Dilthey, citing him: "But it must be acknowledged that the background of these ideas is a kind of a raw power that cannot be overcome by this higher world. And this is always the case. The facticity of race, of space, and of power-relations provides a matrix that can never be wholly brought under the power of spirit" (Marcuse, 16–17). The Dilthey quote is taken from *Der Aufbau der geschichtlichen Welt in den Geisteswissenschaften* (Leipzig: Teubner, 1927), 287–88.

48. Elsewhere, Marcuse makes a similar point directly employing Heideggerian terminology: "Human Dasein does not exist on the basis of knowing,

but rather on the basis of fateful happening in a particular situation in the shared and surrounding world [Mit- und Umwelt]" (Marcuse, 46).

49. Douglas Kellner has also noted this convergence. He writes, "The concept of the *radical act* stands at the center of Marcuse's theory. For Marcuse—and here we see for the first time indications of his synthesis between Heidegger and Marx—the radical act is *existential*: it aims at an alternation of the roots of existence; it intends to bring forth a fundamental change in human existence." *Herbert Marcuse and the Crisis of Marxism* (Berkeley: University of California Press, 1984), 41.

50. E.g., "The resolute taking over of one's factical 'there,' signifies, at the same time, that the Situation is one which has been resolved upon. In the existential analysis we cannot, in principle, discuss what Dasein *factically* resolves in any particular case. Our investigation excludes even the existential projection of the factical possibilities of existence. Nevertheless, we must ask whence, *in general*, Dasein can draw those possibilities upon which it factically projects itself" (BTa §74, 434; SZ §74, 382).

51. As Sartre put it in *Being and Nothingness*, "We choose the world. . . . The value of things . . . does nothing more than outline my image—that is, my choice." Elsewhere: "It is this original choice which originally creates all values and all motives which can guide us to partial actions; it is this which arranges the world with its meaning, its instrumental complexes, and its coefficient of adversity." *Being and Nothingness*, trans. H. Barnes (London: Methuen, 1969), 463, 465.

52. The original quote from Marx is taken from *The German Ideology*, in *The Marx-Engels Reader*, ed. Robert C. Tucker (New York: Norton, 1978), 160.

53. In what follows, I focus primarily on reification. For a reconstruction of alienation in contemporary practical philosophy, see Rahel Jaeggi, *Entfremdung: Zur Aktualität eines sozialphilosophischen Problems* (Frankfurt am Main: Campus Verlag, 2005).

54. We will return to this in greater detail in the concluding chapter (Chapter Seven). However, for now it is at least worth noting that a certain ambiguity slips into Marcuse's account as to whether the pathological nature of alienated or reified praxis under capitalism is located in the praxis itself or in its self-understanding. That is to say, the terms of distorted praxis sometimes refer to the activities themselves (e.g., laboring) and sometimes to the proper apprehension of them (e.g., the consciousness of the proletariat). In the later case, a superordinate distinction is introduced to parallel the one we identified in Heidegger. In Heidegger the superordinate distinction was between (a) a condition in which ontological freedom is disclosed, and (b) a condition in which it is disguised in some nontrivial manner, which remained "superordinate" because while a nontrivial distinction, it nevertheless had no bearing on the "fact" of ontological freedom itself. Instead, it was a distinction between two modes of relating to ontological freedom, not between ontological freedom and

ontological nonfreedom. In a similar manner, Marcuse oscillates between viewing the distortions of capitalism as operating at the level of praxis itself, or the level of the self-conscious apprehension of that praxis.

55. A position that is generally true of all Critical Theory in the 1930s to 1970s, as well as for Foucault. The linkage to Foucault becomes all the more apparent when we note that Marcuse took this "ground-clearing" work to require a "destructive history," akin to Foucault's notion of genealogy. E.g., "Historicity as the basic determination of Dasein demands, moreover, a 'destruction' of history as it has existed up to the present" (Marcuse, 14). Later, I shall argue that this "destructive" impulse in genealogy also has a recuperative and reconstructive dimension. This is perhaps best captured in Foucault's invocation of a critical ethos in which "the high value of the present is indissociable from a desperate eagerness to imagine it, to imagine it otherwise than it is, and to transform it *not by destroying it but by grasping it in what it is* . . . [through] an exercise in which extreme attention to what is real is confronted with the practices of a liberty that *simultaneously respects this reality and violates it*" (*EW1*, 311; *DE2*, 1389; italics added). See Chapter Six.

56. To appreciate the links to Heidegger, we need only cite the overlap between Marcuse's "Dasein '*is*' happening" with the words of *The Metaphysical Foundations of Logic*: "Dasein's transcendence and freedom are identical! Freedom provides itself with intrinsic possibility: a being is, as freed, necessarily in itself transcending" (*MFL*, 184).

57. An alternative route leading from a similar impasse is the "negative dialectics" of Theodore Adorno. However, this would take us too far afield from present concerns.

58. In a retrospective moment, Marcuse did nevertheless acknowledge that Heidegger may have in the end achieved genuine historical insights to complement his earlier fundamental ontology ("The *Frage nach dem Sein* recedes before the *Frage nach der Technik*"; Marcuse, 98), but also admitted to not knowing enough of Heidegger's later work.

59. The general relationship to Hegelian-Marxism is, however, reconsidered here in Chapter Seven through a reading of Lukács and reification theory.

60. The term *ontology of actuality* comes from Gianni Vattimo, who calls for a form of analysis that "starts with Heidegger's teaching and goes on to elaborate what might be called, using a term from Foucault's late period, an "ontology of actuality." "The expression is meant to be taken in its most literal sense: it does not simply indicate, as Foucault thought, a philosophy oriented primarily toward the consideration of existence and its historicity rather than toward epistemology and logic—that is, toward what would be called, in Foucault's terminology, an 'analytic of truth.' Rather, 'ontology of actuality' is used here to mean a discourse that attempts to clarify what Being signifies in the present situation." Gianni Vattimo, *Nihilism and Emancipation*, trans. William McCuaig (New York: Columbia University Press, 2003), 3–4.

CHAPTER FOUR: FOUCAULT CONTRA HEIDEGGER

1. See my discussion in Chapter One, part 2.

2. That is, to those who interpret and self-consciously work within the sets of questions Heidegger developed. Gadamer might be a good example here.

3. Specifically, "Dream, Imagination, and Existence," *Mental Illness and Psychiatry*, *History of Madness*, and *The Birth of the Clinic*.

4. For a detailed study of Foucault's relationship to phenomenology, including a direct relating of his work to that of Husserl and Merleau-Ponty, see Johanna Oksala, *Foucault on Freedom* (Cambridge: Cambridge University Press, 2005).

5. Keith Hoeller, Editor's foreword in *Review of Existential Psychology and Psychiatry* 19.1 (1986): 8.

6. "Interview with Michel Foucault" (*EW3*, 257). In saying this, Foucault is contrasting himself to R. D. Laing who, he says, took up such analysis in a "more Sartrean" manner.

7. Foucault, *Mental Illness and Psychology* (Berkeley: University of California Press, 1987), 46.

8. Hubert Dreyfus, *Being-in-the-World: A Commentary on Heidegger's "Being and Time," Division I* (Cambridge, Mass.: MIT Press, 1991), 177; italics in original.

9. *Traum und Existenz* was originally published in *Neue Schweizer Rundshau* (Zurich: Fretz u. Wasmuth), vol. 23: 673–85, 1930, and reprinted in Ludwig Binswanger, *Ausgewählte Worträge und Aufsätze* (Bern: A. Francke, 1947), 74–97. The French translation for which Foucault wrote "Dream, Imagination and Existence" is *Le rêve et l'existence* (Paris: Éditions Desclée De Brouwer, 1954), published in the series *Textes et Études Anthropologiques*. Information on publication dates comes from Keith Hoeller, editor's foreword, and Forrest Williams, translator's preface in *Review of Existential Psychology and Psychiatry* 19.1 (1986): 7–17 and 19–27.

10. Derrida has also noted this association. See "Être juste avec Freud," in *Penser la folie: Essais sur Michel Foucault*, ed. Michel Delorne (Paris: Galilée, 1992), 180.

11. Foucault continues this line of reasoning in *The History of Madness*, particularly in chapter 1, "*Stultifera Navis*," where he links the rise of a modern conception of madness to transformations in our understanding of death.

12. The standard English translation of *Naissance de la clinique* was first published in 1973 (*BC*) and is based upon a revised version of the original text. Thus, the translation is not based on the original French text, which reads:

> C'est lorsque la mort s'est intégrée épistémologiquement à l'experience médicale que la maladie a pu se detacher de la contre-nature et *prendre corps* dans le *corps vivant* des individus.
>
> Il restera sans doute decisive pour notre culture que le premier discourse scientifique tenu par elle sur l'individu ait dû passer par ce moment de la mort . . .

Et d'une façon générale, l'expérience de l'individualité dans la culture moderne est peut-être liée à celle de la mort: des cadavers ouverts de Bichet à l'homme freudien, un rapport obstiné à la mort prescript à l'universel son visage singulier et prête à la parole de chacun le pouvoir d'être indéfiniment entendue; l'individu lui doit un sens qui ne s'arrête pas avec lui." (NC, 201)

13. John Caputo, "On Not Knowing Who We Are: Madness, Hermeneutics, and the Night of Truth in Foucault," in *More Radical Hermeneutics* (Bloomington: Indiana University Press, 2000), 17–40 at 24.

14. David Hoy, "Heidegger and the Hermeneutic Turn," in *The Cambridge Companion to Heidegger*, ed. Charles Guigon (Cambridge: Cambridge University Press, 1993), 174.

15. In the section the follows, I have deliberately focused on the *juxtaposition* of Foucault and hermeneutic philosophy, to the exclusion of possible overlapping concerns, in order to draw the contrast as starkly as possible. This should not be taken as a commitment to the notion that *no* such overlaps exist, however. For a careful study of such connections, see Hans Herbert Kögler, *The Power of Dialogue: Critical Hermeneutics After Gadamer and Foucault* (Cambridge, Mass.: MIT Press, 1996).

16. In fact, Heidegger readily concedes this "infinite task." The circle of interpretation is not merely a negative loop in his hermeneutic phenomenology. Rather, it is the basis on which understanding unfolds within the condition of ontological freedom. As Heidegger writes,

> This circle of understanding is not an orbit in which any random kind of knowledge may move; it is the expression of the existential *fore-structure* of Dasein itself. It is not to be reduced to the level of a vicious circle, or even of a circle which is merely tolerated. In the circle is hidden a positive possibility of the most primordial kind of knowing. To be sure, we genuinely take hold of this possibility only when, in our interpretation, we have understood that our first, last, and constant task is never to allow our fore-having, fore-sight, and fore-conception to be presented to us by fancies and popular conceptions, but rather to make the scientific theme secure by working out these fore-structures in terms of the things themselves. (BTa §32, 195; SZ §32, 153)

17. For a detailed genealogy of confessional practices, see Chloë Taylor, *The Culture of Confession from Augustine to Foucault: A Genealogy of the "Confessing Animal"* (New York: Routledge, 2008).

18. These practices are discussed in more detail in Chapter Six as "spiritual activities."

19. Hubert Dreyfus and Paul Rabinow, *Michel Foucault: Beyond Structuralism and Hermeneutics*, 2nd ed. (Chicago: University of Chicago Press, 1983), 174.

20. Key to my argument in the final section of this work will be the claim that the function of the "original man" as foundation, corrective tool, and interpretive key is taken over by the transcendental subject in Kant.

CHAPTER FIVE: FOUCAULT'S "AUTOCRITIQUE"

The epigraph to this chapter is drawn from Hannah Arendt, *The Human Condition*, 2nd ed. (Chicago: University of Chicago Press, 1998), 104–5.

1. In Foucault's own words: "Since I started this last type of project [a genealogy of the subject] I had to change my mind on several important points. Let me introduce a kind of autocritique" (*RC*, 161).

2. For instance, Judith Butler's notion of performativity appears to owe a considerable debt to a reading of Foucault along these lines. She defines "performativity" as "a reiteration of a norm or set of norms . . . [that] conceals or dissimulates the conventions of which it is a repetition" and states that her work "accepts as a point of departure Foucault's notion that regulatory power produces the subject it controls, that power is not only imposed externally, but works as the regulatory and normative means by which subjects are formed." *Bodies That Matter* (New York: Routledge, 1993), 12, 22.

3. An example here might be Richard Rorty's reading of Foucault as "an up-to-date version of John Dewey." In other words, as another "good liberal." See his "Moral Identity and Private Autonomy: The Case of Foucault," in *Philosophical Papers*, vol. 2, *Essays on Heidegger and Others* (Cambridge: Cambridge University Press, 1991), 193–94. See also his suggestion that we "assimilate" Foucault's books "into a liberal, reformist political culture." See Richard Rorty, *Contingency, Irony, Solidarity* (Cambridge: Cambridge University Press, 1989), 64.

4. That Foucault saw the metaphor of war as central to the whole of *Discipline and Punish* is evidenced by the concluding lines: "In this central and centralized humanity, the effect and instrument of complex power relations, bodies and forces subjected by multiple mechanisms of 'incarceration', objects for discourses that are in themselves elements for this strategy, we must hear the distant roar of battle" (*DP*, 308; *SP*, 360).

We might also look to the 1976 interview, "Truth and Power," in which Foucault says, "one's point of reference should not be to the great model of language [langue] and signs but, rather, to that of war and battle. The history that bears and determines us has the form of a war rather than that of a language—relations of power, not relations of meaning" (*EW3*, 116).

5. In "Truth and Power," Foucault describes his aim "to dispense with the constituent subject, to get rid of the subject itself, that's to say, to arrive at an analysis that can account for the constitution of the subject within a historical framework. And this is what I would call genealogy, that is, a form of history that can account for the constitutions of knowledges, discourses, domains of objects, and so on, without having to make reference to a subject that is either transcendental in relation to the field of events or runs in its empty sameness throughout the course of history" (*EW3*, 118).

6. A classic example of this from Foucault's work is sexuality. Along with changes in nationalism, capitalism, and imperialism in early modern European governance, the emergence of "biopolitics" saw an increased preoccupation

with how to raise and maintain a large, healthy population from which one could select excellent soldiers, laborers, and the like. This led to the proliferation of a host of political technologies of governance, such as population surveys, birth control methods, infant mortality studies, and so on. In their inception, these practices were really localized, targeted strategies with specific aims. However, into the eighteenth and nineteenth centuries, "the notion of 'sex' made it possible to group together, in an artificial unity, anatomical elements, biological functions, conducts, sensations, and pleasures, and it enabled one to make use of this fictitious unity as a causal principle" (*HS1*, 154; *VS*, 204). "Sexuality," as a central feature of subjectivity and identity, only becomes possible once this transformation has occurred. Now, within this general domain, there has always been a hierarchical ordering of various kinds of sexuality and a differential governance in relation to this ordering. Those marked as "homosexuals" have, for instance, resisted their differential status within the general typology. What Foucault warns us of, however, is that this resistance—insofar as it is a kind of tactical reversal of specific strategies of governance deployed against homosexuals (say, the struggle to decriminalize sex between men)—can simultaneously *reinforce* the general regime of power (i.e., "sexuality" itself), since the general regime depends centrally on the close association of subjectivity and sex-desire (whether it is deployed "for" or "against" any particular, localized governance practice). Cf. Ladelle McWhorter, *Bodies and Pleasures: Foucault and the Politics of Sexual Normalization* (Bloomington: Indiana University Press, 1999).

7. This comprises the heart of Charles Taylor's critique of Foucault. See his "Foucault on Freedom and Truth," in *Philosophical Papers*, 152–84.

8. This appears to be Colin Gordon's reading. He writes, that "the facts of resistance are nevertheless assigned an irreducible role within [Foucault's] analysis. The field of strategies is a field of conflicts: the human material operated on by programmes and technologies is inherently a *resistant* material. If this were not the case, history itself would become unthinkable." Afterword to Foucault, *Power/Knowledge* (New York: Pantheon, 1980), 255. Unfortunately, Gordon never explains the existence of this "resistant material" or how precisely it escapes power. For a study of Foucault's conception of bodies, situated in relation to that of Merleau-Ponty and contemporary feminist theories, see Oksala, *Foucault on Freedom*, part 2.

9. James Miller notes the shift that took place during these lectures, but perhaps overstates the case when he writes, "Foucault begins predictably, by talking about security and bio-politics. But then, abruptly—shortly after the course had started, his associate recalls—'he stopped. He could not go on. And it was clear that this problematic, of bio-politics, was over for him—it was finished. His approach changed. But he still didn't know where he was going.'" James Miller, *The Passion of Michel Foucault* (New York: Simon and Schuster, 1993), 299.

10. Which, Foucault claims, continue on in the Classical age but not under the guise of "governance," but rather under that of security (*STP*, 7–9).

11. For instance, it plays a central role in Foucault's account of the formation of modern sexuality.

12. "Singular generality." Michel Foucault, "Manuscript on Governmentality," quoted in M. Senellart, "Situation des cours" (*SPT2*, 390; *STP*, 490).

13. The fact that Foucault almost immediately began to revise and rework the notion of governmentality seems not to have been fully explored by the "governmentality studies" group predominant in Anglo-American scholarship. This may be due to the fact that the full texts of the 1977–78 and 1978–79 lectures have not been published, much less translated into English, until quite recently. As a result, governmentality studies scholars tend to focus on the 1979 Stanford lectures *"Omnes et singulatim."* On governmentality studies in the Anglo-American context, see especially Graham Burchell, Colin Gordon, and Peter Miller, eds., *The Foucault Effect: Studies in Governmentality* (London: Harvester Wheatsheaf, 1991); Andrew Barry, Thomas Osborne, and Nikolas Rose, eds., *Foucault and Political Reason: Liberalism, Neo-Liberalism and Rationalities of Government* (London: University College, 1996); and Mitchell Dean, *Governmentality: Power and Rule in Modern Society* (London: Thousand Oaks, 1999).

14. In this way, Foucault's rendering signals a clear break with one of its immediate predecessors: Althusser's work on interpellation and/as subjection. In "Ideology and Ideological State Apparatus" (first published in 1970), Althusser developed his highly influential thesis on subjection, which shares a similar field of problematization as Foucault's *aussujettissement*. The key difference highlighted here, however, is that whereas Foucault eventually came to view freedom as a constitutive feature of subjectification, Althusser remained committed to a unidirectional account of interpellation as the mechanism by which ideology "makes" individuals: "The category of the subject is only constitutive of all ideology insofar as all ideology has the function (which defines it) of 'constituting' concrete individuals as subjects." Althusser, "Ideology and Ideological State Apparatus," in *Lenin and Philosophy and Other Essays* (New York: Monthly Review Press, 2001), 85–126, 116.

15. Locating Foucault's use of the term *conduct* here as key to the slow shift described above is supported by the reading given by the editor of Foucault's lectures, Michel Senellart. He writes, "The idea of 'counter-conduct,' in the expression advanced below, represents an essential stage in Foucault's thought, between the analysis of techniques of subjection and that, developed from 1980, of practices of subjectivation" (*STP2*, 217 n. 5; *STP*, 221 n. 5).

16. For evidence that this corresponded with a gradual reintroduction of Heidegger into Foucault's citations and references, see Chapter One.

17. My translation; italics added: "La philosophie peut-elle jouer encore un rôle du côté du contre-pouvoir . . . à condition en somme que la philosophie cesse de poser la question du pouvoir en terme de bien ou de mal, mais *en terme d'existence*." "La philosophie analytique du pouvoir" (April 27, 1978); *DE2*, 540.

18. Marc Djaballah makes a similar argument about late Foucault's reposi-

tioning relative to Kant. See his *Kant, Foucault, and the Forms of Experience* (New York: Routledge, 2008), esp. chaps. 3 and 4.

19. Jana Sawicki has commented on this as well: "It is Heidegger's contention that the Cartesian search for an absolute foundation in the subject of knowledge is itself at the root of the relentless quest for certainty and for mastery that characterizes modernity and culminates in a nihilism in which all of our options increasingly become technological and all of our values instrumental. Heidegger's notion of the "ontological difference," i.e., the difference between the clearing and what shows up in it, guarantees his escaping nihilism, for it guarantees that there are other possibilities for self-understanding (and for understanding nature) to be attained through meditative thinking." Sawicki, "Heidegger and Foucault: Escaping Technological Nihilism," *Philosophy and Social Criticism* 13.2 (1987): 168.

20. A point made by Arpad Szakolczai in *Max Weber and Michel Foucault: Parallel Life Works* (New York: Routledge, 1998).

21. These two problems, which Foucault struggled to resolve, I have referred to in the previous chapter under the headings of (1) historicizing the forms of experience as presented to the subject and (2) studying the relationship between these forms of experience and the techniques of governance within institutional practices.

22. For instance, *The Archaeology of Knowledge* specifically rejected the study of an "experience of madness" by associating it with the philosophy of the transcendental subject. In a different text, *L'ordre du discours*, Foucault restated this. There he said his aim was specifically *not* to study "experience" but rather "une volonté de savoir qui impossait au sujet connaissant (*et en quelque sorte avant toute expérience*)" (*OD*, 18–19). Translation: "a will to know imposed on the knowing subject (*and in some sense prior to all experience*)." My translation; italics added.

23. There is a third sense of "experience" beyond that offered in either early works on madness and psychiatry or late works on ethics and thought. This third sense of the term derives from the tradition that includes Nietzsche, Bataille, Blanchot, and Klossowski. This tradition, also opposed to the phenomenology of everyday life used the term "experience" to refer to a limit-state. The phenomenological tradition had been, according to Foucault, concerned with "a certain way of bringing a reflective gaze to bear on some object of "lived experience," on the everyday in its transitory form, in order to grasp its meanings." By contrast, the understanding of experience with which Foucault worked during his middle writings attempted not to reassemble the phenomenology of "everyday" life, but rather used the term "experience" to refer to an exceptional state or limit. "Experience" in this sense consists in "trying to reach a certain point in life that is as close as possible to the 'unlivable,' to that which can't be lived through." Thus, while the traditional phenomenological concept "attempts to recapture the meaning of everyday experience in order to

rediscover the sense in which the subject that I am is indeed responsible, in its transcendental functions, for founding that experience together with its meaning," Foucault's use of the term signals the "function of wrenching the subject from itself, of seeing to it that the subject is no longer itself, or that it is brought to its annihilation, or its dissolution. This is a project of desubjectivation" ("Interview with Michel Foucault," 241). For a reading of Foucault's work, and his life, as centered around such limit-experiences, see James Miller's biography, *The Passion of Michel Foucault*. Part of my reading here is to demonstrate that although this was one part of Foucault's intellectual and personal development, it certainly did not carry the universal weight that Miller accords it to the whole of his work. Rather, Foucault's understanding of "experience" was more nuanced and fluid, moved beyond the Nietzsche, Bataille, Blanchot, Klossowski reading toward one situated within the question of historical ontology.

24. There are hints that, even at the earliest stages of his work, Foucault was troubled by this question of how to integrate "thought" into an analysis of the conditions for knowledge in a given epoch. In a revealing passage of *Les mots et les choses*, Foucault admits that his analysis as formulated there cannot properly account for the capacity to think differently within *épistémè* and thus effect historical change. He confesses the importance of this question, only to defer it:

> Discontinuity—the fact that within the space of a few years a culture sometimes ceases to think as it had been thinking up till then and begins to think other things in a new way—probably begins with an erosion from outside, from that space which is, for thought, on the other side, but in which it has never ceased to think from the very beginning. Ultimately, the problem that presents itself is that of the relations between thought and culture: how is it that thought has a place in the space of the world, that it has its origin there, and that it never ceases, in this place or that, to begin anew? But perhaps it is not yet time to pose this problem; perhaps we should wait until the archaeology of thought has been established more firmly, until it is better able to gauge what it is capable of describing directly and positively, until it has defined the particular systems and internal connections it has to deal with, before attempting to encompass thought and to investigate how it contrives to escape itself. For the moment, then, let it suffice that we accept these discontinuities in the simultaneously manifest and obscure empirical order wherever they posit themselves. (*OT*, 56; *MC*, 100–101)

25. Translation amended. Original: "savoir dans quelle mesure le travail de penser sa propre histoire peut affranchir la pensée de ce qu'elle *pense silencieusement* et lui permettre de penser autrement" (*UP*, 17; italics added).

26. He even states at one point: "Thought does exist, both beyond and before systems and edifices of discourse. It is something that is often hidden but always drives everyday behaviours. There is always a little thought occurring even in the most stupid institutions; there is always thought even in silent habits.... [It] consists in seeing on what type of assumptions, of familiar notions, of established, unexamined ways of thinking the accepted practices are based"

(*EW3*, 456; *DE2*, 999). The relationship between criticism and thought here appears to reflect closely the relationship between interpretation and understanding in Heidegger.

27. This is discussed in more detail in the previous chapter.

28. Another place where Foucault seems to evoke the language of hermeneutic phenomenology is during his candidacy presentation to the Collège de France. There he poses the question of how to study "knowledge" [*savoir*], and argues that knowledge exists along a spectrum, "going from almost silent habits transmitted by tradition to duly transcribed experimentations and precepts." He states that his task it to "determine the different levels of such a knowledge, its degrees of consciousness, its possibilities of adjustment and correction. Thus, the theoretical problem that appears is that of an anonymous social knowledge [savoir] which does not take individual conscious learning [connaissance] as a model or foundation" ("Candidacy Presentation," *EW1*, 8).

29. On these connections, see Béatrice Han, *Foucault's Critical Project: Between the Transcendental and the Historical* (Stanford, Calif.: Stanford University Press, 2002), 190.

30. For a detailed study of this sort, see Edward McGushin, *Foucault's Askēsis* (Evanston, Ill.: Northwestern University Press, 2007).

31. "Interview with Michael Bess," *History of the Present*, no. 4 (Spring 1988): 2 (italics added). This interview was originally conducted in 1980.

32. Foucault, "About the Beginning of the Hermeneutics of the Self," *RC*, 161 n. 4.

33. In this respect, I diverge from the reading Hubert Dreyfus has offered of the possible similitude between *Being* in Heidegger and *power* in Foucault. Dreyfus argues that *Being* and *power* are roughly equivalent terms since *power* names, for Foucault, that on the basis of which something can appear as an entity at all. This reading seems to gloss over the way that Foucault modifies the use of the term *power* in his late writings, using it to denote a specific kind of relationship existing *within* a field of possibilities. If anything, it is this "field of possibilities" within a "historically singular form of experience" that roughly parallels Heidegger's notion of a clearing [*Lichtung*] and gestures toward ontology. See Hubert Dreyfus, "'Being and Power' Revisited," in *Foucault and Heidegger: Critical Encounters*, ed. Alan Milchman and Alan Rosenberg (Minneapolis: University of Minnesota Press, 2003), 30–54. For a detailed critique of Dreyfus along these lines, see Han, *Foucault's Critical Project*, esp. "Conclusion," 188–96.

34. "Rupture des évidences" (*DE2*, 842).

35. This emphasis on the haphazard, the conflictual, and the singular "events" of history clearly relates back to what Foucault understood by the term *genealogy* in his early works. For instance, in "Nietzsche, Genealogy, History," he stated that genealogy must "record the singularity of events outside of any monotonous finality" and argued that the possibility of change was given

only by the fact of the event; "an event, consequently, is not a decision, a treaty, a reign, or a battle, but the *reversal of a relationship of forces*, the usurpation of power, the appropriation of a vocabulary turned against those who had once used it.... The forces operating in history are not controlled by destiny or regulative mechanisms, but the luck of the battle" (*EW2*, 369, 380–81; *DE1*, 1016).

36. An example of such work might include the historical hermeneutics of Charles Taylor, for instance.

37. Translation has been amended from *UP2*. Original: "les *problématisations* à travers lesquelles l'être se donne comme pouvant et devant être pensé."

38. Han, *Foucault's Critical Project*, 194.

39. For instance, Timothy Rayner sees this "movement of problematization" as the key link to Heidegger, whereas I see it as a break with the notion of pre-ontological understanding and the critique of the constituting subject. Thus, while I focus on the ethical-spiritual transformation as the ground of ontology, Rayner focuses on philosophical activity and the attempt to grasp the historical a priori for a given domain of experience. See Timothy Rayner, *Foucault's Heidegger: Philosophy and Transformative Experience* (New York: Continuum, 2007).

40. In her work, Han hints at this possibility only to decline to take it up:

> The idea that human practices themselves support a non-reflective comprehension of the self and the world, on the basis of which all reflective interpretations are elaborated, would allow Foucault to understand problematizations independently of the intellectual activity of the constituting subject, and thus, by definition, to analyze subjectivation through the practices themselves—"techniques of the self" and "techniques of domination"—indifferently. (Han, *Foucault's Critical Project*, 191)

CHAPTER SIX: THE SUBJECT OF SPIRITUALITY

The first epigraph to this chapter is drawn from Epictetus, *The Art of Living*, trans. Sharon LeBell (New York: HarperOne, 2007), 9.

1. For an alternative account of freedom as "worldly," see Linda Zerilli, *Feminism and the Abyss of Freedom* (Chicago: University of Chicago Press, 2005).

2. Foucault goes on to further designate two main traditions within the modern philosophic tradition, at least insofar as the relationship between the subject and truth is concerned: the "analytics of truth" (associated with Descartes, Kant, and modern positivist science) and the pastoral tradition (associated with Christian confessional practices, psychoanalysis, and modern hermeneutics).

3. Note that in the discussion of spirituality Foucault has not yet differentiated clearly between those activities done on the self by *oneself*, and those done on the self by *others*. If spiritual practices are whatever must be done to the self such that it is transformed into a being capable of apprehending truth, this says nothing of whose evaluation it is of what needs to be done. Part of my reading here is to suggest that practices of care of the self (done to oneself) and disci-

plinary practices (done on oneself by others) are not different *in kind*. They are both "spiritual practices" in the sense that they transform the very being of the subject such that they make a certain form of truth possible, even necessary. This fits into Foucault's analysis of disciplinary practices as always requiring self-oriented practices, opening up a space of possibility for modification of these practices through the *manner* in which one conducts one's conduct. See the discussion of conduct in the previous chapter.

4. This appears to be the central conclusion of Timothy Rayner's study *Foucault's Heidegger: Philosophy and Transformative Experience* (New York: Continuum, 2007), and serves as a point of contrast to the work presented here.

5. A French translation of this interview, modified by Foucault, can be found in *DE2*, 1428–50.

6. It is with respect to the possibility of such a "remainder" or space outside of practical relations to which one does not consent, that Foucault differentiated his project from that of Habermas, for instance. Foucault argued that insofar as Habermas subscribes to the notion that "there could be a state of communication which would be such that the games of truth could circulate freely, without obstacles, without constraint and without coercive effects," his work is "utopian" (*EW1*, 298). In contrast to this, as James Tully has noted, "Foucault drew from his genealogies . . . that this regulative idea is yet another instance of the juridical presupposition that there is some place or procedure in which subjects are "sovereign"—free of power and autonomous—and in which they agree on the conditions of their subjection. . . . To approach communicative games in accord with such a utopian regulative idea is to abstract oneself from what is really going on and the possibilities of concrete freedom *within them*, the only kind of freedom available to humans." See Tully, "To Think and Act Differently: Foucault's Four Reciprocal Objections to Habermas' Theory," in *Foucault Contra Habermas*, ed. Samantha Ashenden and David Owen (London: Sage, 1999), 131.

7. This is discussed in more detail below.

8. There is a huge volume of literature on Foucault's relationship to contemporary feminist philosophy. See, in particular, Susan Hekman, ed., *Feminist Interpretations of Michel Foucault* (University Park: Pennsylvania State University Press, 1996); Cressida Heyes, ed., *Foucault Studies*, no. 16, special issue on Foucault and feminism (September 2013); Cressida Heyes, *Self-Transformations: Foucault, Ethics, and Normalized Bodies* (Oxford: Oxford University Press, 2007); Caroline Ramazanoglu, ed., *Up Against Foucault: Exploration of Some Tensions between Foucault and Feminism* (New York: Routledge, 1993); Diana Taylor and Karen Vintges, eds., *Feminism and the Final Foucault* (Urbana: University of Illinois Press, 2004). A common criticism with respect to Foucault's use of the term *care* has been that his examples of "care of the self" are usually limited to practices performed by elite males on themselves and, to the extent that others are involved, they tend to be used merely instrumentally. Examples of this criti-

cism can be found in Amy Allen, "Foucault, Feminism, and the Self," in Taylor and Vintges, eds., 235–57.

9. This is, for example, one of Levinas's main concerns with Heidegger. For example, in *Totality and Infinity* (Pittsburgh: Duquesne University Press, 1969), Levinas writes that, "to affirm the priority of *Being* over *existents* is to already decide the essence of philosophy; it is to subordinate the relation with *someone*, who is an existent, (the ethical relation) to a relation with the *Being of existents*, which, impersonal, permits the apprehension, the domination of existents (a relationship of knowing), subordinates justice to freedom. . . . In subordinating every relation with existents to the relation with Being the Heideggerian ontology affirms the primacy of freedom over ethics" (45).

10. It is important to note that I am only referring to those rare, specific passages in which critics do make this conflation. I am not claiming that feminist philosophy generally is fixated upon "caring-for" in this narrow, willful sense. In fact, much feminist theory is devoted to precisely the explication of "Care" in the deeper sense, i.e., as fundamental interrelatedness or "relational autonomy." This dimension is touched upon via a discussion of Judith Butler in Chapter Five. For a recent work on the implications of fundamental interrelatedness for legal and political theory, see Jennifer Nedelsky, *Law's Relations: A Relational Theory of Self, Autonomy, and Law* (Oxford: Oxford University Press, 2011).

11. This is discussed in Chapter Two.

12. Friedrich Nietzsche, *Gay Science*, §270. The Cambridge edition of this text states that this passage originates with a victory ode by the early-fifth century (B.C.) poet Pindar, his *Second Pythian Victory Ode* (line 73). See *The Gay Science*, ed. Bernard Williams, trans. Josefine Nauckhoff (Cambridge: Cambridge University Press, 2001), 152. Heidegger uses this expression in *Being and Time* (*SZ* §31, 145; *BTa* §31, 186).

13. The most comprehensive account of this transition remains Charles Taylor's *Sources of the Self* (Cambridge, Mass.: Harvard University Press, 1989).

14. Linda Alcoff, "Feminist Politics and Foucault: The Limits to a Collaboration," in *Crises in Continental Philosophy*, ed. Arleen Dallery and Charles Scott, with Holley Roberts (Albany: State University of New York Press, 1992), 71.

15. For an overview of this "anti-subjectivitist hypothesis," see Amy Allen, "The Anti-Subjectivist Hypothesis: Michel Foucault and the Death of the Subject," *Philosophical Forum* 31.2 (Summer 2000): 113–30.

16. Ibid., 122. See also Ladelle McWhorter, "Subjecting Dasein," in *Foucault and Heidegger: Critical Encounters*, ed. Alan Milchman and Alan Rosenberg (Minneapolis: University of Minnesota Press, 2003), 110–26.

17. In this respect, at least, my reading of Foucault differs from that of Paul Patton, for instance, who argues that Foucault's work does presuppose "a 'thin' conception of the subject of thought and action: whatever else it may be, the human subject is a being endowed with certain capacities." Patton, "Foucault's Subject of Power," *Political Theory Newsletter* 6.1 (1994): 60–71, 61. Later on in

this same article, Patton draws upon the "Nietzschean" foundations of Foucault's work, arguing: "Modernity understood as an ethos of permanent self-criticism presupposes the existence of possible subjects of such activity. Such subjects will necessarily be free in the sense that their possibilities for action will include the capacity to undertake this self-critical activity.... So long as human capacities do in fact include the power of individuals to act upon their own actions, we can see that Foucault's conception of human being in terms of power enables us to distinguish between those exercises of power which inhibit and those which allow the self-directed use and development of human capacities. To the extent that individuals and groups acquire the meta-capacity for the autonomous exercise of certain of their own ... capacities, they will inevitably be led to oppose forms of domination which prevent such activity." Ibid., 68. My general point here is that while a reading of Foucault's account of the subject and agency may begin with Nietzsche, it cannot avoid passing through Heidegger. This passing through Heidegger allows us to see that Foucault's account of the subject does not rely upon an "ontology of the will" à la Nietzsche oriented toward "self-directed use and development of human capacities." Rather, the force and significance of *self*-direction is disclosed *historically* by a preexisting context or field of involvement, not determined universally or transcendentally through reference to the will. Hence, it is to this field of involvement that we must look for an analysis not only of the development of capacities to act but also, more importantly, the context of signification within which action can appear meaningfully at all. It asks: what can *count* as action in this given field of possibilities, what can *count* as *self*-directed action, and attempts to show how this significance is internally related to the development of the capacity to act. This is why, in the previous chapter, I attempted to demonstrate that Foucault's use of the term *power* underwent a modification away from the notion of *capacity* toward one of *relationship*.

18. Amy Allen, for example, specifically glosses over the distinction: "Although Foucault prefers to speak in his late work of a 'self' rather than a 'subject,' it seems clear that the notion of a self-constituting self presupposes some conception of a thinking subject who is capable of reflecting on what kind of self he or she wants to be and deliberating about the best way to become that sort of self, and it also presupposes some conception of an agent who is capable of acting in the world in such a way as to become the sort of self that he or she wants to be." "The Anti-Subjectivist Hypothesis," 118.

19. As James Tully puts this point, "a form of subjectivity is not a limit outside the experience of the subjects themselves; it is the limit of their experience as thinking subjects from the inside, the characteristic way they think through the forms of knowledge, relations of power, and practices of the self through which an aspect of their experience is brought to self-consciousness." Tully, "To Think and Act Differently, 97.

20. Very few commentators have noticed, for example, the irony of the title

L'herméneutique du sujet for the 1981–82 lectures at the Collège de France. In fact, the lectures almost do not deal with the "hermeneutics of the subject" at all. Rather, they study what came *before* the hermeneutics of the subject arose in the West: the care of the self.

21. Foucault's most famous (re)statement of his general project came in "The Subject and Power," where he wrote, "I would like to say, first of all, what has been the goal of my work during the last twenty years. It has not been to analyze the phenomena of power, nor to elaborate the foundations of such an analysis. My objective, instead, has been to create a history of the different modes by which, in our culture, human beings are made subjects . . . it is not power, but the subject, that is the general theme of my research" (*EW3*, 326–27).

22. Perhaps more so than Heidegger, Foucault managed to use classical texts without succumbing to a nostalgia or overly uncritical perspective on them. Some examples of this: "I am not looking for an alternative; you can't find the solution of a problem in the solution of another problem raised at another moment by other people" (*EW1*, 256); "The Greek ethics of pleasure is linked to a virile society, to dissymmetry, exclusion of the other, an obsession with penetration, and a kind of threat of being dispossessed of your own energy, and so on. All that is quite disgusting!" (*EW1*, 258); "I think there is no exemplary value in a period that is not our period . . . it is not anything to get back to" (*EW1*, 259).

23. As quoted by Frédéric Gros, "Situation du cours" (*HS*, 497–526).

24. Of course, in saying "before" we are subjects we are *Da-sein*, "before" is not to be understood in the chronological sense. Foucault's analysis helps to demonstrate that the modes of subjectification are "always already" there, in their historical specificity. What Heidegger is pointing out is that we are not reducible to, or even primarily understandable through, our subjection.

25. For instance, as early as his 1923 lectures at the University of Freiburg, Heidegger claimed, "Dasein is not a "thing" like a piece of wood nor such a thing as a plant—nor does it consist of experiences, and still less is it a subject (an ego) standing over against objects (which are not the ego)" (*OHF*, 37; *GA*, 63: 47).

26. "One of our first tasks will be to prove that if we posit an "I" or subject as that which is proximally given, we shall completely miss the phenomenal content [Bestand] of Dasein. *Ontologically*, every idea of a "subject"—unless refined by a previous ontological determination of its basic character—still posits the *subjectum* (*hupokeimenon*) along with it, no matter how vigorous one's ontical protestations against the "soul substance" or the "reification of consciousness" (*BTa* §10, 72; *SZ* §10, 46).

27. See especially *N4*, chap. 15 ("The Dominance of the Subject in the Modern Age") to the end.

28. This is discussed in more detail in the conclusion to Chapter Three.

29. As Young notes, Heidegger uses the terms *geschont* (taken-care-of) and

schonen (care-for) as two sides of the same modality. Thus, to dwell "is (a) to be cared-for in the dwelling-place and (b) to care for the things of the dwelling-place." Julian Young, *Heidegger's Later Philosophy* (Cambridge: Cambridge University Press, 2002), 64.

30. Foucault speaks in this idiom most explicitly in "Qu'est-ce que les Lumières?" where he defined an "ensemble pratique" as "a homogeneous domain of reference," defined not by "the representations that men give of themselves" (a history of ideas or self-consciousness), nor "the conditions that determine them without their knowledge" (a structuralist historical materialism, for instance), but "the forms of rationality that organize their ways of doing things ... and the freedom with which they act *within these practical systems*" (EW1, 317; DE2, 1395; italics added).

31. I am referring here to the brief historical sketch given in Chapter One.

32. This appears to be part of Heidegger's (arguably unbalanced) characterization of Nietzsche.

33. Béatrice Han, "Foucault and Heidegger on Kant and Finitude," in *Foucault and Heidegger: Critical Encounters*, ed. Alan Milchman and Alan Rosenberg (Minneapolis: University of Minnesota Press, 2003), 127–62. Han gives as an example of such a modification the fact that "the Western understanding of time has been radically modified by Judaism, and later by Christianity" (151).

34. Foucault specifically states that his analysis of the changing relationship of self to self might be read as an another axis in the analysis of forms of *technē* in the West. He states:

> According to some suggestions by Habermas, it seems, one can identify three major types of techniques in human societies: the techniques that allow one to produce, to transform and to manipulate things; the techniques which allow one to use sign systems; and the techniques that allow one to direct [conduire] the behaviour of individuals, to impose certain wills on them, and to submit them to certain ends or objectives. That is to say, there are techniques of production, techniques of signification, and techniques of domination.
>
> However, I became more and more aware that there is in all societies, I think, in all societies whatever they are, another type of technique: techniques which permit individuals to perform, by their own means, a certain number of operations on their bodies, on their own souls, on their own thoughts, on their own conduct, and this in such a way that they transform themselves, modify themselves, and reach a certain state of perfection, of happiness, of purity, of supernatural power, and so on. Let's call this kind of techniques a techniques or technology of the self. ("Subjectivity and Truth," in *The Politics of Truth*, ed. Sylvère Lotringer [New York: Semiotext(e), 1997], 153)

We have already seen (in the previous chapter) that Foucault sees this as an extension of Heidegger's analysis of *technē*, only "turned around": "For Heidegger, it was through an increasing obsession with *technē* as the only way to arrive at an understanding of objects that the West lost touch with Being.

Let's turn the question around and ask which techniques and practices form the Western concept of the subject, giving it its characteristic split of truth and error, freedom and constraint." Michel Foucault, "About the Beginning of the Hermeneutics of the Self," *RC*, 161 n. 4.

35. Foucault calls him "the most decisive modern representative" of the Cartesian system insofar as he continues the "the reduction of discursive practices to textual traces; the elision of the events produced therein and the retention only of marks for a reading: the invention of voices behind texts to avoid having to analyze the modes of implication of the subject in discourses; the assigning of the originary as said and unsaid in the text to avoid placing discursive practices in the field of transformations where they are carried out" (*EW2*, 416; *DE1*, 1135).

36. In the 1982 interview, "On the Genealogy of Ethics: An Overview of Work in Progress," Foucault reiterated: "We must not forget that Descartes wrote 'meditations'—and meditations are a practice of the self. But the extraordinary thing in Descartes's texts is that he succeeded in substituting a subject as founder of practices of knowledge for a subject constituted through practices of the self" (*EW2*, 278). The original interview was conducted in English, but a French translation, checked and corrected by Foucault, is also available: *DE2*, 1202–30.

37. For a detailed, careful explication of Kant's work along these lines—a reading to which my own is indebted—see Ian Hunter, *Rival Enlightenments: Civil and Metaphysical Philosophy in Early Modern Germany* (Cambridge: Cambridge University Press, 2001). There, particularly in chapter 6, Hunter subjects Kant to an analysis not unlike Foucault's reading of Descartes. That is, he reads Kant's moral philosophy, not only in terms of an argument, as an instance of the exercise of reason, but rather as comprised by various steps that "form the architecture of an elaborate spiritual exercise, designed to lead the reader through ascending levels of speculative self-questioning and self-purification" (293). Other readings that proceed along these lines include Edward F. McGushin, *Foucault's Askēsis* (Evanston, Ill.: Northwestern University Press, 2007), chap. 8; and Andrew Cutrofello, *Discipline and Critique: Kant, Poststructuralism, and the Politics of Resistance* (Albany: State University of New York Press, 1994).

38. Discussed in Chapter One as the move to "transcendentalize finitude": redefine the limits of human reason positively as the condition of possibility for knowledge as such.

39. Tully, "To Think and Act Differently," 125.

40. Béatrice Han-Pile has also noted this connection and related it back to Descartes:

> The history of objectification and subjectification in the West thus developed along two increasingly divergent lines: On the one hand, the knowing subject emancipated itself from spiritual demands, first though the framework of Cartesianism, then through Kantian philosophy. On the other, the idea of a necessary transformation of the self through a relation to the truth was first taken up by Christian

pastoralism, then by the disciplines . . . and finally by the internalisation of techniques of subjectivation particular to bio-power. Therefore, to the growing epistemologisation of philosophy chronologically corresponds the progressive disciplinarisation of the constitution of the self." (Béatrice Han-Pile, "The Analytic of Finitude and the History of Subjectivity," in *The Cambridge Companion to Foucault*, 2nd ed., ed. Gary Gutting [Cambridge: Cambridge University Press, 2003], 188)

41. Cutrofello, *Discipline and Critique*, 33.

42. Tully, "To Think and Act Differently," 126.

43. Heidegger, of course, also objects to this humanistic anthropology. This is discussed in the conclusion to Chapter Three and in more detail below.

44. Ian Hacking, "Self-Improvement," in *Historical Ontology* (Cambridge, Mass.: Harvard University Press, 2002), 119.

45. We might even say that when Kant speaks of the courage demanded by the heraldic *Aude sapere* he is invoking the *moral virtue* required to submit oneself to reason: the ethical stance one would have to take—*have courage!*—in order to become a universal subject of reason. Another example of this can be found in Kant's reflections on the French Revolution. For him, the true hope of progress can be seen, not so much in the fact of the revolutionary action, but in the affective response of the onlookers. He writes that "they openly express universal yet disinterested sympathy. . . . This revolution has aroused in the hearts and desires of all spectators who are not themselves caught up in it a *sympathy* which borders almost on enthusiasm. . . . True enthusiasm is always directed exclusively towards the *ideal*." Immanuel Kant, "The Contest of the Faculties," in *Political Writings* (Cambridge: Cambridge University Press, 1991), 182–83. To put this in the idiom we are using here, Kant applauds the necessary ethical-spiritual transformation of the subjects in question as a necessary feature of the philosophical enterprise to which he is contributing.

46. Immanuel Kant, "What Is Enlightenment?" in *Political Writings*, 54.

47. Amy Allen, "Foucault and Enlightenment: A Critical Reappraisal," *Constellations* 10.2 (2003): 180–98 at 189.

48. For instance, Heidegger argues at one point that the "scandal of philosophy" is not that a final proof for the Kantian distinction between transcendental and empirical forms of selfhood—between what is "in me" and what is "outside of me" has yet to be given, but rather that *"such proofs are expected and attempted again and again"* (*BTu* §43, 249; *SZ* §43, 205).

CHAPTER SEVEN: OBJECTIFICATION, REIFICATION, SUBJECTIFICATION

1. Although I have not commented on it directly, it should also be fairly evident by now that I see Foucault's critical historical works as a more successful attempt to realize the historicizing impulse of Heidegger's ontology than, say, the deconstructive work of Jacques Derrida. Despite Derrida's insistence that his work better exemplifies a "deconstructive genealogy" approach, it ap-

pears alongside Foucault's fine-grained works on the actual histories of basic practices of freedom to be precisely the sort of abstract and false historicity Marcuse warned against, i.e., historicity without any real history. On Marcuse's concerns, see Chapters One and Three. For an example of Derrida's use of "deconstructive genealogy," situated in relation to Heidegger, see *Aporias* (Stanford, Calif.: Stanford University Press, 1993).

2. All citations in text to Marcuse here are references to Herbert Marcuse, *Heideggerian Marxism*, ed. Richard Wolin and John Abromeit (Lincoln: University of Nebraska Press, 2005), here, 138, unless otherwise noted.

3. For a survey of such approaches, see Nussbaum, *Sex and Social Justice* (Oxford: Oxford University Press, 1999), chap. 8; and Evangelia Papadaki, "Sexual Objectification: From Kant to Contemporary Feminism," *Contemporary Political Theory* 6 (2007): 330–48.

4. We might also think of Aristotle's famous reference to natural slaves as "animate tools" as the starkest example of this kind of objectification.

5. Georg Lukács, *History and Class Consciousness*, trans. Rodney Livingstone (Cambridge, Mass.: MIT Press, 1971). Hereafter cited in text as "Lukács, [page no.]." Another text of the same era that evinces some of the same concerns as *History and Class Consciousness* is Karl Korsch's *Marxism and Philosophy* (New York: Monthly Review Press, 2008 [1923]).

6. Marx also occasionally employs the term *vergegenständlich* to denote a form of "objecfication" similar to the phenomenon named as *verdinglichkeit*.

7. Karl Marx, *Capital, Vol. 1* (London: Penguin Classics, 1990), 128. Hereafter cited in text as "*Capital*, [page no.]."

8. Honneth also briefly mentions Foucault, but does not pursue his possible contribution to this discussion. Moreover, Honneth promptly assimilates Foucault to a previously formulated conception of Recognition:

> If a subject does not regard her desires and feelings as worthy of articulation, she will not be able to gain access to the mental life that is to be maintained in her self-relationship. This type of recognition is frequently characterized as a kind of "care of the self"—parallel to the Heideggerian notion of care. This notion indicates that a subject takes up the stance of engaged concern toward herself that Heidegger regarded as being characteristic of our dealings with things and other humans. If we don't project any more ethical ambitions onto this activity of self-care than are already implied when a person regards his or her desires and feelings as worthy of articulation, then this activity of self-care is identical with the stance that I would like to designate as "recognition." (Axel Honneth, *Reification: A New Look at an Old Idea* [Oxford: Oxford University Press, 2008], 71–72; see also 92 n. 97. Hereafter cited in text as "Honneth, [page no.]")

9. Perhaps the best known of these was that undertaken by Lukács's student, Lucien Goldman, in his *Lukács et Heidegger* (Paris: Denoël-Gonthier, 1973).

10. Honneth, *Reification*, 30.

11. Adorno has also discussed reification in these terms, which Honneth

notes. Adorno's celebrated phrase "all reification is forgetting" serves as epigraph to Honneth's essay.

12. Honneth also draws upon other thinkers to make his case, including John Dewey and Stanely Cavell. I focused here on his reading of Heidegger since it most directly relates to the issue at hand.

13. For instance, in "Philosophy as a Strict Science" we find Husserl argue, "To follow the model of the natural sciences almost inevitably means to reify consciousness." Edmund Husserl, "Philosophy as a Strict Science," in *Phenomenology and the Crisis of Philosophy*, trans. Quentin Lauer (New York: Harper, 1965), 103.

14. The preface to the 1967 reissue of *History and Class Consciousness* is strikingly critical of the original book. Part of the shift in tone is clearly related to political developments, partially reflecting a general disillusion with Soviet Communism among Western Marxists, but in Lukács's case most obviously related to the crushing of the Hungarian Revolution in 1956. However, another dimension of the self-critique involves a philosophical rethinking. Lukács states that the "ultimate philosophical foundation" of Hegelianism is the "identical subject-object that realises itself in the historical process," and characterizes his own project as an attempt to recast Hegel's "logico-metaphysical construction" in terms of sociohistorical process that "culminates when the proletariat reaches this stage in its class consciousness, thus becoming the identical subject-object of history." He then concedes that this is untenable: "The proletariat seen as the identical subject-object of the real history of mankind is no materialist consummation that overcomes the constructions of idealism. It is rather an attempt to out-Hegel Hegel, it is an edifice boldly erected above every possible reality and thus attempts objectively to surpass the Master himself." (Lukács, "Preface to the New Edition (1967)," xxii–xxiii.

15. See the response essays in Axel Honneth, *Reification*. I have also benefitted greatly from Anita Chari's work. See Chari, "Toward a Political Critique of Reification: Lukács, Honneth, and the Aims of Critical Theory," *Philosophy and Social Criticism* 36.5 (2010): 587–606.

16. Raymond Geuss, "Philosophical Anthropology and Social Criticism," in Honneth, *Reification*, 127. Geuss is echoing here one dimension of the concern first articulated by Adorno in *The Jargon of Authenticity*. Adorno, however, went one step further. For him, Heidegger's existential categories were not merely too general to be of use in social criticism—they were pathologically obscurantist and thus only aided the very instrumentalizing forces they were originally deployed to critique. For instance, he writes that Heidegger "did not foresee that what he named authentic, once become word, would grow toward the same exchange-society anonymity against which *Sein und Zeit* rebelled." Theodor Adorno, *The Jargon of Authenticity* (New York: Routledge, 2003 [1964]), 13.

17. Although my argument here does not depend on this point, it is worth noting that Geuss's rendering of "care" here is at least as problematic as Hon-

neth's. As his examples attest, Geuss reduces "care" to one of two possibilities: (a) a general, "neutral" description of the structure of reality, or (b) a purposeful, deliberate, willful attention (or inattention) to others. In the first case, it is dismissed as denoting no normative implications at all. In the second, it is only one specific normatively loaded behavior (caring-for). This dichotomized structure of "care" is, however, precisely what Heidegger's work is meant to set aside by showing us that the first-order sense of the care/freedom is a bringing forth (disclosing) the field we inhabit, to disclose without determining, to "release," and so on. The second is the care/freedom we enact *in* the *Spielraum* of the care/freedom relationships of the field we inhabit. Moreover, the two are intimately related since care/freedom in the second sense, which "realizes" care/freedom in the most basic sense, is the care/freedom of "receptivity," or the mode of disclosure that brings forth a field in such a way that lets beings be or "show up" in their ownness. This can be contrasted with the dominant modern mode of disclosure as *Gestell*. For a compelling and novel working out of the ethical-political significance of "receptivity," see Nikolas Kompridis, *Critique and Disclosure: Critical Theory Between Past and Future* (Cambridge, Mass.: MIT Press, 2006).

18. For example, "What strikes me is the fact that, in our society, art has become something that is related only to objects and not to individuals or to life. That art is something which is specialized or done by experts who are artists. But couldn't everyone's life become a work of art? Why should the lamp or house be an art object but not our life?" (*EW1*, 261).

19. Michel Foucault, "Truth, Power, Self: An Interview with Michel Foucault," *Technologies of the Self: A Seminar with Michel Foucault*, ed. Luther Martin, Huck Gutman, and Patrick Hutton (Amherst: University of Massachusetts Press, 1988), 9–15, 10.

20. Heidegger does provide a few scattered indications that he recognizes the possibilities for exploring the sociocritical dimensions of his perspective on selfhood in a manner not entirely dissimilar to Foucault. For instance, Heidegger writes that we experience ourselves as who we are in concrete, communal worlds "in a very specific, factical characterization: as a student, a lecturer, as a relative, superior, etc., and *not* as specimen of the natural-scientific species *homo sapiens*, and the like." However, as I have been arguing, he never fully develops these possibilities. *The Phenomenology of Religious Life*, trans. Matthias Fritsch and Jennifer Anna Gosetti-Ferencei (Bloomington: Indiana University Press, 2004), 8.

21. David Owen, "Reification, Ideology, and Power: Expression and Agency in Honneth's Theory of Recognition," *Journal of Power* 3.1 (2010): 97–109.

22. The reference to an expressivist self in Foucault is indebted to, inter alia, David Owen and Nancy Luxon. See Owen, "Reification, Ideology, and Power"; and Luxon, "Ethics and Subjectivity: Practices of Self-Governance in the Late Lectures of Michel Foucault," *Political Theory* 36.3 (2008): 377–402.

WORKS CITED

Abromeit, John. "Herbert Marcuse's Critical Encounter with Martin Heidegger: 1927–1933." In *Herbert Marcuse: A Critical Reader*, ed. John Abromeit and William Mark Cobb, 131–51. New York: Routledge, 2004.
Adorno, Theodor. *The Jargon of Authenticity*. New York: Routledge, 2003 [1964].
Alcoff, Linda. "Feminist Politics and Foucault: The Limits to a Collaboration." In *Crises in Continental Philosophy*, ed. Arleen Dallery and Charles Scott, with Holley Roberts, 69–86. Albany: State University of New York Press, 1990.
Allen, Amy. "The Anti-Subjectivist Hypothesis: Michel Foucault and the Death of the Subject." *Philosophical Forum* 31.2 (Summer 2000): 113–30.
———. "Foucault and Enlightenment: A Critical Reappraisal." *Constellations* 10.2 (2003): 180–98.
———. "Foucault, Feminism, and the Self." In *Feminism and the Final Foucault*, ed. Diana Taylor and Karen Vintges, 235–57. Urbana: University of Illinois Press, 2004.
Althusser, Louis. *L'avenir dure longtemps*. Paris: Stock/IMEC, 1992.
———. *The Future Lasts Forever*. Trans. Richard Veasey. New York: New Press, 1992.
———. "Ideology and Ideological State Apparatus." In *Lenin and Philosophy and Other Essays*. New York: Monthly Review Press, 2001.
Arendt, Hannah. *The Human Condition*. 2nd ed. Chicago: University of Chicago Press, 1998.
Barash, Jeffrey. *Martin Heidegger and the Problem of Historical Meaning*. New York: Fordham University Press, 2003.
Barry, Andrew, Thomas Osborne, and Nikolas Rose, eds. *Foucault and Political Reason: Liberalism, Neo-Liberalism and Rationalities of Government*. London: University College Press, 1996.

Binswanger, Ludwig. *Ausgewählte Vorträge und Aufsätze*. Bern: A. Francke, 1947.
———. *Le rêve et l'existence*. Paris: Éditions Desclée De Brouwer, 1954.
———. "Traum und Existenz." *Neue Schweizer Rundshau* 23: 673–85. Zurich: Fretz u. Wasmuth, 1930.
Burchell, Graham, Colin Gordon, and Peter Miller, eds. *The Foucault Effect: Studies in Governmentality*. London: Harvester Wheatsheaf, 1991.
Butler, Judith. *Bodies That Matter*. New York: Routledge, 1993.
Caputo, John. "On Not Knowing Who We Are: Madness, Hermeneutics, and the Night of Truth in Foucault." In *More Radical Hermeneutics*. Bloomington: Indiana University Press, 2000.
Chari, Anita. "Toward a Political Critique of Reification: Lukács, Honneth, and the Aims of Critical Theory." *Philosophy and Social Criticism* 36.5 (2010): 587–606.
Connolly, William. *Identity/Difference*. Minneapolis: University of Minnesota Press, 1991.
Cutrofello, Andrew. *Discipline and Critique: Kant, Poststructuralism, and the Politics of Resistance*. Albany: State University of New York Press, 1994.
Dallmayr, Fred. "Ontology of Freedom: Heidegger and Political Philosophy." *Political Theory* 12.2 (May 1984): 204–34.
Dean, Mitchell. *Governmentality: Power and Rule in Modern Society*. London: Thousand Oaks: Sage Publications, 1999.
Denker, Alfred. *Historical Dictionary of Heidegger's Philosophy*. Landam, Md.: Scarecrow, 2000.
Derrida, Jacques. *Aporias*. Stanford, Calif.: Stanford University Press, 1993.
———. "Être juste avec Freud." In *Penser la folie: Essais sur Michel Foucault*, ed. Michel Delorne, 141–95. Paris: Galilée, 1992.
Dilthey, Wilhelm. *Der Aufbau der geschichtlichen Welt in den Geisteswissenshaften*. Leipzig: Teubner, 1927.
Djaballah, Marc. *Kant, Foucault, and the Forms of Experience*. New York: Routledge, 2008.
Dreyfus, Hubert. "'Being and Power' Revisited." In *Foucault and Heidegger: Critical Encounters*, ed. Alan Milchman and Alan Rosenberg, 30–54. Minneapolis: University of Minnesota Press, 2003.
———. *Being-in-the-World: A Commentary on Heidegger's "Being and Time," Division I*. Cambridge, Mass.: MIT Press, 1991.
Dreyfus, Hubert, and Paul Rabinow. *Michel Foucault: Beyond Structuralism and Hermeneutics*. 2nd ed. Chicago: University of Chicago Press, 1983.
Dumm, Thomas. *Michel Foucault and the Politics of Freedom*. Lanham, Md.: Rowman and Littlefield, 2002.
Epictetus. *The Art of Living*. Trans. Sharon LeBell. New York: HarperOne, 2007.
Feenberg, Andrew. *Heidegger and Marcuse: The Catastrophe and Redemption of History*. New York: Routledge, 2005.
Figal, Günter. "An Essay on Freedom: Ontological Considerations from a Prac-

tical Point of View." In *For a Philosophy of Freedom and Strife*, trans. Wayne Kline, 13–28. Albany: State University of New York Press, 1998.

Fink-Eitel, Hinrich. "Zwischen Nietzsche und Heidegger: Michel Foucaults 'Sexualität und Wahrheit' im Spiegel neuerer Sekundärliteratur." *Philosophisches Jahrbuch* 97.2 (1990): 367–90.

Forst, Rainer. "Endlichkeit, Freiheit, Indiviualität: Die Sorge um das Selbst bei Heidegger und Foucault." In *Ethos der Moderne: Foucaults Kritik der Aufklärung*, ed. Eva Erdmann, Rainer Forst, and Axel Honneth. Frankfurt am Main: Campus Verlag, 1990.

Foucault, Michel. *Abnormal*. Trans. Graham Burchell. New York: Picador, 2003.

———. *Les anormaux*. Paris: Gallimard, 1999.

———. *L'archéologie du savoir*. Paris: Gallimard, 1969.

———. *The Archaeology of Knowledge*. Trans. Alan Sheridan Smith. London: Routledge, 2002.

———. *The Birth of the Clinic: An Archaeology of Medical Perception*. Trans. Alan Sheridan. London: Routledge, 1989.

———. *Death and the Labyrinth: The World of Raymond Roussel*. Trans. Charles Ruas. Garden City, N.J.: Doubleday, 1986.

———. *Discipline and Punish: The Birth of the Prison*. Trans. Alan Sheridan. New York: Vintage, 1977.

———. *Dits et écrits*. Vols. 1–2. Paris: Gallimard, 1994.

———. "Dream, Imagination and Existence." *Review of Existential Psychology and Psychiatry* 19.1 (1986): 31–78.

———. *Essential Works of Foucault*. Vol. 1, *Ethics, Subjectivity, and Truth*. Ed. Paul Rabinow. New York: New Press, 1997.

———. *Essential Works of Foucault*. Vol. 2, *Aesthetics, Method, and Epistemology*. Ed. James D. Faubion. New York: New Press, 1998.

———. *Essential Works of Foucault*. Vol. 3, *Power*. Ed. James D. Faubion. New York: New Press, 2000.

———. *Il faut défendre la societé*. Paris: Gallimard, 1997.

———. *Foucault Live: Collected Interviews, 1961–1984*. Trans. Sylvère Lotringer. New York: Semiotext(e), 1989.

———. *The Foucault Reader*. Ed. Paul Rabinow. New York: Pantheon, 1984.

———. *The Hermeneutics of the Subject*. Trans. Graham Burchell. New York: Picador, 2005.

———. *L'herméneutique du sujet*. Paris: Gallimard, 2001.

———. *Histoire de la folie à l'âge classique*. Paris: Gallimard, 1972.

———. *Histoire de la sexualité, vol. I: La volonté de savoir*. Paris: Gallimard, 1976.

———. *Histoire de la sexualité, vol. II: L'usage des plaisirs*. Paris: Gallimard, 1984.

———. *Histoire de la sexualité, vol. III: Le souci de soi*. Paris: Gallimard, 1984.

———. *History of Madness*. Trans. Jonathan Murphy and Jean Khalfa. London: Routledge, 2006.

———. *The History of Sexuality*, vol. 1: *An Introduction*. Trans. Robert Hurley. New York: Vintage, 1978.

———. *The History of Sexuality*, vol. 2: *The Use of Pleasure*. Trans. Robert Hurley. New York: Vintage, 1985.

———. *The History of Sexuality*, vol. 3: *The Care of the Self*. Trans. Robert Hurley. New York: Vintage, 1986.

———. "Interview with Michael Bess." *The History of the Present* 4 (Spring 1988): 11–13.

———. *Leçons sur "La volonté de savoir" et "Le savoir d'Oedipe"*. Paris: Seuil, 2011.

———. *Lectures on "The Will to Know" and "Oedipal Knowledge."* Trans. Graham Burchell. New York: Palgrave Macmillan, 2013.

———. *Maladie mentale et psychologie*. 4th ed. Paris: Quadridge/Puf, 2005.

———. *Mental Illness and Psychology*. Trans. Alan Sheridan. Berkeley: University of California Press, 1987.

———. *Les mots et les choses*. Paris: Gallimard, 1966.

———. *Naissance de la clinique*. Paris: Presses Universitaires de France, 1963.

———. *The Order of Things*. London: Routledge, 1989.

———. *L'ordre du discours*. Paris: Gallimard, 1971.

———. *The Politics of Truth*. Ed. Sylvère Lotringer. New York: Semiotext(e), 1997.

———. *Religion and Culture: Michel Foucault*. Ed. Jeremy R. Carrette. New York: Routledge, 1999.

———. *Remarks on Marx: Conversations with Duccio Trombadori*. Trans. R. James Goldstein and James Cascaito. New York: Semiotext(e), 1991.

———. *Sécurité, territoire, population*. Paris: Gallimard, 2004.

———. *Security, Territory, Population*. Trans. Graham Burchell. New York: Palgrave Macmillan, 2007.

———. *"Society Must Be Defended."* Trans. David Macey. New York: Picador, 2003.

———. "Subjectivity and Truth." In *The Politics of Truth*, ed. Sylvère Lotringer, 147–68. New York: Semiotext(e), 1997.

———. *Surveiller et punir: Naissance de la prison*. Paris: Gallimard, 1975.

———. *Technologies of the Self: A Seminar with Michel Foucault*. Ed. Luther Martin, Huck Gutman, and Patrick Hutton. Amherst: University of Massachusetts Press, 1988.

Gadamer, Hans-Georg. *Truth and Method*. 2nd ed. Trans. Joel Weinsheimer and Donald G. Marshall. New York: Continuum, 1989.

Gelven, Michael. *A Commentary on Heidegger's "Being and Time."* Rev. ed. DeKalb: Northern Illinois University Press, 1989.

Geuss, Raymond. "Philosophical Anthropology and Social Criticism." In *Reification: A New Look at an Old Idea*, ed. Axel Honneth, 120–30. Oxford: Oxford University Press, 2008.

Goldman, Lucien. *Lukács et Heidegger*. Paris: Denoël-Gonthier, 1973.

Gordon, Colin. Afterword to Michel Foucault, *Power/Knowledge*, 229–60. New York: Pantheon, 1980.

Gros, Frédéric. "Situation du cours." In *L'herméneutique du sujet*, by Michel Foucault, 497–526. Paris: Gallimard, 2001.
Haar, Michael. "The Question of Human Freedom in the Later Heidegger." *Southern Journal of Philosophy* 28, supplement (1990): 1–16.
Han, Béatrice. *Foucault's Critical Project: Between the Transcendental and the Historical*. Stanford, Calif.: Stanford University Press, 2002.
———. "Foucault and Heidegger on Kant and Finitude." In *Foucault and Heidegger: Critical Encounters*, ed. Alan Milchman and Alan Rosenberg, 127–62. Minneapolis: University of Minnesota Press, 2003.
Han-Pile, Béatrice. "The Analytic of Finitude and the History of Subjectivity." In *The Cambridge Companion to Foucault*, 2nd ed., ed. Gary Gutting. Cambridge: Cambridge University Press, 2003.
———. "Freedom and the 'Choice to Choose Oneself' in *Being and Time*." In *The Cambridge Companion to "Being and Time"*, ed. Mark Wrathall, 291–319. Cambridge: Cambridge University Press, 2013.
Habermas, Jürgen. *The Philosophical Discourse of Modernity*. Cambridge, Mass.: MIT Press, 1987.
———. *Philosophisch-politische Profile*. Frankfurt am Main: Suhrhamp, 1971.
———. *The Theory of Communicative Action*. 2 vols. Boston: Beacon, 1984 [1981].
———. "Work and Weltanschauung: The Heidegger Controversy from a German Perspective." In *The New Conservatism: Cultural Criticism and the Historians' Debate*, ed. and trans. Shierry Weber Nicholsen, 140–72. Cambridge, Mass.: MIT Press, 1989.
Hacking, Ian. "Self-Improvement." In *Historical Ontology*, 115–20. Cambridge, Mass.: Harvard University Press, 2002.
Hegel, G. W. F. *The Philosophy of Mind*. Trans. William Wallace. Oxford: Oxford University Press, 1971.
Heidegger, Martin. *Basic Writings*. Ed. David Farell Krell. New York: Harper and Row, 1977.
———. *Being and Time*. Trans. John Macquarrie and Edward Robinson. New York: Harper and Row, 1962.
———. *Being and Time*. Trans. Joan Stambaugh. Albany: New York Press, 1996.
———. *The Essence of Human Freedom*. Trans. Ted Sadler. London: Continuum, 2002.
———. *The Fundamental Concepts of Metaphysics: World, Finitude, Solitude*. Trans. William McNeill and Nicholas Walker. Bloomington: Indiana University Press, 1995.
———. *Gesamtausgabe*. 77 vols. Frankurt am Main: Vittorio Klostermann, 1975–2000.
———. *An Introduction to Metaphysics*. Trans. James Manheim. New Haven, Conn.: Yale University Press, 1984.
———. *Kant and the Problem of Metaphysics*. Trans. Richard Taft. 5th ed. Bloomington: Indiana University Press, 1997.

———. *The Metaphysical Foundations of Logic*. Trans. Michael Heim. Bloomington: Indiana University Press, 1984.
———. *Nietzsche*. 4 vols. Trans. David Farrell Krell. San Francisco: Harper and Row, 1991.
———. *Of Time and Being*. Trans. Joan Stambaugh. New York: Harper and Row, 1972.
———. *Off the Beaten Track*. Ed. and trans. Julian Young and Kenneth Haynes. Cambridge: Cambridge University Press, 2002.
———. *Ontology: The Hermeneutics of Facticity*. Trans. John van Buren. Bloomington: Indiana University Press, 1999.
———. *Pathmarks*. Ed. William McNeil. Cambridge: Cambridge University Press, 1998.
———. *The Phenomenology of Religious Life*. Trans. Matthias Fritsch and Jennifer Anna Gosetti-Ferencei. Bloomington: Indiana University Press, 2004.
———. *Sein und Zeit*. Tübingen: Max Niemeyer, 1967.
Hekman, Susan, ed. *Feminist Interpretations of Michel Foucault*. University Park: Pennsylvania State University Press, 1996.
Heyes, Cressida, ed. *Foucault Studies*, no. 16, special issue on Foucault and feminism (September 2013).
———. *Self-Transformations: Foucault, Ethics, and Normalized Bodies*. Oxford: Oxford University Press, 2007.
Hoeller, Keith. Editor's foreword in *Review of Existential Psychology and Psychiatry* 19.1 (1986): 7–17.
Honneth, Axel. *Reification: A New Look at an Old Idea*. Oxford: Oxford University Press, 2008.
Hoy, David. "Heidegger and the Hermeneutic Turn." In *The Cambridge Companion to Heidegger*, ed. Charles Guigon, 170–94. Cambridge: Cambridge University Press, 1993.
Hunter, Ian. *Rival Enlightenments: Civil and Metaphysical Philosophy in Early Modern Germany*. Cambridge: Cambridge University Press, 2001.
Husserl, Edmund. "Philosophy as a Strict Science." In *Phenomenology and the Crisis of Philosophy*, trans. Quentin Lauer, 69–147. New York: Harper, 1965.
Ijsseling, Samuel. "Foucault with Heidegger." *Man and World* 19 (1986): 413–24.
Inwood, Michael. *A Heidegger Dictionary*. Oxford: Blackwell, 1999.
Jaeggi, Rahel. *Entfremdung: Zur Aktualität eines sozialphilosophischen Problems*. Frankfurt am Main: Campus Verlag, 2005.
Kant, Immanuel. *Critique of Judgment*. Trans. Werner S. Pluhar. Indianapolis: Hackett, 1987.
———. *Political Writings*. Trans. H. B. Nisbet. Cambridge: Cambridge University Press, 1991.
Katab, George. "Thinking and Human Extinction (II): Nietzsche and Heidegger." In *The Inner Ocean: Individualism and Democratic Culture*, 127–51. Ithaca, N.Y.: Cornell University Press, 1992.

Kellner, Douglas. *Herbert Marcuse and the Crisis of Marxism*. Berkeley: University of California Press, 1984.

Klossowski, Pierre. *Nietzsche and the Vicious Circle*. Trans. Daniel Smith. Chicago: University of Chicago Press, 1998.

———. *Nietzsche et le cercle vicieux*. Paris: Mercure de France, 1969.

Kögler, Hans Herbert. *The Power of Dialogue: Critical Hermeneutics after Gadamer and Foucault*. Cambridge, Mass.: MIT Press, 1996.

Kompridis, Nikolas. *Critique and Disclosure: Critical Theory Between Past and Future*. Cambridge, Mass.: MIT Press, 2006.

Korsch, Karl. *Marxism and Philosophy*. New York: Monthly Review Press, 2008 [1923].

Levinas, Emmanuel. *Totality and Infinity: An Essay on Exteriority*. Pittsburgh: Duquesne University Press, 1969.

Levy, Neil. "The Prehistory of Archaeology: Heidegger and the Early Foucault." *Journal of the British Society for Phenomenology* 27.2 (May 1996): 157–71.

Lukács, Georg. *History and Class Consciousness*. Trans. Rodney Livingstone. Cambridge, Mass.: MIT Press, 1971.

Luxon, Nancy. "Ethics and Subjectivity: Practices of Self-Governance in the Late Lectures of Michel Foucault." *Political Theory* 36.3 (2008): 377–402.

Marcuse, Herbert. *Hegel's Ontology and the Theory of Historicity*. Trans. Seyla Benhabib. Cambridge, Mass.: MIT Press, 1987.

———. *Hegels Ontologie und die Theorie der Geschichtlichkeit*. Frankfurt am Main: Vittorio Klostermann, 1968.

———. "Heidegger's Politics: An Interview." In *Heideggerian Marxism*, ed. Richard Wolin and John Abromeith, 165–75. Lincoln: University of Nebraska Press, 2005.

Marx, Karl. *Capital, Vol. 1*. London: Penguin Classics, 1990.

———. *The Marx-Engels Reader*. Ed. Robert C. Tucker. New York: Norton, 1978.

McCumber, John. *Philosophy and Freedom*. Bloomington: Indiana University Press, 2000.

McGushin, Edward. *Foucault's Askēsis*. Evanston, Ill.: Northwestern University Press, 2007.

McNeil, William. "Care for the Self: Originary Ethics in Heidegger and Foucault." *Philosophy Today* 42.1 (1998): 53–64.

McWhorter, Ladelle. *Bodies and Pleasures: Foucault and the Politics of Sexual Normalization*. Bloomington: Indiana University Press, 1999.

———. "Subjecting Dasein." In *Foucault and Heidegger: Critical Encounters*, ed. Alan Milchman and Alan Rosenberg, 110–26. Minneapolis: University of Minnesota Press, 2003.

Megill, Allan. *Prophets of Extremity: Nietzsche, Heidegger, Foucault, Derrida*. Berkeley: University of California Press, 1985.

Merleau-Ponty, Maurice. *The Phenomenology of Perception*. New York: Routledge, 1945.

Milchman, Alan, and Alan Rosenberg, eds. *Foucault and Heidegger: Critical Encounters*. Minneapolis: University of Minnesota Press, 2003.
Miller, James. *The Passion of Michel Foucault*. New York: Simon and Schuster, 1993.
Mulhall, Stephen. *Heidegger and "Being and Time."* London: Routledge, 1996.
Nancy, Jean-Luc. *L'expérience de la liberté*. Paris: Galilée, 1988.
Nedelsky, Jennifer. *Law's Relations: A Relational Theory of Self, Autonomy, and Law*. Oxford: Oxford University Press, 2011.
Nichols, Robert. "The World of Negative Liberty: Reading Berlin Though Weak Ontology." In *Isaiah Berlin and the Politics of Freedom*, ed. Bruce Baum and Robert Nichols, 216–30. New York: Routledge, 2012.
Nietzsche, Friedrich. *The Gay Science*. Ed. Bernard Williams. Trans. Josefine Nauckhoff. Cambridge: Cambridge University Press, 2001.
Nussbaum, Martha. *Sex and Social Justice*. Oxford: Oxford University Press, 1999.
Oksala, Johanna. *Foucault on Freedom*. Cambridge: Cambridge University Press, 2005.
———. *Foucault, Politics, and Violence*. Evanston, Ill.: Northwestern University Press, 2012.
Owen, David. "Reification, Ideology, and Power: Expression and Agency in Honneth's Theory of Recognition." *Journal of Power* 3.1 (2010): 97–109.
Owen, David S. *Between Reason and History: Habermas and the Idea of Progress*. Albany: State University of New York Press, 2002.
Papadaki, Evangelia. "Sexual Objectification: From Kant to Contemporary Feminism." *Contemporary Political Theory* 6 (2007): 330–48.
Patton, Paul. "Foucault's Subject of Power." *Political Theory Newsletter* 6.1 (1994): 60–71.
Rabinow, Paul. "Modern and Counter-Modern: Ethos and Epoch in Heidegger and Foucault." In *The Cambridge Companion to Foucault*, 1st ed., ed. Gary Gutting, 197–214. Cambridge: Cambridge University Press, 1994.
Ramazanoglu, Caroline, ed. *Up Against Foucault: Exploration of Some Tensions Between Foucault and Feminism*. New York: Routledge, 1993.
Rayner, Timothy. *Foucault's Heidegger: Philosophy and Transformative Experience*. New York: Continuum, 2007.
Ricoeur, Paul. *Memory, History, Forgetting*. Chicago: University of Chicago Press, 2006.
Rockmore, Tom. *Heidegger and French Philosophy: Humanism, Antihumanism, and Being*. London: Routledge, 1995.
Rorty, Richard. *Contingency, Irony, Solidarity*. Cambridge: Cambridge University Press, 1989.
———. *Philosophical Papers*. Vol. 2, *Essays on Heidegger and Others*. Cambridge: Cambridge University Press, 1991.
Sartre, Jean-Paul. *Being and Nothingness*. Trans. H. Barnes. London: Methuen, 1969.

Sawicki, Jana. "Heidegger and Foucault: Escaping Technological Nihilism." *Philosophy and Social Criticism* 13.2 (1987): 155–73.

Schmidt, Alfred. "Existential Ontology and Historical Materialism in the Work of Herbert Marcuse." In *Marcuse: Critical Theory and the Promise of Utopia*, ed. Robert Pippin, Andrew Feenberg, and Charles P. Webel, 47–67. South Hadley, Mass.: Bergin and Garvey, 1988.

Schwartz, Michael. "Critical Reproblematization: Foucault and the Task of Modern Philosophy." *Radical Philosophy*, no. 91 (September–October 1998): 19–31.

Sloterdijk, Peter. *The Critique of Cynical Reason*. Minneapolis: University of Minnesota Press, 1987 [1983].

Sluga, Hans. "Foucault's Encounter with Heidegger and Nietzsche." In *The Cambridge Companion to Foucault*, 2nd ed., ed. Gary Gutting, 210–39. Cambridge: Cambridge University Press, 2003.

Spanos, William V. *Heidegger and Criticism: Retrieving the Cultural Politics of Destruction*. Minneapolis: University of Minnesota Press, 1993.

Szakolczai, Arpad. *Max Weber and Michel Foucault: Parallel Life Works*. New York: Routledge, 1998.

Taylor, Charles. "Engaged Agency and Background in Heidegger." In *The Cambridge Companion to Heidegger*, ed. Charles Guigon, 202–21. Cambridge: Cambridge University Press, 2006.

———. *Hegel and Modern Society*. Cambridge: Cambridge University Press, 1979.

———. *Philosophical Arguments*. Cambridge, Mass.: Harvard University Press, 1995.

———. *Philosophical Papers*. Vol. 2, *Philosophy and the Human Sciences*. Cambridge: Cambridge University Press, 1985.

———. *Sources of the Self*. Cambridge, Mass.: Harvard University Press, 1989.

Taylor, Chloë. *The Culture of Confession from Augustine to Foucault: A Genealogy of the "Confessing Animal."* New York: Routledge, 2008.

Taylor, Diana, and Karen Vintges, eds. *Feminism and the Final Foucault*. Urbana: University of Illinois Press, 2004.

Thiele, Leslie. *Timely Meditations: Martin Heidegger and Postmodern Politics*. Princeton, N.J.: Princeton University Press, 1995.

Thomson, Iain. "Heidegger and National Socialism." In *A Companion to Heidegger*, ed. Hubert Dreyfus and Mark Wrathall, 32–48. London: Blackwell, 2005.

Tully, James. "To Think and Act Differently: Foucault's Four Reciprocal Objections to Habermas' Theory." In *Foucault Contra Habermas*, ed. Samantha Ashenden and David Owen, 90–142. London: Sage, 1999.

Vattimo, Gianni. *Nihilism and Emancipation*. Trans. William McCuaig. New York: Columbia University Press, 2003.

Veyne, Paul. *Foucault: Sa pensée, sa personne*. Paris: Albin Michel, 2008.

Visker, Rudi. "From Foucault to Heidegger: A One-Way Ticket?" *Research in Phenomenology* 21 (1991): 116–40.
Williams, Forrest. Translator's preface in *Review of Existential Psychology and Psychiatry* 19.1 (1986): 19–27.
Wittgenstein, Ludwig. *Culture and Value*. Trans. Peter Winch. Chicago: University of Chicago Press, 1980.
Wolin, Richard, and John Abromeit, eds. *Heideggerian Marxism*. Lincoln: University of Nebraska Press, 2005.
Young, Julian. *Heidegger's Later Philosophy*. Cambridge: Cambridge University Press, 2002.
Yovel, Yirmiahu. *Kant and the Philosophy of History*. Princeton, N.J.: Princeton University Press, 1980.
Zerilli, Linda. *Feminism and the Abyss of Freedom*. Chicago: University of Chicago Press, 2005.
Ziarek, Krzysztof. "Powers That Be: Art and Technology in Heidegger and Foucault." *Research in Phenomenology* 28 (1998): 162–94.

INDEX

Absolute Being or Spirit, 95–96, 200, 220
actuality: freedom in space between potentiality and, 31–32; mode of, 36–39; ontology of, 97, 185, 194, 239n60
Adorno, Theodor, 256–57n11
Alcoff, Linda, 172–73
alētheia, 25, 161
alienation, 55, 92, 96–97, 135, 200, 214
Allen, Amy, 173, 192, 251n18
Althusser, Louis, 26, 244n14
analytics of finitude, 119–27, 128
anticognitivism, 220
antihumanism of Heidegger, 26, 76–78
Arendt, Hannah, 81, 129, 235–36n38
Aristotle, 226n22, 256n4
as-structure, 29–30, 32, 41, 42, 43, 45, 54
assujettissement (subjectification). *See* subjectivity
Aufklärung (Enlightenment), 186–87, 190–91
authenticity in *Being and Time*: defined, 50–51; historicity and authentic historicizing, 80–87; inauthentic/authentic distinction, 48–54, 55; limitations of, 55–56; Marcuse on authentic and inauthentic praxis, 92

Bachelard, Gaston, 26

Bacon, Francis, 119
Bataille, Georges, 245–46n23
Beaufret, Jean, 22, 26, 101
Befindlichkeit (disposition) in Heidegger, 36–39, 230–31n4
Being: Absolute Being or Spirit, 95–96, 200, 220; Dasein, concept of, 15, 16, 19–20, 31–32, 177 (*See also entries at* Heidegger); as experience in Foucault, 148; Foucault's history of subjectivity and Heidegger's history of Being, 193–94; Heidegger's concept of Being-in-the-world, 32–36, 37, 59, 101, 229n2; power in Foucault and Being in Heidegger, 247n32
Berlin, Isaiah, 234n24
Binswanger, Ludwig, 22, 103
Blanchot, Maurice, 245–46n23
Boss, Medard, 22, 103
Burke, Edmund, 1
Butler, Judith, 216, 242n2, 250n10

capitalism as primary obstacle to self-realization, 87, 92, 96, 202. *See also* Marx, Karl, and Marxism; reification theory
Caputo, John, 107
care: Being and, 30, 85, 86; in *Being and Time*, 80, 81, 85; defined, 69; dwelling

and, 179; importance in Heidegger and Foucault, 5, 9, 17–18, 169–71; Marcuse and, 88–89; as recognition, 216; reification theory and, 211–12, 214–16, 219, 257–58n17; social criticism and concept of, 201; as vocabulary for relationship to present, 169–71, 191–92
Cassian, 113–14
Cavell, Stanley, 257n12
Christianity, early: confessional practices in, 113–14, 119, 136, 248n2; *oikonomia psuchōn*, 134, 136–37; the self in, 176; time, Western understanding of, 253n33
classicism: Foucault and Heidegger's use of classical texts, 252n22; Foucault on threshold between modernity and, 119–21
cognitive, 29, 86, 90, 162, 167, 177, 208, 209, 215–21
commodity fetishism, 203–6
conduct in Foucault: governmentality and, 133–40; as relationship to our field of practical involvement, 179; as space between possibility and constraint, 169, 179
confessional or pastoral power, 113–14, 119, 136, 248n2
Connolly, William, 71
contingent eventalization, principle of, 130, 149, 155–56
"Copernican turn," 8
Critical Theory, 207, 217, 227n26, 239n55
Cutrofello, Andrew, 188

Dallmayr, Fred, 57
Dasein, concept of, 15, 16, 19–20, 31–32, 177. *See also* entries at Heidegger
Daseinsanalysis, 22, 25, 26, 103
death: Foucault's analysis of, 104–5, 107, 108; Heidegger on finitude and awareness of, 47, 48, 73, 108, 231n15; historicity and, 81, 83, 103, 104, 107, 108; natality and, 235–36n38
Derrida, Jacques, 183–84, 255–56n1
Descartes, René: "analytics of truth," 248n2; *cogito* of, 121, 122–23; Foucault's initial critique of Heidegger and, 119, 120, 122–23; Heidegger on Being-in-the-world and, 229n2; Heidegger's analysis of, 194–95; Heidegger's critique of metaphysics and, 76; history of subjectivity and, 18, 181, 182–86, 189, 191–96, 254–55n40, 254n35–37; Kant and, 185–86, 254n35; "le moment cartésien," 182–84; nihilism and, 245n19; ontological understanding of freedom and, 7; philosophy of the constituting subject and, 15, 146; reification theory and, 219, 220; spirituality and, 162, 172–73, 184, 192, 195; world as present-at-hand in, 35
Dewey, John, 242n3, 257n12
Dilthey, Wilhelm, 82, 107, 120, 237n47
disposition (*Befindlichkeit*) in Heidegger, 36–39, 230–31n4
doubles in Foucault's analytic of finitude, 119–27
Dreyfus, Hubert, 24, 46, 103, 117–18, 186, 247n32
Dumm, Thomas, 13, 227n23

embedded subjectivity, 101, 103, 175, 219
Enlightenment (*Aufklärung*), 186–87, 190–91
Epictetus, 161
epistemological indeterminacy, 60–65, 67–69, 71, 72, 74, 85, 96
ethical-spiritual transformation, freedom as, 130, 149, 155, 160, 167–69, 184–86, 189. *See also* spirituality
excess of the signified, 111–13, 118–19
existentialism: Being-in-the-world, as existential analytic, 32–36; Dasein, analysis of, 31–32; distinguishing experiential, existential, and ontological levels of analysis, 29–31; experience as existential-phenomenological category, 100–108; freedom as fundamental existential condition of world-disclosure, Heidegger on, 59–66; Marcuse on social criticism and, 20; ontological analysis and, 14; potentiality as existential a priori, 28; Sartre,

Heidegger's critique of, 26; Sartre's appropriation of existential analytic in *Being and Time*, 58. *See also* preparatory existential analytic of freedom in *Being and Time*

experience: as Being in Foucault, 148; equivocation in Foucault's use of thought and, 140–48; existential, experiential, and ontological levels of analysis distinguished in *Being and Time*, 29–31; as existential-phenomenological category, 100–108; historicizing phenomenology of, 100–108, 123–24; as limit-state, 245–46n23

facticity, 38–39, 82, 91, 93, 95, 234n21, 237n47

feminist scholarship, 170, 203, 249–50n8, 250n10

finitude and freedom, 6–9, 12–15; Foucault's initial critique of Heidegger and analytics of, 119–27, 128; in Heidegger's middle period works, 69, 71, 72, 73; in Kantian philosophy, 192; overcoming gap between objective knowledge and finite subject, different approaches to, 220; in preparatory existential analytic of freedom in *Being and Time*, 47–48

fore-grasping, fore-having, and fore-seeing, 41–42

fore-structure, 32, 41–42, 43, 241n16

Foucault, Michel: *The Archaeology of Knowledge* (*L'archéologie du savoir*), 112, 142, 245n22; *The Birth of the Clinic* (*Naissance de la clinique*), 101, 103–6, 111, 112, 240–41n12; classicism and modernity, threshold between, 119–21; combining historical and ontological forms of critical analysis and, 19, 20, 21; *Discipline and Punish* (*Surveiller et punir*), 116, 117, 131, 134, 135, 142, 150, 242n4; on genealogy, 242n5, 247–48n35; Habermas versus, 249n6; Heidegger's insights, as means of concretizing, 200–201; *The Hermeneutics of the Subject* (*L'herméneutique du sujet*), 14, 23, 154, 162, 164, 171, 252–53n20; *The History of Sexuality* (*Histoire de la sexualité*), 114–15, 116, 129, 134, 135, 141, 143, 144, 158, 168, 242–43n6; influence of Heidegger on, 21–26, 228–29n40; Kompridis on, 227n26; on language, 119–21; madness/mental illness and psychiatry, works on, 100, 103, 107, 117, 127, 240n11, 245n22; Marcuse and, 88, 97, 239n55; *The Order of Things*, 106, 112, 119; on problematization, 148, 149, 156–59, 162, 163, 166, 178, 200, 221, 244n14, 248n39; reification and, 217–22, 256n8; *Security, Territory, Population* (*Sécurité, territoire, population*), 134, 136, 149; sexuality, interest in, 168, 175, 242–43n6; "The Subject and Power," 149–55; on subjectivity and subjectification, 18, 101, 102, 152–53, 155, 217–22, 252n24; on technologies of the self, 154–55, 253–54n34. *See also* conduct in Foucault; history of subjectivity; power in Foucault; spirituality

Foucault's "autocritique" and ontological concept of freedom, 17, 129–60; contingent eventalization, principle of, 130, 149, 155–56; ethical-spiritual transformation, freedom as, 130, 149, 155, 160, 167–69; experience and thought, equivocation in use of, 140–48; governmentality and conduct, 133–40, 169; irreducibility of thought, principle of, 130, 149, 155, 156–60; power and freedom, 149–55; three stages in analysis of freedom, 130, 149, 155; war model, 131–33, 150, 155, 242n4

Foucault's initial critique of Heidegger, 99–129; analytics of finitude, 119–27, 128; historicizing of phenomenology of experience, 100–108, 123–24; interpretation, 109–10, 115, 118, 119; original man, 110, 119, 124–27, 241n20; the unthought, 119, 121–24. *See also* hermeneutics, Foucault's critique of

Frankfurt school, 227n26. *See also* Critical Theory

Frankl, Viktor, 22, 103

freedom. *See* ontological understanding of freedom
French Revolution, 1, 255n45
fundamental ontology: defined, 14; Heidegger's move to, 15–16, 29, 30, 40; Heidegger's move to historical ontology from, 79–80; unfolding into historical ontology, 180

Gadamer, Hans-Georg, 107–8, 240n2
genealogy, Foucault's concept of, 242n5, 247–48n35
Geuss, Raymond, 216–17, 257–58n16–17
Goldman, Lucien, 202, 211, 256n9
Gordon, Colin, 243n8
governance and governmentality: conduct in Foucault and, 133–40, 169; governmentality studies, 244n13; juridical subject and model of law-governance in Kant, 187–90
Gregory of Nazianzen, 136

Habermas, Jürgen, 3, 10, 12, 58, 227n26, 233n10, 249n6, 253n34
Hacking, Ian, 190
Han/Han-Pile, Béatrice, 8, 79, 159, 182, 248n40, 253n33, 254–55n40
Hegel, G. W. F.: Foucault's reading of, 24, 25; Heidegger compared, 3; historical teleology and, 146; on idea of freedom, 1; on intersubjectivity, 2; Kant influencing, 10; Lukács on, 257n14; Marcuse and, 88, 95–97; ontological understanding of freedom and, 6; overcoming gap between objective knowledge and finite subject, 220; the unthought and, 124
Hegelian-Marxism, 96–97, 199–200, 203
Heidegger, Martin: antihumanism of, 26, 76–78; combining historical and ontological forms of critical analysis and, 19–20; Dasein, concept of, 15, 16, 19–20, 31–32, 177; Descartes analysed by, 194–95; Foucault as means of concretizing insights of, 200–201; Foucault influenced by, 21–26, 228–29n40; fundamental ontology, move to, 15–16, 29, 30, 40; historical ontology, move to, 79–80; historicity and authentic historicizing in *Being and Time*, 80–87; Honneth on reification theory and, 210–17; Kompridis on, 227n26; *Letter to Jean Beaufret on Humanism*, 26; Marcuse building on ontological freedom as laid out by, 56, 59, 80, 87–97, 199–200, 210; Marx and, 59, 88; Nazis, involvement with, 52–53; on objectification, 152; on philosophy, 76, 235n34, 255n48; power in Foucault and Being in, 247n32; selfhood, sociocritical dimensions of, 258n20; on *Spielraum*, 46–47, 62–64, 67, 169; on subjectivity, 218, 252n24; thought, Foucault on, 158–59; thought, Foucault's relationship of freedom to, 161–62; on values, 235n33. *See also* authenticity in *Being and Time*; Foucault's initial critique of Heidegger; history of subjectivity; preparatory existential analytic of freedom in *Being and Time*; spirituality
Heidegger's middle period works on freedom, 16–17, 57–80; background understanding as feature of world-disclosure, 60–62; (self)concealment, 72–74, 195; contradictory interpretations of, 57–58; epistemological indeterminacy, 60–65, 67–69, 71, 72, 74, 85, 96; finitude, 69, 71, 72, 73; historical ontology, move to, 79–80; "letting-be," "releasement," or "open comportment," 66–72; Marcuse influenced by, 56, 59; metaphysics and humanism, critique of, 74–79; ontological understanding stressed in, 58; *Spielraum*, 46–47, 62–64, 67, 169, 178; world-disclosure, freedom as fundamental condition of, 59–66
hermeneutics, Foucault's critique of, 108–19; in candidacy presentation, 247n28; excess of the signified, 111–13, 118–19; interpretation, 109–10, 115, 118, 119, 241n16; power dynamics and, 113–18, 119; thought, relationship of freedom to, 161–62; the unthought and, 124

historical ontology: combining historical and ontological forms of critical analysis, 18–21; conduct, Foucault's concept of, 179; defined, 14–15; distinguishing selves and subjects in Foucault, 172; Foucault on historical ontology of ourselves, 159; fundamental ontology unfolding into, 180; Heidegger's move to, 79–80; history of subjectivity and, 179–82; Kant's importance for, 184–85; practical involvement and, 180; social criticism and, 201–2; spirituality, read through lens of, 181–82

historical teleology, 146

historicity: death and, 81, 83, 103, 104, 107, 108; experience, historicizing phenomenology of, 100–108, 123–24; Heidegger's *Being and Time*, historicity and authentic historicizing in, 80–87; Marcuse on, 89–90, 95–96; thought and, 246n24; translation of Heidegger's term for, 236–37n39; the unthought and, 123–24

history of subjectivity, 179–97; consequences of Kantian-Cartesian model, 194–97; Descartes and, 18, 181, 182–86, 189, 191–96, 254–55n40, 254n35–37; Enlightenment (*Aufklärung*), Kant's reflections on, 186–87, 190–91; Heidegger's history of Being and, 193–94; historical ontology and, 179–82; humanism and, 189–90; juridical subject and model of law-governance in Kant, 187–90; Kant and, 184–97; "le moment cartésien" in, 182–84; objectification and, 193–95; selves and subjects, distinguishing, 172, 176; spirituality and, 179, 181–82, 184–86, 189, 190–92, 195

Hobbes, Thomas, 234n24

Hoeller, Keith, 101

Hölderlin, Friedrich, 126

Honneth, Axel, 18, 202, 209–17, 219, 220, 256–57n11–12, 256n8

Hoy, David, 109

humanism: Foucault's concerns regarding, 190–91; Heidegger's critique of, 26, 76–78

Hume, David, 122

Hunter, Ian, 254n37

Husserl, Edmund, 15, 29, 101, 107, 122, 124, 146, 228n40, 257n13

indeterminacy, epistemological, 60–65, 67–69, 71, 72, 74, 85, 96

interpretation, Foucault's critique of Heidegger's concept of, 109–10, 115, 118, 119, 241n16

intersubjective and relational nature of freedom, 2–3, 161, 225n4

Jaspers, Karl, 22, 103

Kant, Immanuel: "analytics of truth," 248n2; autonomy model of, 168; *Critique of Judgment*, 11; Descartes and, 185–86, 254n35; Enlightenment (*Aufklärung*), reflections on, 186–87, 190–91; Foucault's "autocritique" and, 140, 146, 153, 158; Foucault's history of subjectivity and, 18, 184–97; Foucault's initial critique of Heidegger and, 100, 121, 122, 123, 124; on French Revolution, 1, 255n45; Heidegger's middle period work on freedom and, 64, 67, 76, 77, 78, 237n28; historical ontology of freedom, importance for, 184–85; history of subjectivity and, 184–97; Hunter's reading of, 254n37; juridical subject and model of law-governance in, 187–90; Marcuse's bridging of Heidegger and Marx and, 95; "le moment cartésien" and, 185–86; ontological understanding of freedom and, 7–12, 18; original man and transcendental subject in, 241n20; philosophy of the constituting subject and, 15, 146; preparatory existential analytic of freedom in *Being and Time* and, 35, 48, 229n2; reification theory and, 203, 219, 220; spirituality and, 162, 168, 172, 181, 182, 184–86, 189, 190–91, 192, 195, 255n45

Kateb, George, 13, 227n23

Kellner, Douglas, 238n49

Klossowski, Pierre, 25–26, 229n42, 245–46n23
Kompridis, Nikolas, 225n5, 227n26

labor, Marcuse on, 88–90
Laing, R. D., 22, 240n6
language, Foucault on, 119–21
Lear, Jonathan, 216
"letting-be," "releasement," or "open comportment," 66–72
Levinas, Emmanuel, 250n9
liberty. *See* ontological understanding of freedom
Locke, John, 8
Lukács, Georg: Honneth's use of Heidegger and, 210, 211, 212–14, 217; reification theory of, 18, 92, 202, 203, 206–8; self-critique of, 257n14

madness/mental illness and psychiatry, Foucault's works on, 100, 103, 107, 117, 127, 240n11, 245n22
Mallarmé, Stéphane, 120, 121
Marcus Aurelius, 113
Marcuse, Herbert: on capitalism as primary obstacle to self-realization, 87, 92, 96, 202; on combining historical and ontological forms of critical analysis, 19–21, 79; on Dilthey, 237n47; efforts to bridge Heidegger and Marx, 87, 88, 90, 94, 96, 199–200; Foucault and, 88, 97, 239n55; Heidegger's concept of freedom and, 56, 59, 80, 87–97, 199–200, 210; on historicity, 89–90, 95–96; Kompridis on, 227n26; on labor, 88–90; location of pathology of reified praxis under capitalism in, 238–39n54; Marxism of, 20, 56, 87, 90, 91, 92, 93, 95–97; on necessity, 93–96; on praxis, 87–97; on radical action, 90–96, 200, 236n38, 238n49; on reification, 92–96, 202, 203, 217
Marx, Karl, and Marxism: alienation, 55, 92, 96–97, 135, 200, 214; Althusser and, 26; commodity fetishism, 203–6; Foucault's reading of Marx, 24, 25; Hegelian-Marxism, 96–97, 199–200, 203; Heidegger and, 19, 26; historical teleology and, 146; Kant influencing Marx, 10; Lukács and, 206, 207; of Marcuse, 20, 56, 87, 90, 91, 92, 93, 95–97; Marcuse's efforts to bridge Heidegger and, 87, 88, 90, 94, 96, 199–200; reification theory of, 92, 203–5, 246n6; teleological freedom and, 10; the unthought and, 124; on world experienced as practical relation, 59, 88, 202
McCumber, John, 225n3
meaning, as aspect of understanding, 43
mental illness/madness and psychiatry, Foucault's works on, 100, 103, 107, 117, 127, 240n11, 245n22
Merleau-Ponty, Maurice, 26, 57, 65, 101, 105, 228n40, 240n4, 243n8
metaphysics, Heidegger's critique of, 74–79
Miller, James, 243n9, 246n23
modernity: Enlightenment (*Aufklärung*), 186–87, 190–91; Foucault on threshold between classicism and, 119–21; technology, problem of, 195–97, 253–54n34
Montaigne, Michel de, 137
Mulhall, Stephen, 60

natality, 81, 235–36n38
Nazis, Heidegger's involvement with, 52–53
necessity, Marcuse on, 93–96
neo-Kantian rationalism, 43, 187, 231n10
Nietzsche, Friedrich: Dumm on, 227n23; on experience as limit-state, 245–46n23; Foucault and, 23–26, 117, 133, 229n40, 251n17; *Genealogy of Morals*, 117; Heidegger's characterization of, 253n32; ontological understanding of freedom and, 6; original man and, 126; overcoming gap between objective knowledge and finite subject, 220; self-care in, 171; unity of general grammar, breakup of, 120, 121; war model and, 133

objectification: Foucault on, 218; Heidegger's focus on, 152; history of subjectivity and, 193–95; reification

theory and, 203 (*See also* reification theory)
oikonomia psuchōn, 134, 136–37
Oksala, Johanna, 4, 13, 58
Olafson, Fredrick, 20
ontological truth and ontological freedom, 62, 67
ontological understanding of freedom, 1–26; combining historical and ontological forms of critical analysis, 18–21; concept of freedom, importance and power of, 1–2; defined, 5–6, 13–14, 58; distinguishing experiential, existential, and ontological levels of analysis, 29–31; finitude and, 6–9, 12–15; history of subjectivity and, 179–97 (*See also* history of subjectivity); importance of Heidegger and Foucault to, 3–5 (*See also entries at* Heidegger *and* Foucault); intersubjective and relational nature of freedom, 2–3, 161, 225n4; Kant and, 7–12, 15; reification theory, 18, 202–22 (*See also* reification theory); social criticism and, 18, 199–202 (*See also* social criticism); spirituality, ontological presuppositions of, 17–18, 161–79 (*See also* spirituality); teleological freedom, 9–12; transcendental freedom, 8–9. *See also* fundamental ontology; historical ontology; situated freedom
ontology of actuality, 97, 185, 194, 239n60
"open comportment," "releasement," or "letting-be," 66–72
original man, 110, 119, 124–27, 241n20

pastoral or confessional power, 113–14, 119, 136, 248n2
Patton, Paul, 250–51n17
performativity, 242n2
philosophy: of the constituting subject, 2–3, 7, 9, 15, 106, 131, 146, 159, 175, 178, 197, 220; Heidegger on, 76, 235n34, 255n48; implicit thought made explicit by, 144; spirituality versus, 164
"play-space" (*Spielraum*), 46–47, 62–64, 67, 169, 178

potentiality: authentic/inauthentic distinction and, 54; as existential a priori, 28; freedom in space between actuality and, 31–32; mode of the possible, 36, 39–40; Understanding, grounded in, 43–48
power in Foucault: Being in Heidegger and, 247n32; *Discipline and Punish* (*Surveiller et punir*), 116, 117, 131, 134, 135, 142, 150, 242n4; freedom involved in, 155; governmentality and conduct, 133–40, 169; pastoral or confessional power, 113–14, 119, 136, 248n2; as relationship, 150–52, 155; (re)statement of general project of, 252n21; in "The Subject and Power," 149–55; war model, 131–33, 150, 155, 242n4
praxis, Marcuse on, 87–97
preparatory existential analytic of freedom in *Being and Time*, 15–16, 27–56; authentic/inauthentic distinction, 48–54; authenticity, critique of, 55–56; Being-in-the-world, 32–36, 37, 229n2; disposition (*Befindlichkeit*) and mode of the actual, 36–39, 230–31n4; distinguishing experiential, existential, and ontological levels of analysis in, 29–31; fundamental ontology, move to, 15–16, 29, 30; historicity and authentic historicizing, 80–87; mode of the possible, 36, 39–40; in space between actuality and potentiality, 31–32; Understanding, 36, 40, 41–49, 60, 74, 109–10, 241n16
present-at-hand, 34–35, 49
problematization, 148, 149, 156–59, 162, 163, 166, 178, 200, 221, 244n14, 248n39
psychiatry: Foucault on pastoral power in, 114–16, 119; Foucault's works on madness/mental illness and, 100, 103, 107, 117, 127, 240n11, 245n22

Rabinow, Paul, 24, 117–18, 186, 229n46
radical action, Marcuse on, 90–96, 200, 236n38, 238n49
Rayner, Timothy, 248n39
ready-to-hand, 34–35, 41
recognition thesis, 225n4

reification theory, 18, 202–22; alienation and, 92, 96–97, 200, 214; care and, 211–12, 214–16, 219, 257–58n17; defined, 202–3; dual use of reification, 208–9; Foucault and, 217–22, 256n8; Heidegger as used by Honneth on, 210–17; Heidegger on philosophy and, 235n34; Honneth on, 18, 202, 209–17, 219, 220, 256–57n11–12, 256n8; of Lukács, 18, 92, 202, 203, 206–8; Marcuse and, 92–96, 202, 203, 217; of Marx, 92, 203–5, 246n6; "nonreified" defined for purposes of, 209; of Sartre, 105, 202, 217; as social theory, 202–3

relational and intersubjective nature of freedom, 2–3, 161, 225n4

"releasement," "letting-be," or "open comportment," 66–72

Ricoeur, Paul, 235–36n38

right relation, pre-modern formulations of freedom as, 226–27n22

Rorty, Richard, 70–71, 235n29, 242n3

Sartre, Jean-Paul: on choice, 91, 238n51; existential analytic in *Being and Time* appropriated by, 58; Foucault's reading of, 101, 228n40; Heidegger's influence on Foucault and, 22, 26; reification theory of, 105, 202, 217

Sawicki, Jana, 245n19

Schleiermacher, Friedrich, 107, 120

Schopenhauer, Arthur, 6, 124, 220

selfhood: capitalism as primary obstacle to self-realization, 87, 92, 96, 202; (self) concealment in Heidegger's middle period works, 72–74, 195; distinguishing selves and subjects, 171–79; freedom and selfhood, Heidegger on, 162, 167, 177–79; Kant, juridical subject and model of law-governance in, 187–90; ontological commitments of Foucault's analysis of, 162–64, 177, 178; self-objectification, 159, 218, 221; sociocritical dimensions of, Heidegger on, 258n20; technologies of the self, 154–55. *See also* reification theory

Senellart, Michel, 244n15

sexuality, Foucault's interest in, 168, 175, 242–43n6

signified, excess of the, 111–13, 118–19

situated freedom: concept of, 6–7, 9, 12–15; Foucault's initial critique of Heidegger and, 99; preparatory existential analytic of freedom in *Being and Time* and, 29, 31, 36, 46; social criticism and, 199, 200, 201, 202; spirituality and, 169, 185

Sloterdijk, Peter, 1

social criticism, 18, 199–202; combining historical and ontological forms of critical analysis and, 19–21; Foucault as means of concretizing Heideggerrian insights, 200–201; Heidegger's "the They" and, 52–53; historical ontology and, 201–2; Marcuse's use of Heidegger's concept of ontological freedom, 56, 59, 80, 87–97, 199–200; situated freedom and, 199, 200, 201, 202. *See also* reification theory

Socrates, 164

spatiality, 35

Spielraum ("play-space"), 46–47, 62–64, 67, 169, 178

spirituality, 17–18, 161–79; care, Foucault's and Heidegger's concepts of, 169–71; conduct in Foucault and, 169, 179; defined, 164–66; Descartes and, 162, 172–73, 184, 192, 195; differentiating activities done to oneself versus done on the self by others, 248–49n3; distinguishing selves and subjects, 171–79; ethical-spiritual transformation, freedom as, 130, 149, 155, 160, 167–69, 184–86, 189; freedom and selfhood, Heidegger on, 162, 167, 177–79; historical ontology read through lens of, 181–82; history of subjectivity and, 179, 181–82, 184–86, 189, 190–92, 195; Kant and, 162, 168, 172, 181, 182, 184–86, 189, 190–91, 192, 195, 255n45; "le moment cartésien" and, 184; ontological commitments of Foucault's analysis of selfhood and, 162–64, 177, 178; philosophy versus, 164; situated freedom and, 169; thought and, 166–67

Stirner, Max, 6
Strauss, Leo, 58
subjectivity: distinguishing selves and subjects, 171–79; embedded, 101, 103, 175, 219; Foucault on, 18, 101, 102, 152–53, 155, 217–22, 252n24; Heideggerian, 218, 252n24; inter-subjective and relational nature of freedom, 2–3, 161, 225n4; Lukács' reification theory and, 206–8; reification theory and Foucault on, 217–22. *See also* history of subjectivity

Taylor, Charles, 6, 28, 225n4, 233n16, 234n24
technē, 22, 23, 126, 181, 182, 221, 253–54n34
technologies of the self, 154–55, 253–54n34
technology, problem of, 195–97, 253–54n34
teleological freedom, 9–12, 187
teleology, historical, 146
"the They," 52–53
Thiele, Leslie Paul, 76
thing-in-itself and thing-under-description, 66
thought: continuous existence of, 246n26; critique as principle of, 147, 247n26; equivocation in Foucault's use of experience and, 140–48; free relations made possible by, 161–62; historical change and, 246n24; irreducibility of, 130, 149, 155, 156–60; problematization and, 148, 149, 156–59, 162, 163, 166, 178, 200, 221, 244n14, 248n39; singularity, principle of, 146; spirituality and, 166–67; the unthought, 119, 121–24, 144
thrownness, 38–39, 59
transcendental freedom, 8–9
truth and freedom, 61, 176, 192, 195
Tully, James, 187, 249n6, 251n19

Understanding in Heidegger's *Being and Time*, 36, 40, 41–49, 60, 74, 109–10, 241n16
the unthought, 119, 121–24, 144

values, Heidegger on, 235n33
Vattimo, Gianni, 239n60
verdinglichkeit. See reification theory

war model, 131–33, 150, 155, 242n4
Wittgenstein, Ludwig, *Culture and Value*, 50

Yorck, Count, 82
Young, Julian, 75, 179, 252–53n29

The authorized representative in the EU for product safety and compliance is:
Mare Nostrum Group
B.V Doelen 72
4831 GR Breda
The Netherlands

www.ingramcontent.com/pod-product-compliance
Lightning Source LLC
Chambersburg PA
CBHW030611230426
43661CB00053B/1934